Hitler's and Hirohito's 'Kamikaze' Flying Bombs

Hitler's and Hirohito's 'Kamikaze' Flying Bombs

The Axis' Manned Suicide Attack Aircraft of WW2

William Wolf

First published in Great Britain in 2025 by
Air World
An imprint of Pen & Sword Books Limited
Yorkshire – Philadelphia

ISBN 978 1 03611 927 0

A CIP catalogue record for this book is available from the British Library.

Typeset by Mac Style
Printed in the UK by CPI Group (UK) Ltd, Croydon, CR0 4YY.

The Publisher's authorised representative in the EU for product safety is Authorised Rep Compliance Ltd., Ground Floor, 71 Lower Baggot Street, Dublin D02 P593, Ireland.
www.arccompliance.com

For a complete list of Pen & Sword titles please contact

PEN & SWORD BOOKS LIMITED
47 Church Street, Barnsley, South Yorkshire, S70 2AS, England
E-mail: enquiries@pen-and-sword.co.uk
Website: www.pen-and-sword.co.uk
or
PEN AND SWORD BOOKS
1950 Lawrence Road, Havertown, PA 19083, USA
E-mail: uspen-and-sword@casematepublishers.com
Website: www.penandswordbooks.com

Contents

Preface

There have been many books and articles over the years concerning the Fieseler V-1 flying bomb and the devastating Japanese kamikaze attackers, but little has been presented on the enemy's manned parasite suicide flying bombs to be carried by bomber motherships to the vicinity of their intended target. Some fervent Nazis, such as famed aviatrix Hanna Reitsch and Mussolini rescuer Otto Skorzeny, favoured the conversion of the V-1 pulsejet into the Fi 103R Reichenberg manned German kamikaze to be carried under the wing of the Heinkel He 111 bomber. However, the scheme would never become operational as even Hitler deemed the idea not to be compatible with Teutonic ideals. However, during the final 10 months of the war in the Pacific the Samurai credo led the desperate Japanese war machine to unleash 2,800 aircraft in kamikaze attacks, and with them the lives of 4,000 airmen (kamikazes and their fighter escorts) were lost. The kamikazes sank 36 US Navy ships, damaged 368 others, killed 4,907 sailors, and wounded 4,874 more. Relatively unknown are the rocket-propelled Ohka kamikaze aircraft that were carried under the wing of a G4M2 Betty mothership and used operationally.

Acknowledgments

My lifelong hobby has been Second World War aerial combat and over the past 45 years I collected more than 27,000 books and magazines, along with hundreds of reels of microfilm on the subject. I probably have nearly every book written on Second World War aviation and complete collections of every aviation magazine published since 1939. Also included in my collection are hundreds of aviation unit histories; intelligence reports; pilot, crew, flight, and training manuals; and technical, structural, and maintenance manuals for aircraft ordnance, armament, engines, and equipment. My 2 million-page microfilm collection includes vintage intelligence reports; hundreds of USAF, USN and USMC group and squadron histories and After Combat Reports; complete Japanese Monograph series; complete US Strategic Bombing Surveys as well as complete USAF Historical Studies. I have made many multi-day expeditions to various military libraries, museums, and photo depositories with my copy machine and

Author Bill Wolf in his office surrounded by the covers of his 28 (now 30) published books.

camera, accumulating literally reams of information and many thousands of photographs. I also had a photo darkroom where I developed thousands of rare photos from microfilm negatives. But, as I am 83 I needed to find a good home for all my 'stuff' described above. During October 2023, I donated my 27,000-book Second World War aviation and air combat library and my entire extensive autograph, lithograph, model aircraft, and memorabilia collection to the National Museum of WWII Aviation in Colorado Springs.

For the twenty-ninth time, thanks also go to my persevering wife, Nancy, who allowed me to spend many hours researching and writing, and patiently (mostly) waited while I browsed bookstores and visited air museums in search of new material and photos.

Photos: Much of the information and many of the photos and drawings were gathered from the Albert F. Simpson Historical Research Center (AFSHRC) for research for articles I wrote on the V-1 for the March 1978 *Airpower* magazine and for the Ohka, *Suicide Samurai*, for the February 1977 *Wings* magazine. I also amassed many Ohka and kamikaze over Okinawa photos for my book *Death Rattlers: Marine Squadron VMF-323 Over Okinawa*. Many of the Japanese photos and drawings in my collection were gathered and shared by my friend and acknowledged Japanese Second World War aircraft and air combat expert Jim Lansdale. I was fortunate to find a folder and photos on the Fi 103 Reichenberg and Me 328 during one of my visits to the National Museum of the United States Air Force (NMUSAF) Research Center. Some of the included photos are not of the best quality because of their age and sources, especially those copied from microfilm and from sixty to eighty-five-year-old contemporary publications from my library, but they were used because of their importance to this narrative.

Photo Credits

AFSHRC: Albert F. Simpson Historical Research Center
JMSDF: Japanese Maritime Self-Defense Force
LoC: Library of Congress
NARA: National Archives
NMUSAF: National Museum of the US Air Force Research Center
PASM: Pima Air and Space Museum
SNASM: Smithsonian National Air & Space Museum
TAIU: Technical Air Intelligence Unit
USAF: United States Air Force
USAAF: United States Army Air Force
USAGF: United States Army Ground Forces
USMC: United States Marine Corps
USN: United States Navy

Introduction

A composite aircraft consists of a larger mother aircraft carrying a smaller parasite that takes off and flies initially as a single aircraft, with the parasite able to separate in flight and continue as an independent aircraft to either conduct its own assigned mission or support the primary mission of the carrier. The first military aircraft to prove the composite concept was the large Felixstowe Porte Baby flying boat carrying the smaller Bristol Scout, which was attached to the Baby's upper fuselage at the wing junction. On 17 May 1916, the incongruously named Baby carried the Scout aloft and released it, with the Scout making a successful landing back at base.

Between the world wars, US Navy composite experiments used the giant *Los Angeles*, *Akron*, and *Macon* airship/biplane composites. Both the *Akron* and *Macon* airships featured internal aircraft hangars opening to a bay on the underside of the hull through which protecting or reconnaissance Curtis F9C Sparrowhawk biplane fighters could be launched and then recovered using a large mechanical arm and sling assembly known as a 'trapeze'. The aircraft were fitted with docking hooks to attach themselves to the trapeze mechanism so they could be retrieved and stored in the hangar. Both airships were destroyed in weather-related accidents.

The Zveno was a military composite developed by aviation engineer Vladimir Vakhmistrov for the Soviet Union during the late 1930s. It consisted of a Tupolev TB-1 or TB-3 heavy

Felixstowe Porte Baby flying boat carrying the smaller Bristol Scout. (*NARA*)

US Navy Airship *Akron* carrying a Curtis F9C Sparrowhawk fighter on its trapeze. (*USN*)

bomber mothership and two to five Polikarpov I-5 or I-16 biplane fighter parasites. Depending on the specific Zveno variant, the fighters were either launched with the mothership or docked in flight and were able to refuel from the bomber. The ultimate composite was a Zveno-SPB employing a TB-3 and two Polikarpov I-16s, each carrying two 550lb (250kg) bombs, which were successfully used operationally against targets in Romania during the initial phases of the German–Soviet War.

Like all 'exotic' enemy air weapons developments during the Second World War, primarily those of the Nazi regime, manned composite suicide weapons carried by a mother bomber aroused Allied interest at the end of the war. Of particular interest were two manned composite aircraft: the parasite German Fi 103R Reichenberg, the manned version of the V-1 'buzz bomb' carried by a mothership Heinkel He 111, which did not enter combat, and the Japanese Ohka parasite rocket kamikaze, carried by a Betty bomber mothership, a composite that did see combat.

Zveno-SPB composite employing a TB-3 and two Polikarpov I-16s. (*NARA*)

Part I

German Manned Parasite Suicide Aircraft

Chapter One

Me 328 Manned Parasite Suicide Aircraft, Reichenberg Precursor

Development and Testing

Sometime during 1941, Messerschmitt began the Me 328 design as Projekt P.1073 to fulfil the role of an inexpensive parasite bomber escort using Argus As 014 pulsejet engines. Since the pulsating engine did not produce static thrust for self-take-off, the Me 328 escort was to be carried by and launched from a modified Heinkel He 177 or Junkers Ju 388 heavy bomber mothership then under development, either by tow or from a launch apparatus installed on the bomber's fuselage or underwing. Messerschmitt emphasized that the Me 328 would be particularly inexpensive, with the projected cost of four being produced for the cost of one Bf 109!

On 31 March 1942, Messerschmitt submitted designs for three basic variants each of the Me 328A fighter and Me 328B fighter-bomber for consideration:

> Me 328A-1, armed with two 20mm MG151 guns, Me 328A-2, armed with two MG151, two 30mm MK 103 guns and having a larger wing area, as well as the Me 328A-3, resembling the previous A-2, but having equipment for refuelling in the air. Me 328B-1, B-2, and B-3, armed with bombs weighing 1,100/2,200/3,086lb (500/1,000/1,400kg), respectively.

The Junkers Ju 388 was a late-war, multi-role, twin-engine bomber based on the Ju 88 airframe, being intended for high-altitude operation as a highly advanced reconnaissance aircraft. (*Author's collection*)

The Heinkel He 177 *Greif* (Griffin) was a twin-engine, long-range heavy bomber whose introduction to combat operations was delayed significantly by both problems with the development of its engines and frequent changes to its intended combat role. (*Author's collection*)

The Heinkel He 274 four-engine variant of the He 177 was purpose-designed for high-altitude operations. A prototype was captured and refurbished by the French and carried the SNCOSA SO.M1 parasite aircraft circa 1946. (*Author's collection*)

Me 328 scale model used for wind tunnel testing. (*NMUSAF/ Messerschmitt AG*)

Later in 1942, after initial scale model wind tunnel testing, two viable glider prototype variants were developed and ready for testing: the Me 328A fighter and the Me 328B fighter-bomber versions. To be cost-effective, the Me 328 airframe would be only slightly modified between the two variants and the design kept small enough to still be considered as a parasite fighter. The project received low priority as the Luftwaffe leadership believed that the war could be won without these 'eccentricities' as at the time the war was going well on all fronts and Allied bombing of the Third Reich remained at a small, ineffective scale.

Test flights finally began during the autumn of 1943 at the Hörsching Airbase near Linz, Austria. The Dornier Do 217E twin-engine, medium-bomber mothership was allocated to carry the Me 328 glider parasite, which had measuring instruments installed. It was mounted in *Mistelschlepp* (Mistletoe) dorsal fuselage configuration on two struts; the forward struts supported the Me 328 under its wing roots while the rear strut supported its tail. During testing the Me 328 was launched at 9,842 to 19,685ft (3,000 to 6,000m). To simulate the mass of fuel and combat armament and equipment, the glider parasites were loaded with on-board water ballast, which was jettisoned before landing. During the flights, controllability issues were revealed but considering the Me 328's mission, control was considered sufficient.

Mounting the Me 328 on the Do 217E-5

(*Author's model*)

(*NMUSAF/Messerschmitt AG*)

(*NMUSAF/Messerschmitt AG*)

(*NMUSAF/Messerschmitt AG*)

Famed aviatrix and test pilot Hanna Reitsch conducted a successful test programme at DFS Hörsching, flying the two glider prototypes at altitudes between 10,000 and 20,000ft (3,048–6,096m), by using a Do 217E bomber to carry the unpowered aircraft aloft. Reitsch found that, regarding the requirement for the Me 328 to be flown as a glide bomb, it exhibited good vision, manoeuvrability, and stability. Even with its short wingspan, tests demonstrated that the Me 328 had good stability and controllability in the range of speeds from 86 to 452mph (140 to 730kmph). Ground launches, using both cable-type catapults and rocket-assisted carriages on rails, were also successful. The aircraft's 'satisfactory' performance led to a proposal to build as many as 1,000 for use as disposable suicide bombers to be flown by volunteers from a projected suicide squadron. The next step was to test a pulsejet-powered version.

While Me 328 glider testing continued slowly, Dr-Ing. (Professor) Walter Georgii of the Deutsche Forschungsanstalt für Segelflug (DFS/German Research Institute For Sailplane Research) and gliding specialist Heinz Kensche, DFS Technical Director of the Me 328 programme, met Reitsch to evaluate the technical and tactical aspects of the type in relation to her plan for a suicide aircraft.

There were two Me 328 glider prototypes: the Me 328A fighter (shown) and the Me 328B fighter-bomber versions. (*NMUSAF/Messerschmitt AG*)

Hanna Reitsch conducted a successful test programme at DFS Hörsching, flying both glider prototypes by using a Do 217E bomber to carry the unpowered aircraft aloft and then landing on its skids. (*NMUSAF/ Messerschmitt AG*)

After completing his university degree in 1913, Georgii specialised in academic meteorology and from 1926 onward concentrated on aviation meteorology. During the 1930s he became interested in glider aircraft and headed the German Research Institute for Gliding (DFS), which he developed into one of Germany's largest aviation research institutes. Besides heading the DFS, Georgii was one of the four directors of the influential German Aeronautical Research Council. In this role he was able to convene a panel of aircraft radio, navigation, explosives, and design experts, and, importantly, representatives from the Luftwaffe and Reichsluftfahrtministerium (RLM/Reich Aviation Ministry), the Transportation Ministry's successor, to further discuss Reitsch's plan to form a squadron of suicide volunteers and their proposed aircraft.

Professor Walter Georgii, Hanna Reitsch, and German gliding pioneer and sailplane designer Wolf Hirst visited South America during January 1934, to study thermal conditions, and take part in the international sailplane competition (seen here in Rio de Janeiro). (*Author's collection*)

Heinz Kensche. (*Author's collection*)

Heinz Kensche, a mechanical engineer and aircraft construction engineer, was initially employed by the Reich Ministry of Aviation (RLM), where he served as a test pilot and was mutually responsible for the certification of all mass-produced gliders. Later, in this position at the RLM, Kensche would become involved in the testing of the Fi 103R (V-1), the manned V-1.

During the evaluation meeting it was determined that the suicide Me 328 was to carry a 2,000lb (907kg) bomb or torpedo in its nose, which was to be steered into the water at an appropriate angle so that the torpedo or bomb would explode directly under the keel of an enemy warship. A twin Argus As 014 pulsejet-powered Me 328 was to be tested but this powered version was still in the late developmental stage at the DFS, although two glider prototypes were available. The meeting members concluded that since the glider

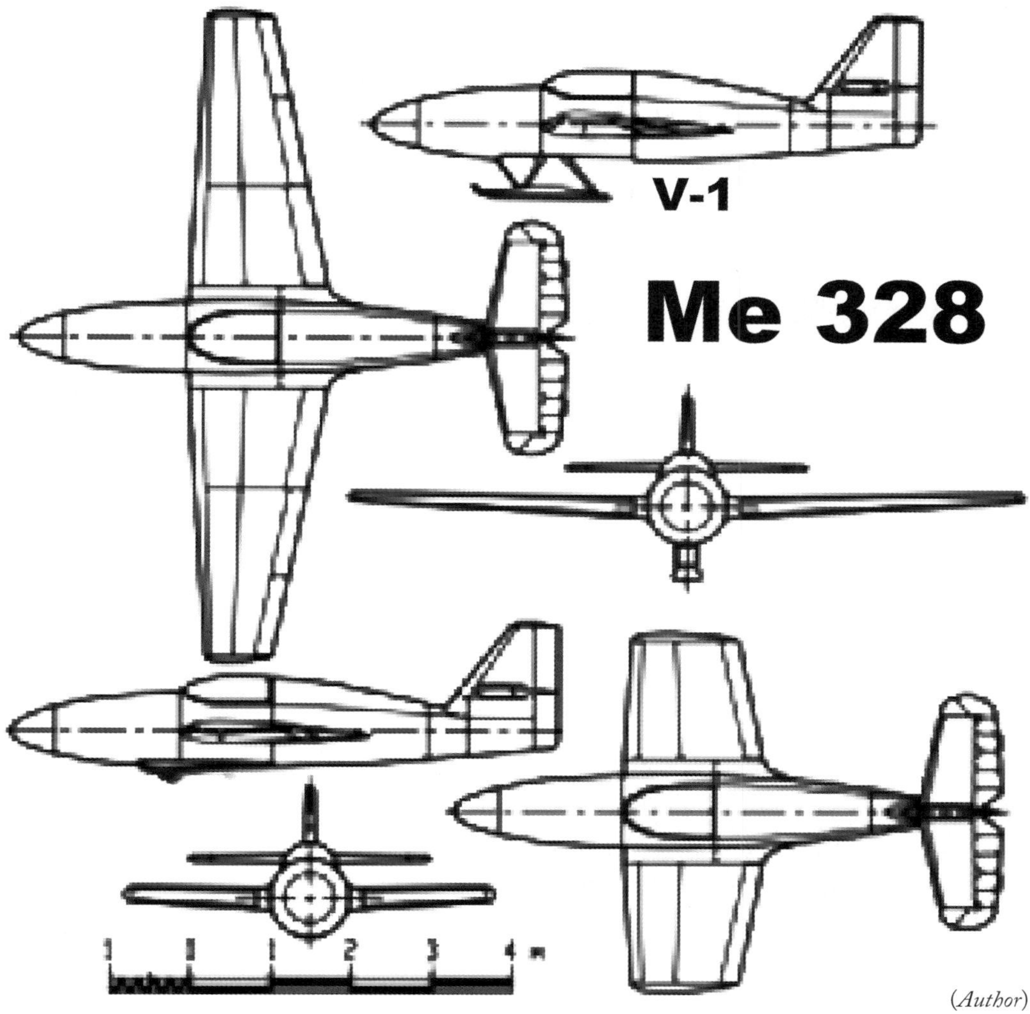

(*Author*)

aircraft were available, valuable development and construction time could be bypassed and that a suicide squadron seemed to be operationally viable.

Glider manufacturer Jacobs-Schweyer Flugzeugbau GmbH of Darmstadt built the seven Me 328 prototypes, V1 to V7. In 1938 Hans Jacobs designed the classic Weihe, which would become the pre-eminent performance sailplane of its time, winning many championships, setting many records, and extending its dominance post-war with a Focke Wulf-built version. Jacobs was also known for his design of the DFS 230 military troop-carrying glider used in the Battle of Fort Ében-Émael.

The Me 328 prototypes were powered by two Argus As 014 pulsejets installed on the rear of the fuselage for ground-based launching without having to rely on a tow or carrying aircraft. This was the same pulsejet engine used in the German V-1 flying bomb and will be described in detail next with the Reichenberg manned V-1 version. It was intended for use as a fighter aircraft version, to be armed with two nose-mounted 20mm MG 151/20 cannon. However, during static testing it soon became apparent that excessive engine vibration, the same problem that was to plague the early development of the V-1 flying bomb, could possibly cause the Me 328 pilot to lose control or the aircraft to disintegrate during the rapid acceleration of an assisted ground launch. It became apparent that the relocation of the pulsejets was necessary, and they were moved to underwing consoles fastened by lifting brackets with shock absorption. This version was to be air-launched but there is no reliable information available substantiating air-launched testing of the Argus-powered version or any vibration reduction during static testing.

Despite the continued vibration problems of the pulsejet version, a manned unpowered variant was suggested for the suicide aircraft role equipped with a nose-mounted 2,000lb (907kg) explosive payload. It was to be carried to the target area on the back of a Dornier Do 217E-5 and be released in a dive at speeds of up to 452mph (730kmph) to crash the target. The pilot was to direct his aircraft to the target, release the rear fuselage, and bail out, which probably was unlikely and so it was synonymous to a suicide mission.

During late 1943, flight tests of the Messerschmitt Me 328 V3, the prototype of the future Me 328A, the fighter-bomber version, carried on a Do 217E began at Hörsching-Linz airfield. During the testing, the Do 217E entered a shallow dive at 18,000ft to expedite the ignition of the two experimental Argus VSR-7 pulsejets attached to both sides of the fuselage of the prototype. After the launch, the Argus engines quickly lost thrust and were unable to maintain altitude until descending to 9,000ft, when they returned to normal. Ensuing tests established that engines were only effective when the parasite was flying at relatively low altitudes and speeds, causing the RLM to determine that the Me 328 was unqualified as a fighter. Consequently, Fieseler used the new series of VSR-9a pulsejets to power the V-1 missiles. Mass production of 32,000 engines of this model, officially called Argus As 109-014, completely monopolised the manufacturer's resources, but research to improve the performance of pulsejets would continue until the end of the war. The Argus As 014 will be described in detail as part of the Reichenberg description.

Description of the Proposed Me 328 Production Version

The Me 328 was to be an inexpensive, relatively simple, small aircraft, designed with more effort to further reduce the amount of metal in series manufacture. The small fuselage frame was welded from steel pipes, to which the wing, landing devices, pilot armour plates, as well as wooden nose and tail sections were attached. The fuselage skin was a glued wooden veneer and reinforced with plywood frames and pine stringers. The wooden keel was glued intact with the fuselage.

The high-mounted trapezoidal solid wood wing was attached to either side of the cockpit walls. Both the leading and trailing edges exhibited some sweep, giving the wings a tapered aspect. Each wing displayed dihedral (upward angle) away from the fuselage and were equipped with ailerons and metal flaps, which were fixed in three positions: flight (0 degrees), take-off (15–20 degrees) and landing (50 degrees). The ailerons had a Duralumin frame and linen cladding. Automatic slats were installed on the outer parts of the wing, behind the engines. The wing skin above the engines was protected from overheating

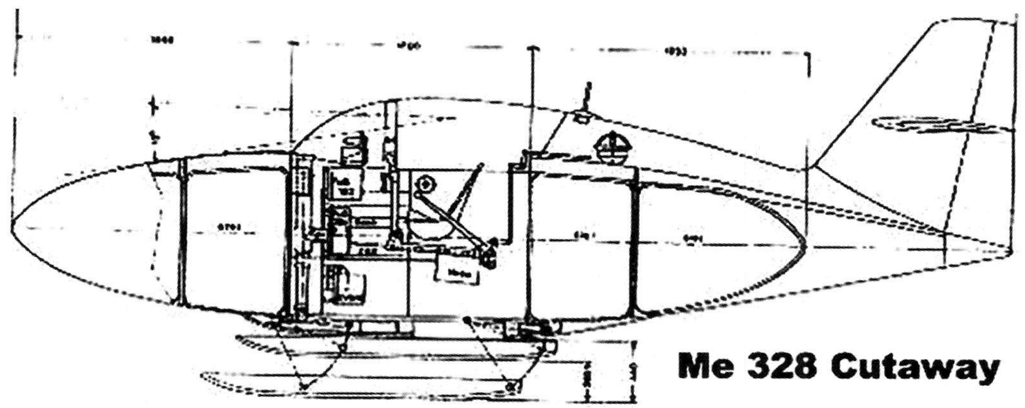

(*NMUSAF/Messerschmitt AG*)

by asbestos thermal insulation. The short empennage included a rounded vertical tailfin with small horizontal planes offset to either fin side. The vertical tail fin was swept only along the leading edge, while the empennage base swept upwards towards the tail fin. The metal stabiliser was commandeered unchanged by Messerschmitt from its Bf 109.

The pilot sat in a cockpit covered by a framed, multi-piece canopy behind rudimentary controls and instruments: compass, speedometer, altimeter, air horizon and fuel gauge. The electrical system provided power to the cockpit equipment, the fuel pumps, and the release of the landing ski. A raised spine along the top of the fuselage made rearward vision rather poor but other perspectives were mostly considered as good. Frontal pilot protection was provided by armour plates 0.6in (15mm) thick and 10–11.8in (255–300mm) wide, separating the cockpit from the fuel compartment, as well as a 3.15in (80mm) windshield with armoured glass. Another 0.6in (15mm) thick armour plate with a headrest protected the pilot from behind. Since it was impossible to install an ejection seat into the small cockpit, pyrobolts (also called explosive bolts) were provided to jettison the aircraft's tail to facilitate the pilot's emergency escape. Just a few seconds before impacting the target, the pilot blasted off the tail section, fell out of the cockpit, and opened his parachute.

The landing gear was a steel skid called a ski by the Germans. (*NMUSAF/Messerschmitt AG*)

The landing gear was a steel skid, called a ski in German literature, and had a shortened shock absorber taken from the landing gear of the Focke-Wulf Fw 200C transport/bomber. For take-off in tow, the ski allowed the suspension of the bomb between the split ski runners. When perched on top of the mother aircraft's fuselage,

To cushion the hard landings, a shortened shock absorber taken from the landing gear of the Focke-Wulf Fw 200C transport/bomber was installed. (*NMUSAF/Messerschmitt AG*)

the ski had the bomb suspended directly on it. The ski was released electrically but had an emergency manual release. The tail was protected during landing by a small extension installed in a half-recessed position at the bottom of the tail compartment.

The aircraft was to be propelled by two 660lb thrust (each) Argus As 014 pulsejets that displayed a bulbous forward compartment and a smooth tubular rear housing underslung along each wing, extending out past the wing trailing edges. The pulsejets were supplied fuel from two Duralumin 132-gallon (500-litre) gas tanks in front of the cockpit and by two of the same tanks located behind the cockpit. These engines were originally planned to be mounted on a pylon on the sides of the fuselage behind the wing with the exhaust pipe extending beyond the tail unit. Because of the vibration of the pulsating engines during operation, this plan was shortly abandoned as the issue created too much distress on the wooden structure of the tail section. It was then decided to install the engines under the wing using pyrobolts to jettison the pulsejets in case of emergency. Initial ground tests were conducted using an early Argus As 014 pulsejet placed under the wings of Me 328V.

To assist air launching using a mothership, it was proposed to use accelerator engines to increase the parasite's acceleration immediately after uncoupling, and then for continued flight it was proposed to install ramjet engines at the ends of the wings to assist the pulsejets. Alternative methods of launch were also proposed, including the Madelung KL 12 catapult, or a launch trolley with solid-fuel rocket boosters manufactured by Rheinmetall Borsig Lippisch.

Early Tests Using the Argus As 014 Pulsejet

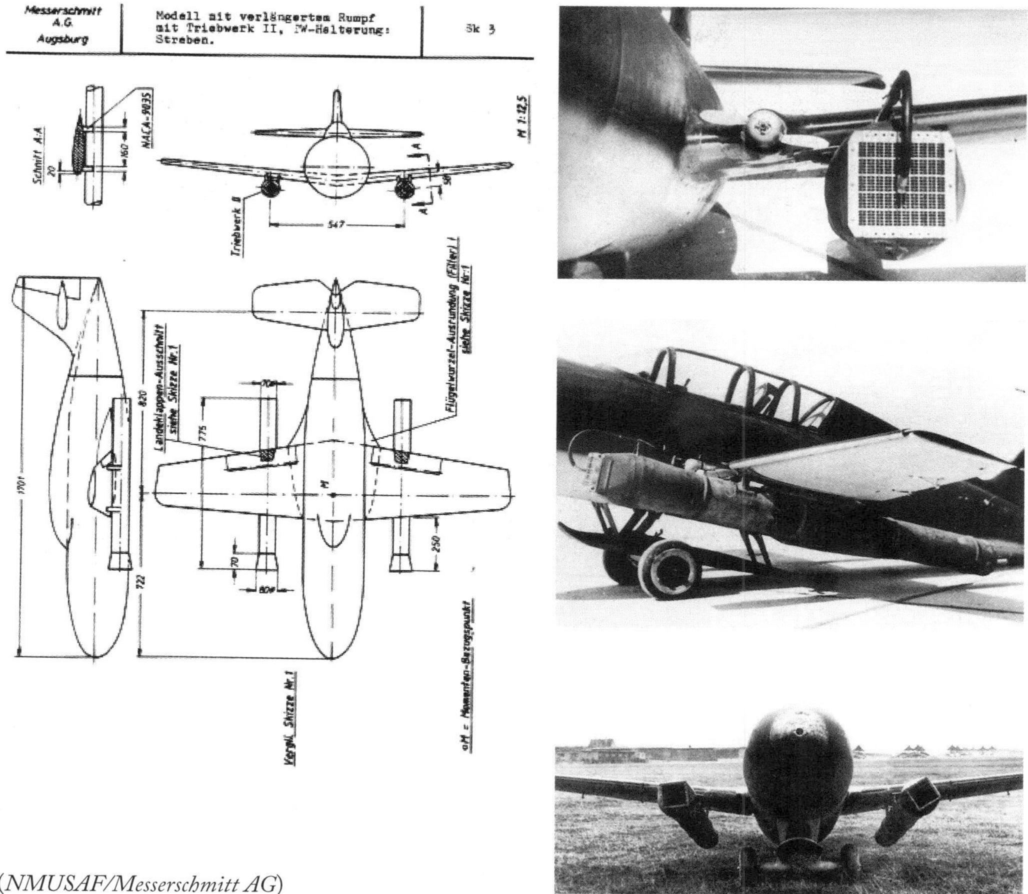

(NMUSAF/Messerschmitt AG)

Proposed Versions

As the Me 328 escort fighter concept faltered, the main efforts were shifted to the creation of a fighter-bomber version that could get close to the target at low altitude and high constant speed, strike, and afterward, if necessary, become a lightweight fighter. Both versions were drawing board proposals that led to other designs.

There are unsubstantiated reports of the Me 328A being proposed as a parasite to be part of the intrinsic defence system of the optimistically planned 'Amerika' super bombers to be carried by or towed behind either an Me 264 or a Ju 390 to attack New York City. After release, the Me 328A pilot would bomb Manhattan and then ditch in the sea, hopefully near a waiting U-boat.

The Me 328B was a proposed bomber variant. The Me 328 V1 to V7 were seven pre-production prototypes of the Me 328B, built by Jacobs-Schweyer, to be powered by Argus As 014 pulsejet engines.

A Me 328C fighter derivative was to have been utilised as a ground-attack fighter powered by a Junkers Jumo 004 turbojet, whose use was to finally solve the Argus vibrations problem.

The Jumo 004 was proposed to be installed inside the fuselage tail, but this meant that a very expensive engine would be combined with an inexpensive disposable airframe, which would have mediocre aerodynamics when powered with this engine. Therefore, this option was abandoned, and the Jumo's priority was wisely given to the excellent Messerschmitt Me 262 jet fighters.

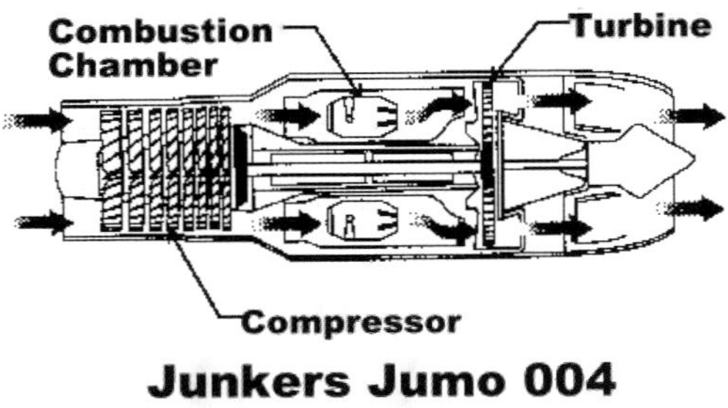

Junkers Jumo 004 turbojet. (*NMUSAF*)

While the Me 328A and 328C were all proposed versions, there were other proposals that did not receive a 328 letter suffix. These proposals would have been low-cost point defence interceptors but did not leave the drawing board stage, as shown on the Messerschmitt factory drawings.

Other late Me 328 designs were a navalised fighter with folding wings to be carried in a large cannister on the deck of a U-boat and be launched from there. There was also a projected high-speed reconnaissance version with four Argus engines, two engines mounted under the wings and two on the sides of the fuselage in the tail.

Me 328V prototype of the Me 328B with standardised pre-production As 014 pulsejets. (*NMUSAF/ Messerschmitt AG*)

Me 328B Fighter-Bomber Production Model

Although the Me 328 glider version's test flight performance was satisfactory, in anticipation of accepting rather than resolving the vibration problems, the first pre-production aircraft was to be the Me 328B fighter-bomber, with mass production recommended for April 1944. However, with war materials and manpower in short supply and then with the future Jacobs-Schweyer Me 328 production facilities at Darmstadt damaged in air raids, the Me 328 programme essentially ended by the middle of 1944, with the pulsejet vibration issue never fully resolved.

Me 328B: Specifications
Crew: 1
Length: 23ft 6in (7.17m)
Wingspan: 22ft 8in (6.9m)
Height: 5ft 3in (1.6m)
Wing Area: 91 sq ft (8.5 sq m)
Empty Weight: 3,527lb (1,600kg)
Gross Weight: 9,921lb (4,500kg)
Powerplant: 2 × Argus As 014 pulsejet, 660lb thrust each

Performance
Maximum Speed: 500mph (805kmph)
Range: 301 miles (485km)

Armament
1,102.3lb (500kg) explosive warhead
2 × nose-mounted 20mm MG 151/20 cannon (proposed)

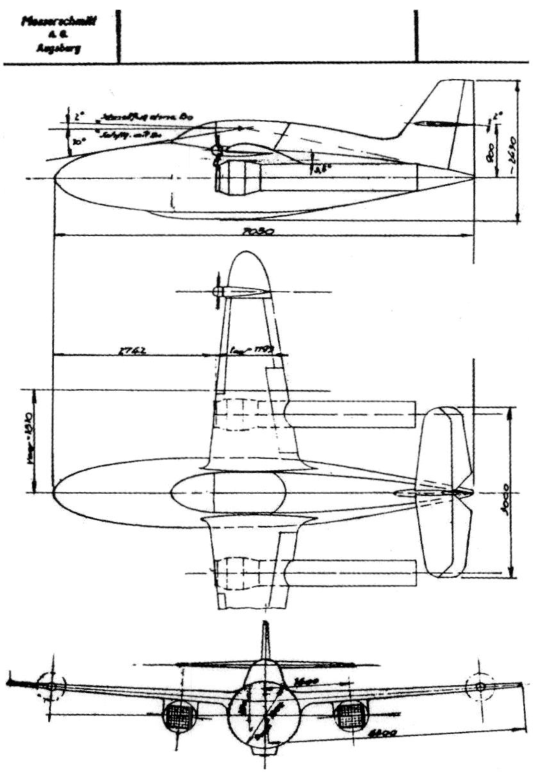

Proposed Me 328B. (*NMUSAF/Messerschmitt AG*)

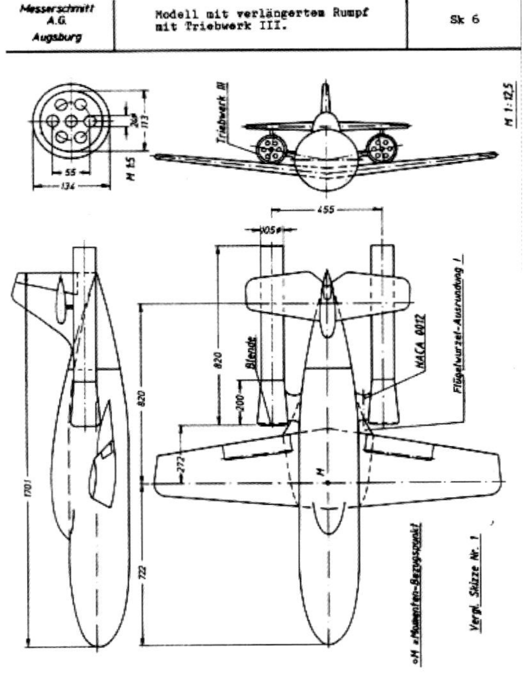

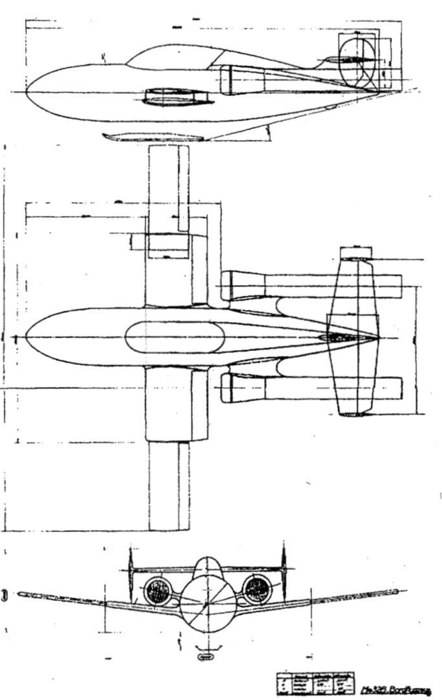

Two As 014 pulsejets mounted on pylons attached to the rear fuselage single-tail empennage. (*NMUSAF/ Messerschmitt AG*)

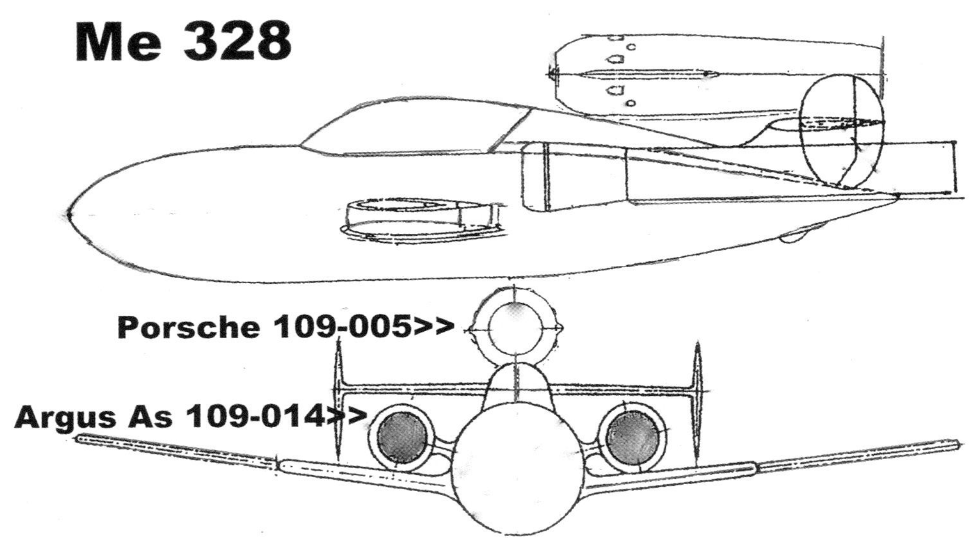

Dorsal Porsche 109-005 turbojet and two Argus engines mounted to the side of the fuselage refitted with a new twin-tail empennage. Another proposal had a new twin-tail design and was to use the proposed Porsche 109-005 located in the same dorsal rear V-1-type location. (*Drawing adapted from NMUSAF/Messerschmitt AG*)

Variants

Me 328 Glider: Two prototype glider aircraft built by Jacobs-Schweyer. Carried piggy-back on a Dornier Do 217 and released for flight test, at times by Hanna Reitsch.

Me 328 V1 to V7: Seven pre-production prototypes of the Me 328B, built by Jacobs-Schweyer, powered by Argus As 014 pulsejet engines.

Me 328A: The proposed parasite fighter intended for carriage by the Amerika bomber.

Me 328B: The proposed bomber variant.

Me 328C: Jumo 004-powered fighter derivative proposed in 1944.

Chapter Two

Fi 103R Reichenberg: Manned Suicide V-1 Parasite

Section One: The Conventional Fi 103 Flying Bomb: Manned Reichenberg Precursor

The first of Germany's 'V-weapons' to be launched on England, the Fieseler Fi 103 was a small pilotless aircraft powered by an Argus pulsejet engine and carrying a 1-ton explosive warhead. From 13 June 1944 when the first V-1 'buzz bomb' was launched against London, until 29 March 1945, when its last launch site was overrun, the Nazis sent 9,500 to 10,000 V-1s at Britain and approximately 2,500 at Belgium.

Design, Development, and Testing

During 1935, powerplant engineer Paul Schmidt and aeronautical engineer and academic Dr-Ing. Georg Hans Madelung, Director of the Deutsche Akademie der Luftfahrtforschung (German Aviation Research Academy), proposed an innovative design for a pulsejet engine-powered flying bomb to the Luftwaffe and received a development contract from the RLM. Meanwhile, while at the Argus Motoren Company, Dr-Ing. Fritz Gosslau assisted in the development and construction of the Argus As 410 and 411 air-cooled inverted V-12 light aircraft engine and then developed a remote-controlled target drone, the FZG 43 (Flakzielgerat-43), in early 1939. During November 1939, Gosslau proposed a motorised, wing-mounted, radio-navigated missile using a pulsejet engine that provided a range of several hundred kilometres with high accuracy. During 1940, Schmidt and Argus began the development of a pulsejet engine, which was finalised as the Argus As 109-014 during 1941. On 27 February 1942, using his previous experience developing the FZG 43 drone, Gosslau joined Robert Lusser in developing the design of the P35 Erfurt, powered by a pulsejet above the tail, and gyroscopically controlled, which was to be the basis for the future V-1.

Dr-Ing. Fritz Gosslau. (*AFSHRC*)

Lusser was an accomplished aeronautical designer and joining Messerschmitt in 1933, where he was instrumental in the design of the Messerschmitt Bf 108 Taifun (Typhoon), a single-engine sport and touring aircraft, which was the basis of the company's renowned Bf 109 fighter aircraft. By 1934, Lusser was head of Messerschmitt's design bureau and in charge of the Bf 110 heavy twin-engine fighter project. Lusser left Messerschmitt in 1938 and joined Heinkel, where he designed the He 280, the first German jet fighter, which was rejected by the RLM in favour of the Me 262, and the pioneering He 219 night fighter, which also was rejected by the RLM in August 1941 as being too complex to order into production because of its many innovations. Ernst Heinkel immediately dismissed Lusser and resubmitted a simplified He 219 design that ultimately went into limited production. After Lusser was discharged by Heinkel he was hired by Fieseler.

Dr-Ing. Robert Lusser. (*AFSHRC*)

Lusser and Gosslau submitted their refined P35 Erfurt design to the Luftwaffe on 5 June 1942. The impressive specifications included a range of 186 miles (300km), an impressive maximum speed of 435mph (700kmph), and the capability of delivering a 1,100lb (500kg) warhead. On 19 June 1942, Argus and Fieseler delegates met at the Air Ministry with RLM head Field Marshal Erhard Milch, who ordered development to proceed with the highest priority under the inhouse RLM designation Fieseler Fi 103; Fieseler made responsible for the airframe, Argus for the pulsejet engine, and Askania for the guidance system. Another reason for the Luftwaffe to assign a high priority to the flying bomb was their rivalry with the Wehrmacht (Army), which at this time had just begun test launches of its radical, rocket-powered A-4 ballistic missile, the future V-2.

Testing commenced at Peenemünde, the joint Wehrmacht/Luftwaffe experimental facility on the island of Usedom, on the Baltic coast, where the A-4 (future V-2) was also

A replica of a Fieseler Fi 103 flying bomb on a Walter launching ramp in front of the Peenemünde Historical-Technical Museum with a V-2 in the background. The first Fi 103 ground-launch test using a ramp was made at Peenemünde-West on 24 December. (*Peenemünde Archive*)

being developed. By 30 August, Fieseler had completed the first fuselage and wings, but delays postponed the Fi 103's first flight until 10 December, when a four-engine Focke-Wulf Fw 200 Condor dropped an unpowered prototype to test its glide characteristics. The first ground-launch test, using a concrete ramp, was made at Peenemünde-West on 24 December 1942, during which the missile flew 1,000 yards (900m) for sixty seconds. During late 1942 and early 1943, work on the V-1 progressed slowly as its three component manufacturers were completing the design. Production in the German aircraft industry slowed during this time as there was an increase of new, desperately needed, aircraft designs, as well as continued shortages of aircraft raw materials and engines. During 1943 Albert Speer, using his close relationship with Hitler, took control of the RLM from Milch, resulting in an immediate improvement in the aircraft industry. Although production did finally catch up with the Allies in 1944, the RLM could never surmount its raw material and fuel supply shortages, a lack of experienced pilots, technical problems, and shortfalls in the workforce, which relied on slave labour.

In later tests, ranges of 150 miles were realised with accuracies of a half a mile, but only after a long and problem-plagued series of flight tests, during which numerous technical problems with the pulsejet and the Askania guidance system occurred. On 26 May 1943, Germany decided to put both the V-1 and the impressive but expensive and overrated V-2 rocket into production. Although the V-1 was contracted for production, its development and production remained unhurried until autumn 1943, when it was again decided to fast track the V-1's development as Hitler had become infuriated by the heightened Allied bombing of the Fatherland and wished to retaliate with a new 'blitz' on England.

Production

The heavy Allied bombing of Kassel interrupted production of the Fi 103 at the Gerhard Fieseler Werke (GFW), with deliveries held up that delayed its testing of modifications. It was not until early spring 1944 that mass production began, with some parts supplied by the massive Fallersleben Volkswagen factory, which also was under heavy bombing attacks. Consequently, the V-1 was only considered operational by late May 1944 and on 12 June 1944, six days after D-Day, the first V-1 attacks on London were launched.

Gerhard Fieseler Werke (GFW)

The Gerhard Fieseler Werke (GFW), located in Kassel, the largest city in the south-western Germany, was known mostly for its military aircraft built for the Luftwaffe during the Second World War. The company was founded on 1 April 1930 as Fieseler Flugzeugbau Kassel by First World War flying ace and aerobatic champion Gerhard Fieseler. Fieseler had previously been a manager/designer for the Raab-Katzenstein Aircraft Company, but after it declared bankruptcy in 1930, he bought a sailplane factory in Kassel. He soon began building powered sport aircraft but continued to make custom sailplanes for some of Germany's most prominent designers and pilots. In 1934, Fieseler won the World Aerobatics Championship in the F2 Tiger, an aircraft his company had built. The F2 was followed by the highly successful F5, a classic among sports planes. With Fieseler's

Willy Fiedler in the cockpit of his iconic short take-off and landing (STOL) observation and liaison aircraft Fieseler Fi 156 Storch, which was instrumental in the Skorzeny Mussolini rescue. (*Fieseler*)

new prominence, in 1936 his design won an offer over aircraft from both Messerschmitt and Siebel for a new short take-off and landing (STOL) observation and liaison aircraft for the Luftwaffe. Designated the Fieseler Fi 156 Storch (Stork), Fieseler would produce 2,867 during the war and it would gain fame as the aircraft that rescued Mussolini from the Italian Alps. On 1 April 1939 the company name changed to the Gerhard Fieseler Werke GmbH (Gesellschaft mit beschränkter Haftung), similar to a limited liability company (LLC) in the United States. Fieseler's other wartime production at the time would largely consist of building other companies' aircraft under licence, including the Luftwaffe's front-line fighters, the Messerschmitt Bf 109 and Focke-Wulf Fw 190. During 1941, however, a Fieseler project for an unpiloted flying bomb (Fi 103) drew the interest of the RLM. The Fi 103 went into production as the Fieseler FZG 76, the V-1, at the company's Rothwesten Kaserne (Fritz-Erler-Kaserne) factory. Although the Fieseler factories were the target of many Allied air raids, they continued production throughout the war. Following the war, the Storch (manufactured by Mraz in Czechoslovakia and by Morane-Saulnier in France) and the V-1 continued to be produced by foreign companies. Part of the Fieseler factory continued in business for a few years after the war, producing automotive components.

V-1 Etymology

The V-1 (Vergeltungswaffe Eins, or Vengeance Weapon One), was the name given to it by Josef Goebbels' Propaganda Ministry and made popular by *Das Reich* journalist Hans Schwarz Van Berk in June 1944. *Das Reich* was a weekly newspaper founded by Goebbels and had a huge circulation of more than 1.4 million by 1944. The original Air Ministry designation was Fi 103 after its Fieseler (Fi) airframe designer. As an intelligence code,

Fieseler Rothwesten Kaserne (Fritz-Erler-Kaserne) factory before and after Allied bombing. (*Fieseler*)

the Germans named it Flakzielgerät (Flak Target Device) 76 (FZG 76) to deceive Allied intelligence about its purpose. The missile also had the code names of *Kirschkern* (Cherry Stone) in reports by German spies in London to the Abwehr military intelligence service. This name refers to the idea of spitting cherry stones and successively improving the hit accuracy by monitoring the impact points. Powered by a simple but very noisy pulsejet, the British named it the 'buzz bomb'. 'Diver' was its code name as part of the British countermeasures consisting of AA guns, barrage balloons and fighter aircraft. The Germans called it 'Maikäfer' (Maybug), while the Americans in Britain named them 'Doodle Bugs' after a rather large, sometimes 2in-long, native American antlion flying insect species with four membranous wings, often mistaken for dragonflies or damselflies. Contemporary historical British accounts have referred to it as a 'robot bomb'.

Description

The basic mid-wing monoplane Fi 103 V-1 flying bombs were constructed of mild steel, although later long-range, lighter models had a plywood nose cover and wooden wings on a tubular metal spar. The cylindrical fuselage body was 2ft 7in (0.8m) at its greatest body diameter and tapered sharply toward its stern. The fuselage was constructed of six sections shaped from welded 16-gauge mild steel sheet. From nose to tail, it measured 21ft 5in (6.5m) and its overall length (which included its extended tail section with the Argus As 014) was 25ft 4in (7.7m). The operational colours were usually a mottled camouflage pattern of greens and light blue or a green upper fuselage and pulsejet tube with a light blue lower separated by a wavy demarcation. Despite post-war museum reconstructions, there were no Swastikas or Balkenkreuz applied as the V-1 was a weapon not an aircraft.

The fuselage was divided into six compartments individually containing the aluminium alloy nose fairing containing the small air-log propeller for determining range, the magnetic compass, the 1,874lb (855kg) Amatol (mixture of TNT and ammonium nitrate) warhead, the fuel tank, two circular, wire-bound, compressed air bottles for the pneumatic control servos, the autopilot and height- and range-setting controls, and the servo mechanisms controlling the rudder and elevators.

The 17ft 6in wings were attached by sliding the wing panel over the tubular wing spar and then locking it in place with a pin. (*USAGF*)

The 17ft 6in span (5.3m) monoplane wings were located midway on the missile's fuselage, were squared off at their tips and had no ailerons. The wing had a tubular spar and metal ribs covered with plywood sheeting. The wings were attached by sliding the wing panel over the tubular wing spar and then locking it in place with a pin. The tail assembly was conventional, consisting of a horizontal and vertical stabiliser with

FIG. 1.

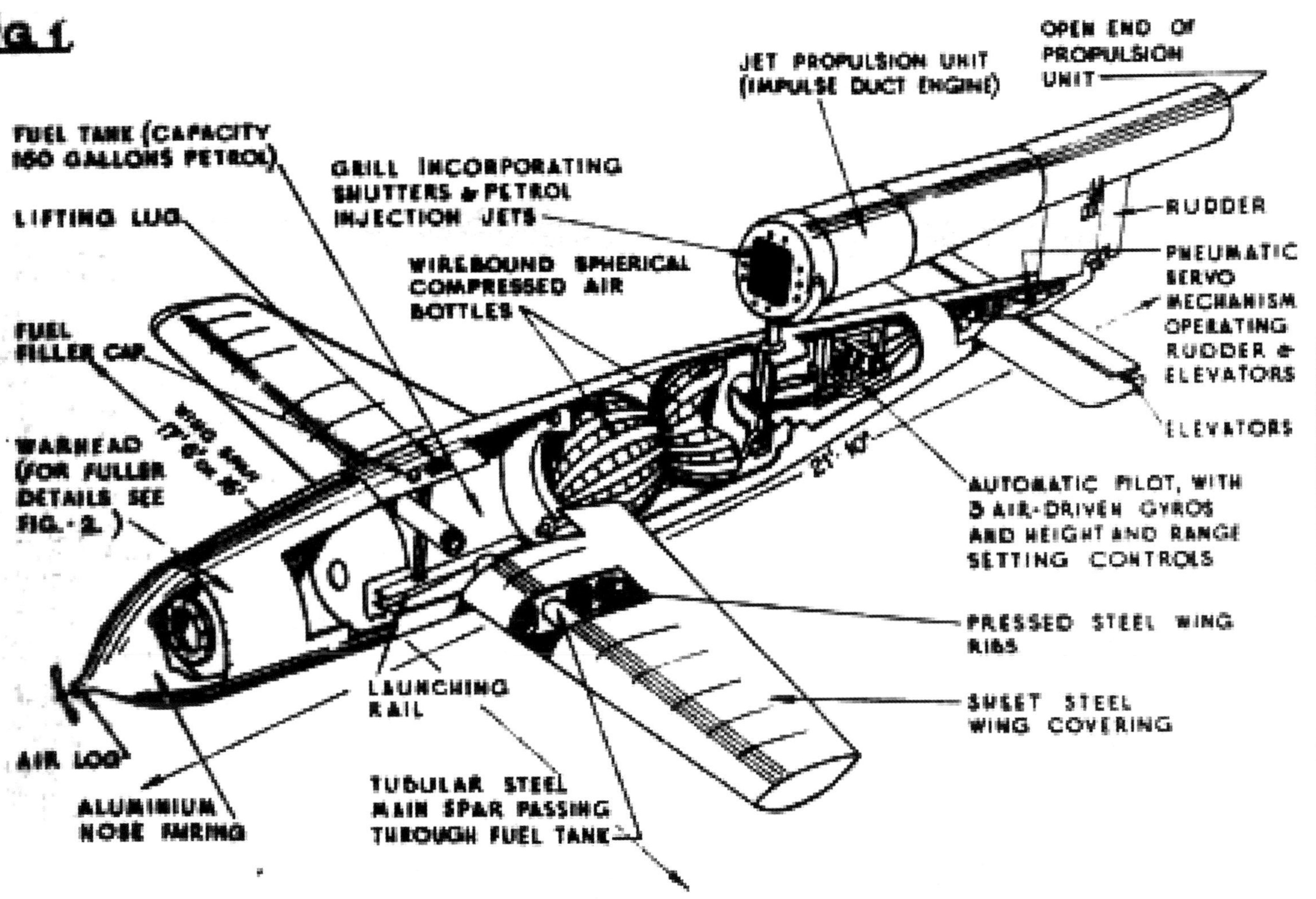

FLYING BOMB - GENERAL ARRANGEMENT | FIG. 1

An odometer (counter) driven by a vane anemometer (propeller) on the V-1's nose tip determined when target area had been reached by the number of revolutions counted. (*USAF*)

a rudder and elevators. The vertical tail did support the Argus pulsejet at a point at the beginning of the tailpipe.

The V-1 did not use a radio-controlled guidance system but had a pre-set system that consisted of a magnetic compass monitoring an automatic pilot, which had a displacement gyro and two rate gyros as its basis. These gyros sent pneumatic signals that were converted to mechanical forces, opening valves for high-pressure compressed air that moved the pistons in the rudder and elevator actuators. The simple autopilot developed by Askania, Berlin, was used to regulate altitude and airspeed. A weighted pendulum system provided fore-and-aft attitude measurement to control pitch, which was damped and stabilised by a gyrocompass. Operating power for the gyroscope platform and the flight control actuators (and also the fuel tank) was provided by two large, spherical, compressed air tanks charged to 150 atmospheres (2,200 psi).

An odometer (counter) driven by a vane anemometer (propeller) on the V-1's nose tip determined, by the number of revolutions, when the target area had been reached, with sufficient accurately for area bombing. Before launch, the counter was set to a value that would reach zero upon the V-1's arrival at the target considering the prevailing wind conditions. With the counter determining how far the missile would fly, it was only necessary to launch the V-1 with the ramp pointing in the approximate direction, and the autopilot controlled the flight. As the missile flew toward the target, the airstream turned the propeller, with every thirty rotations counted down one number on the counter. This counter triggered the arming of the warhead after approximately 37 miles (60km). When the counter reached zero, two detonating bolts were fired in the tail, jamming the linkage between the elevator and servo causing a guillotine-type apparatus to sever the control hoses to the rudder servo, setting the rudder in neutral, locking the elevator in the neutral position, stopping rudder control and deploying two hinged spoilers from the underside of the tailplane. This caused the missile to enter a steep dive, stopping the fuel flow, which stopped the buzzing engine. The sudden silence alerted and triggered fear in those below of the imminent deadly explosion.

Specifications of the Conventional V-1 Fi 103

General Characteristics

Length Fuselage Nose to Tail: 21ft 5in (6.5m)
Length Overall (to end of Argus tailpipe): 25ft 4in (7.7m)
Fuselage Diameter: 2ft 9in
Wingspan: 17ft 6in (5.3m)
Empty weight: 1,360lb (617kg)
Fully loaded weight: 4,750lb (2,155kg)
including fuel: 1,050lb (476kg) and warhead: 1,870lb (848kg)

Performance

Speed: 400mph (640kmph) flying between 2,000 and 3,000ft (600 and 900m)
Speed at Target Approach: 500mph (800kmph)
Range: 160 miles (250km)
Range from air launch at 8,200ft (2,500m): 205 miles (330km)

The Fieseler Flying Bomb is Mated with the Argus Pulsejet

Argus As 014 Pulsejet

Argus Motorenwerke

Argus Motorenwerke was formed in Berlin in 1906 manufacturing auto and boat engines but increasingly focused on the aviation market and by 1910 aero engines were mostly produced. During the First World War Argus produced aero engines for the German army and air corps. After the war, Argus manufactured automobile engines and during 1919 acquired a majority interest in Horch Automobile, a predecessor of the present-day Audi company. In 1926 they resumed aircraft engine design, producing a series of inverted inline and V engines. Although all Argus aero engines were of low horsepower, by the onset of the Second World War they were used extensively in training and light utility aircraft, including the Arado Ar 96 and the Focke-Wulf Fw 189. Most notable (with 28,700 built) of Argus engine designs was the air-cooled, 90-degree cylinder bank-angle, inverted V8 Argus As 10, used in small, short-range reconnaissance and communications aircraft including the Fieseler Fi 156 Storch. However, the company is best known for its Argus As 014 pulsejet, which would be the unique powerplant for the equally unique Fi 103 flying bomb.

Development of the Argus As 014 Pulsejet

Although several pulsejet patents were issued previously to Russian Victor de Karavodine in 1907 and Belgian Georges Marconet in 1909, it was Frenchman René Lorin who wrote well-publicised articles on ram and pulsejet engines between 1907 and 1913 and advocated the development of long-range missiles for bombarding targets 'like Berlin'. Lorin was unable to test his engines as at the time aircraft were unable to fly fast enough for the ram or pulsejet to function properly. The first practical pulsejet design originated in Munich during 1928 when inventor Paul Schmidt, who was familiar with Lorin's work, began work on promising air-breathing jet-propulsion technology with the design of pulsejet engines for aircraft. Without sufficient funding, Schmidt's work progressed slowly but he received a patent on his design in 1931 and conducted experiments at the Munich-Wiesenfeld Airfield with support from the Research Division of the Ministry of Transportation. He constructed a motor with a duct that produced a thrust of 1,000lb (450kg) but it self-destructed after only thirteen minutes of operation. Even so, Schmidt continued to receive support from the Transportation Ministry. In 1935, he and Dr-Ing. Georg Madelung had proposed a 'flying bomb' to be powered by his pulsejet and received a development contract from the RLM. Work proceeded slowly and Schmidt would lose control of his project in 1938 when his pulsejet-powered pilotless bomber project was cancelled by the Air Ministry as the prototype lacked range and accuracy and was expensive to construct. However, Schmidt would be provided additional funding from the Heereswaffenamt (Army Weapons Office), allowing him to continue his work and he established a research group at Munich. Work continued slowly on his promising SR 500 model and its innovative flap valve.

Meanwhile, in 1939, the RLM initiated a second pulsejet programme at the Argus Motorenwerke, under Dr-Ing. Fritz Gosslau. Other German manufacturers were also working on similar pulsejets and flying bombs: the Askania Company, Fieseler's Dr-Ing. Robert Lusser, and the Siemens company, which were all combined to work on the V-1 flying bomb. Initially, unaware of Schmidt's work, Gosslau began the design of a similar pulsejet motor using a flow valve. But the Argus group soon became aware of Schmidt's flap valve advances and in February 1940 Scmidt's pulsejet shutter system design was integrated with Argus' atomised fuel injection system and then was further developed and finally perfected as the Argus As 109-014 (*Pulsationsschubrohres*) in 1940. Argus then pursued its own pulsejet design and there was no further cooperation between Schmidt and Argus, although by 1943 the V-1 pulsejet was known as the Argus-Schmidtrohr, or Argus-Schmidt tube.

Testing

Beginning during January 1941, the pulsejet engine was first tested on a variety of vehicles, including automobiles and an experimental attack boat known as the Tornado. The unsuccessful Tornado prototype was a version of a *Sprengboote*, a boat loaded with explosives, which was guided towards a target vessel during which the driver would hopefully leap out of the back in time not to become a 'Self-Sacrifice Commando'. The Tornado prototype was a noisy underachiever and was cancelled for the more conventional piston-engined powerplant. A prototype Argus VSR-9a engine made its first flight piloted by Flugkapitän Staege while slung below a Luftwaffe biplane training Gotha Go-145 (D-IIWS) on 30 April 1941 at E-Stelle Diepensee. The pulsejet was attached so that it would be close to the fuselage underside during take-off and landing and could be swung down into place when in use. The aircraft was fitted with a sheet-metal cover over its fuselage bottom to protect it from the pulsejet's very hot exhaust. The first V-1 prototype

The Gotha Go 145 (D-IIWS) training biplane with the Argus As 014 engine suspended from the fuselage for the first airborne ignition test on 30 April 1941. (*AFSHRC*)

was ground-launched from a concrete ramp on 24 December 1942 at Peenemünde-West using its Argus pulsejet for about a minute.

Description

There are three main advantages to using a pulsejet engine. First, its simple mechanism and its basic body made it easy and inexpensive to manufacture. Secondly, it used low-grade fuel. Third, the maintenance was simple and not as complicated as piston or turbojet engines. However, the pulsejet has significant weaknesses, specifically its poor fuel efficiency and very noisy flight.

The first V-1 prototype was ground-launched from a concrete ramp on 24 December 1942 at Peenemünde-West propelled by its Argus pulsejet for about a minute. (*AFSHRC*)

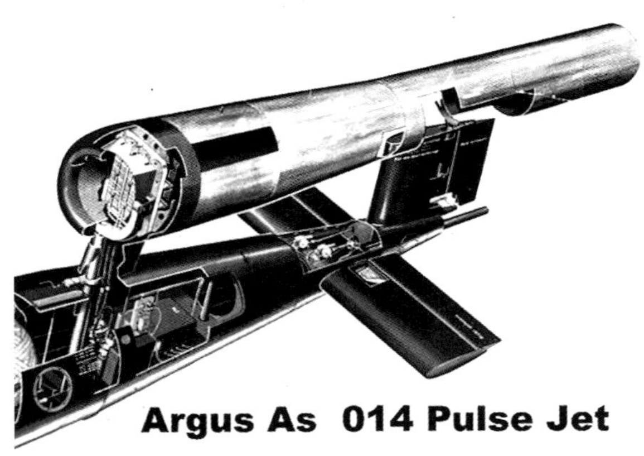

The Argus As 014 Schmidt pulsejets, measuring 25ft 4in (7.7m) long, were fabricated from a sheet of mild steel rolled into a tube. The pulsejet tube with a recessed intake circular grille in front and open exhaust exit at the rear was mounted on top of the rear of the fuselage. The front of the tube had a larger diameter to accommodate the grille, internal flappers, and a combustion chamber with fuel injectors and spark plug, while the rear gradually tapered down to the straight, elongated exhaust. It was comprised of a nacelle (a sheet of mild steel rolled into a tube), 169-gallon (640-litre) fuel tank, fuel jets, flap valve grid, mixing chamber venturi, tail pipe, and a spark plug. At the front of the engine there was a flat spring flap valve grid (shutters) arranged in a cylindrical pattern to match the Argus' air intake, a fuel inlet valve, and an igniter.

The pulsejet did not need a fuel pump because of its pressurised fuel system. Since the pulsejet was elementary, low-grade petrol could be used, as its shutter system was intended for only a one-way flight, having an operational life of approximately one hour. The low-grade fuel created sufficient thrust 660lb (300kg), but was inefficient, as it limited the V-1's range to 150–250 miles (240–400km).

The fuel jets consisted of three banks of atomizers with three nozzles each, which were located ahead of the air inlet valve system and connected to an external source of high-pressure air. Fuel from these nine atomising nozzles mixed with air from the inlet valve system before entering the chamber. A throttle valve, which was connected to the altitude and ram pressure instruments, controlled fuel flow. An effective straight path for the incoming air was provided by Schmidt's ingenious spring-controlled flap valve grid (shutters) system.

Air intake showing shutters with grill behind and three vertical banks of fuel atomisers. (*AFSHRC*)

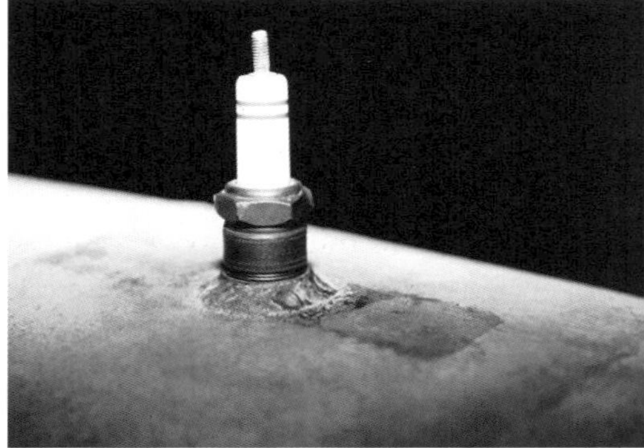

Spark plug. (*AFSHRC*)

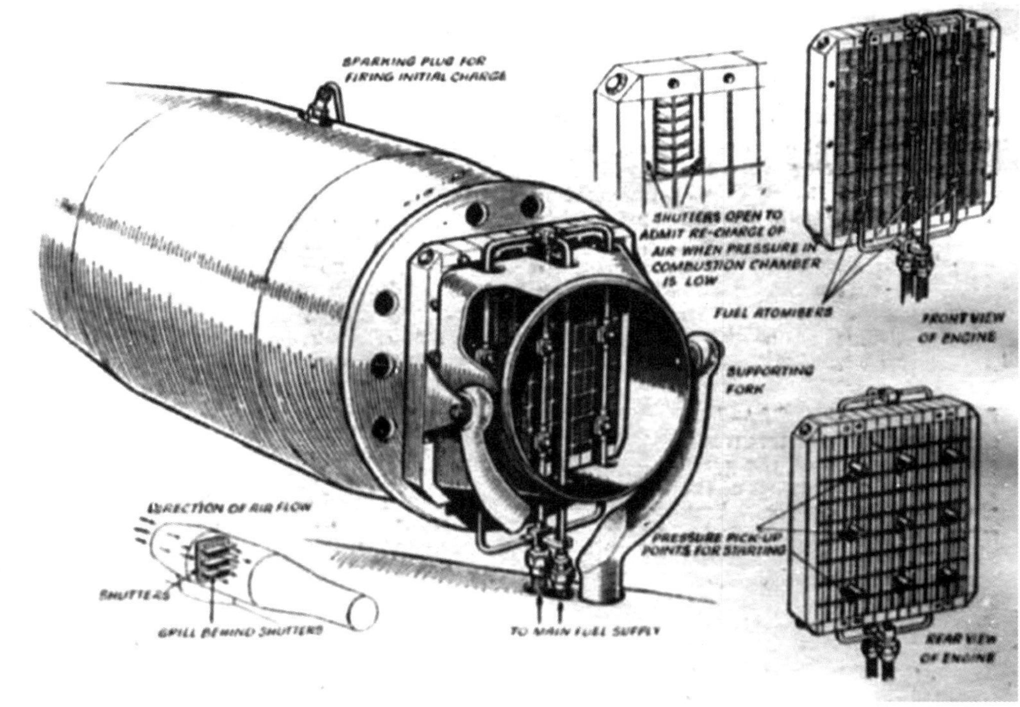

An automotive-type spark plug, located about 2ft 6in (0.75m) behind the shutter system, detonated the acetylene used for ignition. Electricity to the plug was provided from a portable starting unit. Three air nozzles in the front of the pulsejet were connected to an external high-pressure air source, which was used to start the engine. A panel, usually wood, was commonly placed across the end of the tailpipe to prevent the fuel from diffusing and escaping before ignition was complete. Since the V-1's electrical ignition system was needed only to start the engine, it carried no coils or magnetos to power the spark plug once launched and flying.

Contrary to popular belief, the V-1's pulsejet did not need a minimum airspeed of 150mph (241kmph) for operation but could operate after attaining its minimum operating temperature while the V-1 was stationary on its launch ramp. It could operate at zero airspeed due to the character of its intake vane system and acoustically tuned resonant combustion chamber. However, the pulsejet's low static thrust and the very high stall speed of the V-1's wings meant that it could not take off under its own power in a practically short distance, and thus take-off speed was attained by launching from a ground ramp, using a chemical or steam catapult that accelerated the V-1 to 200mph, or from a modified Heinkel He 111 bomber.

Once the pulsejet had been started and the temperature rose to the minimum operating level, the external air hose and connectors were removed, and the resonant tailpipe design kept the pulsejet firing without any further need for the electrical ignition system, which was used only to ignite the engine when starting. Each cycle or pulse began with the

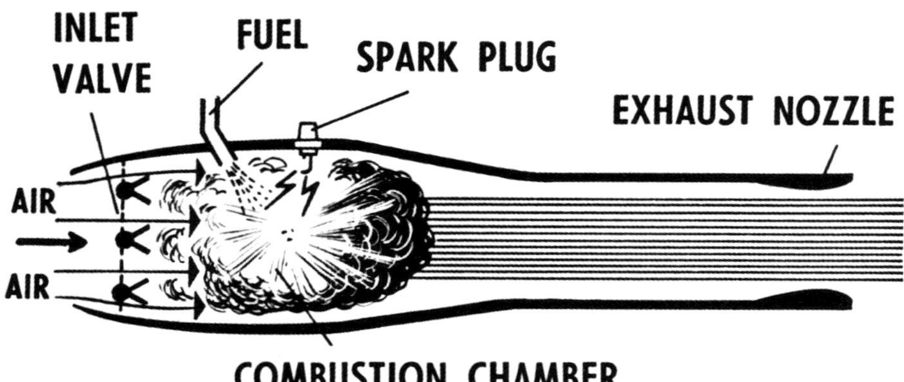

shutters open; with fuel injected behind them and ignited, and the resulting expansion of gases forced the shutters to close. These flaps momentarily closed after each explosion, with the resultant gas partially compressed by the venturis (a short tube with a tapering constriction that affects fluid flow and pressure), with the tapered tail pipe additionally compressing the exhaust gases generating thrust. As the pressure in the engine dropped following each combustion, the shutters reopened and the cycle was repeated, at a rate of 45 to 55 cycles per second, with the resonant frequency of the combustion process being approximately 45Hz. This is the actual low end where sound is more felt than heard (human hearing ranges from 20Hz up to 20,000Hz) and caused the distinctive buzzing sound of its air-breathing pulsejet engine, and thus its 'buzz bomb' tag by those who were under its approach. All was safe until the pulsejet's buzzing stopped and the missile headed downward to its destruction.

Specifications Argus As 014 Pulsejet

General Characteristics
Unit length: 144in (3.66m)
Unit diameter: 22in (0.59m)
Tailpipe length: 69in (1.75m)
Tailpipe diameter: 15in (0.38m)
Weight: 344lb (153kg)
Fuel: Petrol consumed @ 3.4lb/hour
Fuel cell length: 4ft 6in (1.4m)
Fuel capacity: 180 gallon (681 litre)

Performance
Speed (max): 373mph (600km) @ 8,200ft (2,500m)
Range (max): 146 miles (235km)

Porsche 109-005 Turbojet Replacement for the Argus As 014

Because the production V-1 flying bomb's Argus As 014 pulsejet was relatively fuel inefficient, the small, single-use Porsche 005 design (RLM designation 109-005) was initiated in late 1944 with the intention of providing a more fuel-efficient turbojet, delivering longer range and higher speed, without the vibration. The projected increase in the V-1's range was to be from 150 miles (245km) to 435 miles (700km) and, importantly, would allow launching without ramps. The model TL-300 turbojet (Porsch designation) was designed by Ferdinand Porsche and his design team and resembled the Junkers Jumo 004 jet engine used to power the Me 262 jet fighter. Shortly before the end of the war, the turbojet project was transferred to Eng. Max Adolf Mueller. Mueller had contributed to the design of the BM 003 (used in the Heinkel He 162 and Arado Ar 234C) and Junkers Jumo 004, which were Germany's only jet engines to reach production during the war. Due to its small size, low thrust of only 1,100lb (500kg), and little power, it was not suitable for jet aircraft use but could be adaptable for V-1 use. By the war's end the 005 design had not been finalised nor any components fabricated. Porsche did not continue work on gas turbines or jet engines for the promising post-war commercial aviation market. Mueller was captured by the Americans at the end of the war and later supplied them with information on the Porsche 005.

Pulsejet Operation

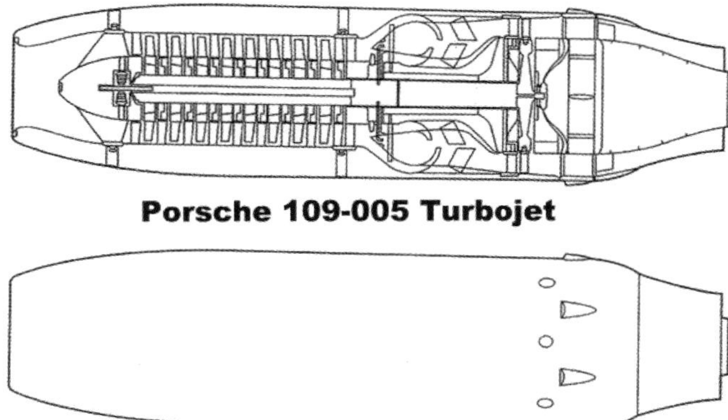

Porsche 109-005 Turbojet

Specifications*
General Characteristics
Type: Turbojet
Length: 9.33ft (2.85m)
Diameter: 2.1ft (0.65m)
Dry weight: 441lb (200kg) for complete power

Performance
Maximum thrust: 1,102lb (500kg) static
Overall pressure ratio: 2.8:1
Thrust-to-weight ratio: 2:5
Compressor: Axial flow

* Because the Porsche 005 had undergone only limited development by the time the war ended, these figures are based on known engine data and intended performance.

Summary of Unmanned V-1 Operations

Launching

On 18 June 1943, Hermann Göring decided on launching the V-1, using the Walter catapult, in both large permanent launch bunkers, called *Wasserwerk*, and smaller, quickly built installations, called the Stellung system. V-1 launching and depot sites in France were in nine general areas, four of which had the ramps aligned toward London, and five towards other English coastal and southern inland cities. Flakregiment 155 (W) was formed and trained at Zinnowitz, near Peenemünde, to test fire the missiles and was then dispatched to construct ninety-six permanent launch sites along the occupied northern French coast for launching the weapons across the Channel. Some of the launch sites were built as bomb-proof concrete bunkers, however, the first easy to build and set up launch facilities were nicknamed 'ski sites' by the Allies because of the inclined shape of the ramps. The Allies became aware of seventy-two of the permanent sites at an early stage and these ramps had to be abandoned after repeated Allied Operation Crossbow air attacks by fighter-bombers and medium bombers, further delaying V-1 deployment before they came into use before D-Day. Germany then began constructing modified V-1 launch sites with limited structures that could be built and repaired quickly after bombing. The mobile launch sites could theoretically launch about fifteen V-1s per day, but this rate was difficult to achieve on a consistent basis; however, the maximum rate achieved was eighteen.

The V-1 was normally ground launched from a firing tube mounted on an inclined metal ramp 150ft (45.75m) long, reaching 16ft (4.9m) high at its end. Pressurised hydrogen peroxide caused a piston on the ramp to thrust forward, propelling the flying bomb into the air, where its pulsejet would be activated at an initial operational speed of 200mph (322kmph). The usual flight time for the V-1, which used low-grade aviation fuel, was

V-1 abandoned on its launching ramp in a woods near the town Ardouval, south of Dieppe. (*AFSHRC*)

The basic, lightweight design and small size of the V-1 launching base was quick to build and used few scarce building materials, as well as being designed to be concealed from Allied bombers. (*AFSHRC*)

about half an hour at altitudes of between 2,000 and 3,000ft (610 to 914m) and at speeds of up to 400mph (644kmph).

At 0418 on 13 June 1944, the first of four buzz bombs fell on Swanscombe, Kent, and on 1 September 1944, Flakregiment 155 (W) fired its last round of V-1s from French soil against Great Britain. About 9,500–10,000 V-1s, including more than 2,000 abortive missiles or misses, had been fired against England but the V-1 campaign against Antwerp and other Belgian cities continued from launch sites in Germany and the Netherlands. The last V-1 was launched against Antwerp on 30 March 1945.

Effectiveness

Almost 30,000 V-1s were manufactured, each requiring 350 hours (including 120 for the autopilot) to construct, which was at a cost of just 4 per cent of fabricating a huge V-2 rocket, which delivered a comparable and just as inaccurate payload. Of the approximately 9,500 to 10,000 V-1s fired at England, 2,419 reached London, killing about 6,184 people and injuring 17,981. Croydon, on the south-east fringe of London, received the greatest density of hits. After the cessation of French coast launches, the vital Allied port of Antwerp, Belgium, was hit by 2,448 V-1s from October 1944 to March 1945. Overall, only about 25 per cent of the V-1s hit near their intended targets, the majority being lost because of a combination of mechanical unreliability, guidance errors, and Allied defensive countermeasures.

Countermeasures

Operation Diver was the British code name for countermeasures used against the V-1 flying bomb campaign and consisted of anti-aircraft gun batteries, barrage balloons, and

Dramatic photo of a 'buzz bomb' with its pulsejet off and diving silently near its central London target. (*AFSHRC*)

eight RAF fighter squadrons, equipped with Hawker Typhoons, Supermarine Spitfire IXs and XIVs, Hawker Tempest Vs, and the RAF's new jet-powered Gloster Meteor, flying standing patrols. These anti-Diver fighters were modified to catch the 400mph+ (645kmph) flying bombs by removing all protective armour plate and excess weight and polishing the leading edges of the wings and empennage. The engines were finely tuned and overhauled. It was found that to have AA guns sited south of London to defend against the V-1s would be dangerous to the English population living in the towns and villages below and would restrict the intercepting fighters. Instead, a belt of 800 AA guns were positioned along the Channel coast from Newhaven to Dover, which gave the AA guns unrestricted fields of fire and allowed their shells to explode safely out to sea. The newly developed VT proximity-fuse AA shells also increased the effectiveness of AA gunfire against the easy to hit, straight-and-level-flying V-1s as they crossed the coast. Radar equipment also functioned more effectively on the coast than inland. Meanwhile, intercepting fighters positioned near the coast were more able to catch the V-1s between the coast and southern London, where 1,000 balloons were floating in wait to ensnare the approaching buzz bombs. However, the leading edges of the V-1's wings were equipped with balloon cable cutters and fewer than 250 V-1s are known to have been destroyed by hitting such cables. Pursuing fighter pilots soon determined that the V-1's sheet steel skin deflected standard RAF .303 calibre machine gun bullets and so cannon fire was most effective. However, a 20mm cannon had a much shorter effective range than a .303 calibre machine gun, causing the attacking pilot to fly to a closer firing range. Hitting

A Hawker Tempest closes on a V-1 approaching London to place its wingtip under the V-1's wing tip and then roll it off course by quickly banking away. The pilot had to take care not to fire too closely on the target to avoid being demolished by the explosion of its 2,000lb warhead. A longer-range deflection shot and banking immediately away was the preferred attack method. (*AFSHRC*)

the 1,874lb (855kg) explosive warhead from too close behind could be devastating as an exploding V-1 scattered large hunks of metal everywhere. The prescribed V-1 attack method was to allow it to pass on one side, then fire a deflection shot once it was at a safe distance, not less than 200 yards (183m), and then bank quickly away to be safe from the resulting huge explosion. Another method was for the fighter pilot to place a wing tip under the V-1's wing tip and then roll it off course by quickly banking away, or also to fly in front of it to have the slipstream destabilise it so that it would spin out of control. These measures were so successful that between June 1944 and March 1945, 3,957 V-1s (about 80 per cent launched) were claimed to have been destroyed: 1,979 by fighters, 1,866 by AA guns, 232 by balloons, and 12 by naval guns.

While a few early experimental versions of the unmanned V-1s were air launched, the majority of operational V-1s were launched from static, land-based 'ski' catapults. However, after these launch sites along the French coast were overrun by the Allies after D-Day, for many months the only method for the Luftwaffe to attack Britain with V-1s was by air launching. The first air launch of a V-1 took place on 9 July 1944, when Heinkel He 111 H-22s of III./KG 3 began attacking London. However, due to fuel shortages, battle

He 111H-2 Air Launch of the Unmanned F-103s

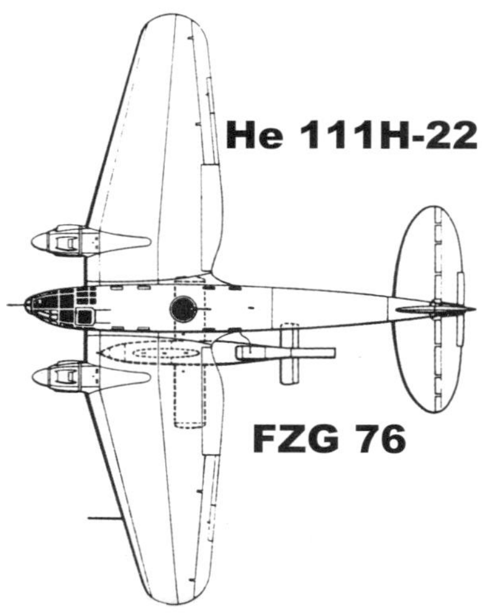

For the optimum launch procedure, the Heinkel was to climb to approximately 2,000ft, before entering a shallow dive to achieve a launch speed of 150mph, which was required for the R-4 pulsejet to sustain flight. The He 111 crew initiated preliminary heating of the combustion chamber before igniting the spark plug to start the pulsejet once this speed was reached. After the pulsejet engine was started and allowed to run for a few seconds, the V-1 was released. (*AFSHRC*)

A Scheuch-Schlepper (tractor) on a specialised tricycle trolley equipped with a hand-pumped hydraulic lifting device was to load the Fi 103R-4 under the left wing. The V-1, with its wings and wing spars removed, arrived at the parked Heinkel so that it could be backed into position under its carrying pylon under the wing, past the Heinkel's landing gear and propellers, which would block a winged version from being backed and attached. V-1 loaded for take-off. (*AFSHRC*)

The V-1 was held in place by a standard bomb shackle that attached to the T-shaped lifting lug on the top of the V-1's fuselage. The suspension point on the Heinkel carrier was located behind its rear spar and the weight of the V-1 was distributed between the front and rear spar by a connecting structure. The area under the bomber where the bomb doors were located were faired over with metal plating. (*AFSHRC*)

During the He 111 transport portion of the flight, the V-1 was steadied by two telescoping adjustable rods that projected from the Heinkel's under-wing surface. (*AFSHRC*)

fatigue, and combat losses from Allied fighters, the Luftwaffe's campaign over Great Britain finally ended on 14 January 1945.

Kampfgeschwaders 3 and 53 were chosen to fly the motherships to carry the conventional Fi 103s to attack England. Their Heinkel He 111H-22s were of a variant that was a modified and redesignated H-6, H-16 and H-21, equipped with Junkers Jumo 213E-1 engines. After a ten-day-long aircrew training course at Peenemünde, bases were readied at Gilze-Rijen, southern Netherlands, for air launches against southern England until 15 September 1944, and at Venlo in the south-eastern Netherlands close to the border with Germany for launches after the first week in December 1944. Aircrews and the V-1s were sheltered nearby for secrecy from marauding Allied fighter-bombers.

III./KG 3, the sole surviving group of KG 3 (3rd Bomber Wing, the 'Blitz Wing') after Eastern Front operations, was reformed on 6 February 1944 in Poland and was trained to use the Heinkel He 111H-22 in night operations as the Fi 103 weapon platform. It began operations in late June 1944 under Fliegerkorps IX from Venlo and Gilze-Rijen with nine He 111H-22s. From 18 to 20 July 1944, it launched approximately fifty V-1s, then continued its Fi 103 carrying sorties into mid-October 1944, when the group's He 111 numbers increased to twenty-five. However, KG 3 continued to lose its heavily V-1 burdened aircraft to RAF night fighters and attrition and then fuel shortages caused it to discontinue operations by the end of the year. From July 1944 to January 1945 KG 3 mainly night-launched approximately 1,176 V-1s from modified Heinkels over the North Sea. Afterward there is no further mention of III./KG 3 V-1 activity. Post-war research estimated a 40 per cent failure rate of air-launched V-1s, and the launching Heinkel motherships were particularly vulnerable to prowling Allied night fighter attack as the flash of the missile launch exposed the bomber for several seconds. Even after a successful air launch over the English coast, the British had increasingly developed effective aircraft interception and AA defensive methods. The Luftwaffe lost 77 He 111 carrying aircraft to all causes during 1,200 sorties.

During August 1944 I/II/III./KG 53 was withdrawn from the Eastern Front and soon after was also outfitted with the He 111H-22 variant. The H-22s of I/II/III./KG 53 similarly started buzz bomb operations over Britain beginning in October 1944, launching 1,200 V-1s of which 562 were seen to crash (46.8 per cent). However, little information is available on the unit's V-1 operations. Its Heinkels also suffered heavy losses to Allied interceptors and then fuel shortages, causing the Kampfgeschwader to suspend all V-1 carrying operations on 25 January 1945 after only limited success.

The combat potential of air-launched V-1s against England dwindled into 1945 at about the same rate as that of the ground-launched missiles against the country, as the British gradually developed increasingly effective defensive tactics.

Arado Jet Ar 234C Motherships Considered

During late October 1944, just as the Heinkel He 111H-22/Fi 103 composite was entering operations, the Arado company correctly anticipated that the inferior performance of the Heinkel motherships would result in severe losses. Arado then submitted several proposals

Because of the inferior performance of the He 111 motherships and their anticipated high losses, in late 1944 Arado submitted several proposals regarding the towing or carrying of the V-1 by its Ar 234C Blitz (Lightning), the world's first operational jet bomber. (*Author's model kit box cover collection*)

regarding the towing or carrying of the Fieseler Fi 103 flying bomb by their Ar 234C Blitz (Lightning), the world's first operational jet bomber and reconnaissance aircraft.

Arado submitted four drawing board proposals using the Ar 234C as the mother aircraft. The first two involved towing the Fi 103 bomb by a non-flexible boom attached to the bomber just below the vertical tail surfaces. For the third proposal, the Ar 234/Fi 103 composite was mounted on a simple two-wheeled take-off trolley, which was jettisoned immediately as the combination left the ground. The fourth, most sophisticated, proposal involved mounting the Fi 103 on top of the Ar 234C, in a so-called reverse Mistel installation (parasite on top of mother) in which the parasite V-1's under-fuselage fairing was attached to the mother Arado's dorsal fuselage as well as by stabilising struts positioned between the twin turbojets and at the rear fuselage. The composite was placed on a special jettisonable, three-wheeled, jet-assisted, take-off trolley. For aerial launching, the Fi 103 was raised above the Ar 234 by a pilot-controlled, hydraulically operated dorsal trapeze mechanism that would elevate the Fi 103 on the trapeze's launch cradle about 8ft (2.4m) clear of the 234's upper fuselage to avoid damaging the launch aircraft's fuselage and tail surfaces when the pulsejet ignited, as well as to ensure a clean airflow for the Argus motor's intake.

The American Composite Buzz Bomb: JB-2/B-17

During early July 1944, only three weeks after the first German V-1s were fired on England, American engineers at Wright Field, Ohio, succeeded in 'reverse-engineering' a German V-1 Argus pulsejet engine and body from crashed German V-1 buzz bombs. The USAAF prioritised the JB-2's completion for them to participate in the final destruction of Nazi Germany. By October 1944, the first launch of an American buzz bomb, designated as the JB-2 (Jet Bomb-2), occurred at Eglin Army Airfield, Florida. Despite the realisation that America's first unmanned guided missile was inherently inaccurate, contracts were let for production of 2,000 weapons. Republic Aircraft Corporation was awarded the contract for the overall airframe (later subcontracted to Willys-Overland), Ford Motor Company was to manufacture the Ford IJ-15-1 770lb thrust pulsejet engine, and Jack and Heintz the control apparatus.

Early test flights were failures, but finally on 5 June 1945 the USAAF JB-2 flew successfully for the first time. However, by this time the war was quickly nearing an end and the need for a JB-2-type weapon had diminished. During September 1945, production finally ceased, with only 1,385 JB-2s delivered to the USAAF. However, the USAAF continued the development of the JB-2 as Project MX-544, with two versions: one with preset internal guidance and another with radar control. The AAF's newly created First Experimental Guided Missiles Group developed, tested and evaluated the missiles at Eglin Field.

Several launch platforms were developed for the JB-2, including German-style permanent and portable ramps, and air launching from under the wings of B-17 or B-29 bombers. Motivated by the Luftwaffe's successful operational He 111H-22 aerial V-1 launches during first months of 1945, a scheme to air launch the missiles from B-17 bombers began a trial phase. The JB-2's 17ft 8in wingspan and 5,000lb weight required it to be carried externally under the B-17's wing, instead of internally. A second JB-2 had to be carried under the opposite wing for balance and symmetry to prevent the mother from going into a stall. Launching in flight eliminated the need for the sometimes-unreliable Rocket Assisted Take-Off (RATO) units to accelerate the buzz bombs to a speed that allowed the missile to attain lift, as the B-17 simply had to maintain an indicated airspeed between

The re-engineered American 'buzz bomb', designated as the JB-2, tested as an air-launched missile from B-17 bombers for anticipated use against Germany and Japan. Republic Aircraft Corporation was awarded the contract for the overall airframe and Ford Motor Company was to manufacture the Ford IJ-15-1 pulsejet engine. (*AAF*)

The JB-2's 17ft 8in wingspan and 5,000lb weight required it to be carried externally under the B-17's wing, instead of internally, and a second JB-2 had to be carried under the opposite wing for balance and symmetry to prevent the mothership from going into a stall. (*AAF*)

180 and 220mph prior to the release. The bomber's airspeed also eliminated the need for the air compressor required during ground launches to provide forced air into the pulsejet engine to allow ignition, which was from controls inside the bomber just before release. Tests in December 1944 determined that a B-17 could carry two JB-2s over a combat radius of 1,000 miles, but it was not until 2 March 1945 that the first successful air launch took place. Bomber crews launched a total of ten JB-2s during March and April, however, five of the missiles launched from the bomber experienced engine starting malfunctions, resulting in aborted launches. Of the remaining air launches, four proved successful and one experienced a control malfunction, causing it to nose dive into the Gulf of Mexico. The test report concluded that JB-2s could be launched successfully from a B-17, and that the engine failures could be eliminated by the installation of a motorised fuel valve. The JB-2's air-launch capability increased its limited range to over 1,000 miles, which was sufficient to reach targets in Germany. However, once Germany surrendered during May 1945, the JB-2's range was far too short for deployment in the Pacific. Using the B-29 to air launch the JB-2 was considered but was not possible as the bomber would require extensive modification, and besides, it was unavailable because the XXI Bomber Command was unwilling to divert any from its bombing of Japan.

Section Two: The Fi 103R-4 Reichenberg, Manned V-1

Interest in the Manned V-1 Begins

After Hanna Reitsch and Heinz Kensche finished testing the unsuccessful twin pulsejet Me 328, Reitsch became interested in converting the Fieseler Fi 103 V-1 into a manned suicide aircraft. Heinrich Himmler had informed Waffen SS Obersturmbannführer (Lt Col) Otto Skorzeny, the head of Hitler's SS Kommando, about Reitsch's new interest in a manned V-1. Skorzeny had also recently become interested in the concept of the

Otto Skorzeny escorts overthrown Italian dictator Benito Mussolini outside the Campo Imperatore Hotel after a daring rescue from the Abruzzi Italian Alps on 12 September 1943. (*NARA*)

piloted V-1 for his SS Selbstopferkommando (SS Self-Sacrifice Commando) *Leonidas* suicide squadron. The squadron was named after the Spartan king Leonidas I, who led the famed 300 Spartans that fought to the death at Battle of Thermopylae (480 BCE) while attempting to defend a narrow pass from the invading Persian army. By 16 January 1944, some seventy to eighty volunteers from various air transport units had been recruited for Skorzeny's SO Squadron (Self Sacrifice Squadron) and were required to sign a pledge stating; 'I hereby declare my accession to the suicide squadron as a pilot of the flying bomb that I am fully aware that joining this unit is synonymous with my own death.'

Reitsch describes her first meeting with Skorzeny:

> Otto Skorzeny introduced himself to me over the telephone and said he was anxious to meet me. This was the man whose name had become a by-word as the pilot who had rescued Mussolini by helicopter from a hotel in the Abruzzi Mountains where he was held prisoner by the Badoglio Government. Skorzeny, it appeared, had recently been told by Himmler about our project and had himself been concerned in the development of special weapons. He was already in contact with those in the Navy who saw in the use of one-man torpedoes and frogmen a chance of bringing about a last-minute change in the courses of the war in Germany's favour. Quite independently of us, Skorzeny had also come on the idea of the piloted V-1 and had been anxious to meet me in order to discuss it. When he saw how the situation lay, Skorzeny set to work in characteristic fashion, sweeping aside all objections and

March 1941: Hitler awards the Iron Cross Second Class to Captain Hanna Reitsch and on 28 February 1944 she was awarded a second Iron Cross Second Class, becoming the first and only woman to do so. She was also the only woman to receive the Military Air Badge of Gold with Diamonds. (*NARA*)

> obstacles with the same simple pretext, Hitler had vested him with full powers and had expressly called for a daily progress report.
>
> From Reitsch memoir, *The Sky My Kingdom*

During their discussions, Skorzeny and Reitsch both concurred that the war would be lost unless a decisive assault could be launched against the Allies' warships and transports during their anticipated invasion of occupied France. On 28 February 1944 Reitsch met Hitler at the Berghof mountain retreat as she was to be awarded her second Iron Cross Second Class. Reitsch used the occasion to present the 'Self-Sacrifice Operation' to Hitler and his trusted Luftwaffe adjutant, Nicolaus von Below. Hitler initially rejected the proposal, believing instead that the introduction of new jet aircraft would change the downturn in Germany's war situation. However, Reitsch and Skorzeny, two ardent Nazis and Hitler favourites, were able to cajole him into granting top priority to their secret project to modify the V-1 into a manned flying bomb with the proviso that the pilot would escape before

impact. The project was assigned to Gen. Günther Korten, Chief of the General Staff of the Luftwaffe. Korten, in turn, delegated the project to the 2nd Group of Kampfgeschwader 200 (KG 200) which had provided pathfinders, radar-jamming aircraft, Mistel composite aircraft, and flown refurbished downed USAAF aircraft.

Willy Fiedler. (*AFSHRC*)

In the summer of 1944, the Fieseler plants were at their development and production capacity producing the first of over 30,000 Fi 103 flying bombs and manufacturing other aircraft under licence, including the Messerschmitt Bf 109 and Focke-Wulf Fw 190. Feldmarschall Erhard Milch, the Chief of Air Force Special Supply and Procurement Service, assigned the Henschel Flugzeug-Werke (HFW) at Berlin Schönefeld for the development of the manned V-1, under the direction of engineer Dipl. Ing. Willy Fiedler and Dipl. Ing. Robert Lusser.

The official RLM name of the Reichenberg was Fieseler Fi 103, renumbered with the operational version and a serial number. The vengeance weapon designation V-4 is occasionally attributed to it by some sources, but this is a mistake as the Reichenberg was not a weapon of reprisal as was its progenitor the V-1. The Reichenberg code name originated from Reichenberg (Liberec, Czech Republic today), the capital of the Reichsgau Sudetenland (an annexed part of Germany since 1938). The manned Fi 103 Reichenberg workshop at Berlin Schönefeld was later named 'Segelflug Reichenberg GmbH' (*Segelflug* = Glider).

From 1942 on Willy Fiedler directed the overall testing of the Fi 103 V-1 flying bomb at Peenemünde. In the spring of 1944, once the V-1 became operational, Fiedler and Lusser were transferred to the new manned V-1 project at Berlin Schönefeld. After leaving the Reichenberg project, Fiedler developed the exotic vertical take-off Bachem Ba 349 Natter rocket interceptor together with Erich Bachem.

The Reichenbergs Described

The Fi 103R-4 combat version's structural parts: fuselage, wings, and engine were identical to the late models of the conventional Fi 103 V-1 flying bomb except for the following:

1) The V-1 was transformed into the Reichenberg by adding a small, cramped cockpit inside the fuselage area that was immediately forward of the pulsejet's intake, at the previous location of the conventional V-1's compressed-air cylinders.
2) A single-piece hinged canopy incorporated a thick armoured front glass plate and opened to the right side to allow entry. However, there are later photos that show the canopy also opening by sliding it forward.

Reichenberg Gallery

Small cramped cockpit with a starboard hinged canopy. (Note: US Army 'pilot' wearing German life preserver). (*USAGF*)

Forward-sliding canopy. Other canopies were hinged, opening to the right. (*USAGF*)

The cockpit with controls, and flight instruments were installed just forward of the Argus As 014 pulsejet unit. (*USAGF*)

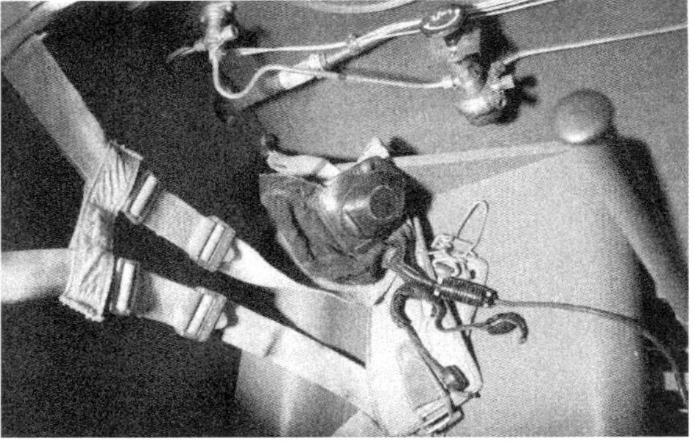

Plywood seat with shoulder and lap belts, leather helmet with radio earphones and microphone. (*USAGF*)

Wings were attached by sliding each wing panel over the pipe-like tubular spar. The photo shows the spar attached alongside the trolley. (*USAGF*)

Full-length ailerons were added to the rear of the standard wings. (*Author's collection*)

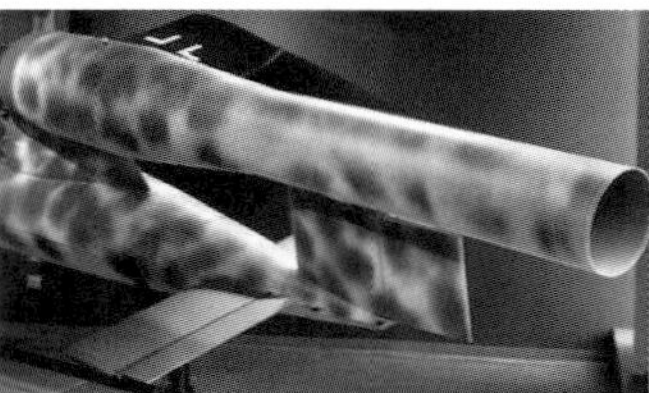

The empennage comprised a horizontal stabiliser with a full-length elevator and a rudder that was increased in size from the unmanned V-1. (*Author's collection*)

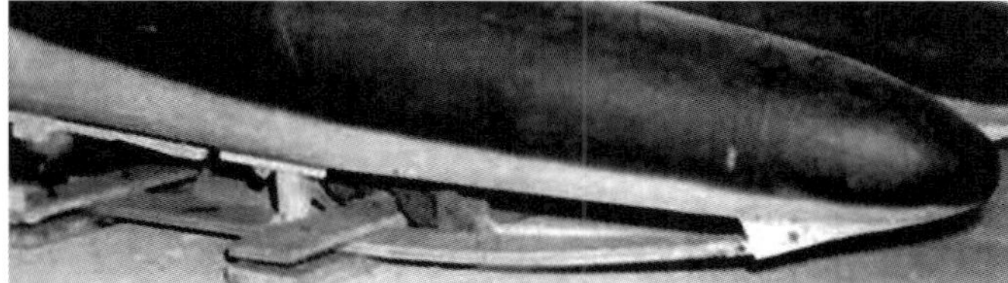

The four training versions were equipped with a curved plywood skid. (*Author's collection*)

3) The cockpit with controls, and flight instruments were installed just forward of the Argus As 014 pulsejet unit. As a result, the remaining compressed air cylinder and wings were moved forward slightly, as was the aircraft's neutral point (the position of centre of mass where the aircraft would be neutrally stable). Therefore, the shifting in weight caused by adding a pilot and cockpit equipment and a different payload were mostly compensated for. A 9.8in (25cm) addition to the fuselage was appended to the centre section aft of the fuel tank to create the required feet area for the pilot.
4) Plywood seat with shoulder and lap belts.
5) Wings were attached by sliding each wing panel over the pipe-like tubular spar. The spar could be detached from the fuselage and attached along the fuselage for shipping.
6) Full-length ailerons were added to the rear of the standard wings.
7) Horizontal stabiliser had a full-length elevator supplemented by trim weights.
8) The area of the rudder had to be increased and the control stick and pedals had to be connected to the rudders by cables. The rudder was moved by a small-diameter wire cable attached to the articulating rudder lever located near the piano-type rudder hinge. This cable then passed along the outside of the tapered fuselage through a small-diameter round hole and then on to the pilot's small foot-operated left and right pedals.

9) To house the different payloads, the bow and load compartment remained connected to the centre section by Frydag couplings. A tapered warhead with two fuse cells and a plywood cover replaced the standard olive-shaped warhead. This configuration also made it possible to use a nose warhead section as a space for accommodating a flight instructor for training flights of prospective pilots.
10) The two stern steering gears and the compass in the bow were omitted.
11) Deleted was the compressed air cylinder, which was no longer required for control, as were the pneumatic control servos, the autopilot, the height and range setting controls, and the servo mechanisms controlling the rudder and elevators. The other air cylinder was then relocated in the rear space that normally accommodated the V-1's autopilot and the electrical panel, which were removed.
12) The air log propeller on the tip of the nose that 'guided' the V-1 to its target by the number of revolutions was deleted.

Reichenberg Cockpit

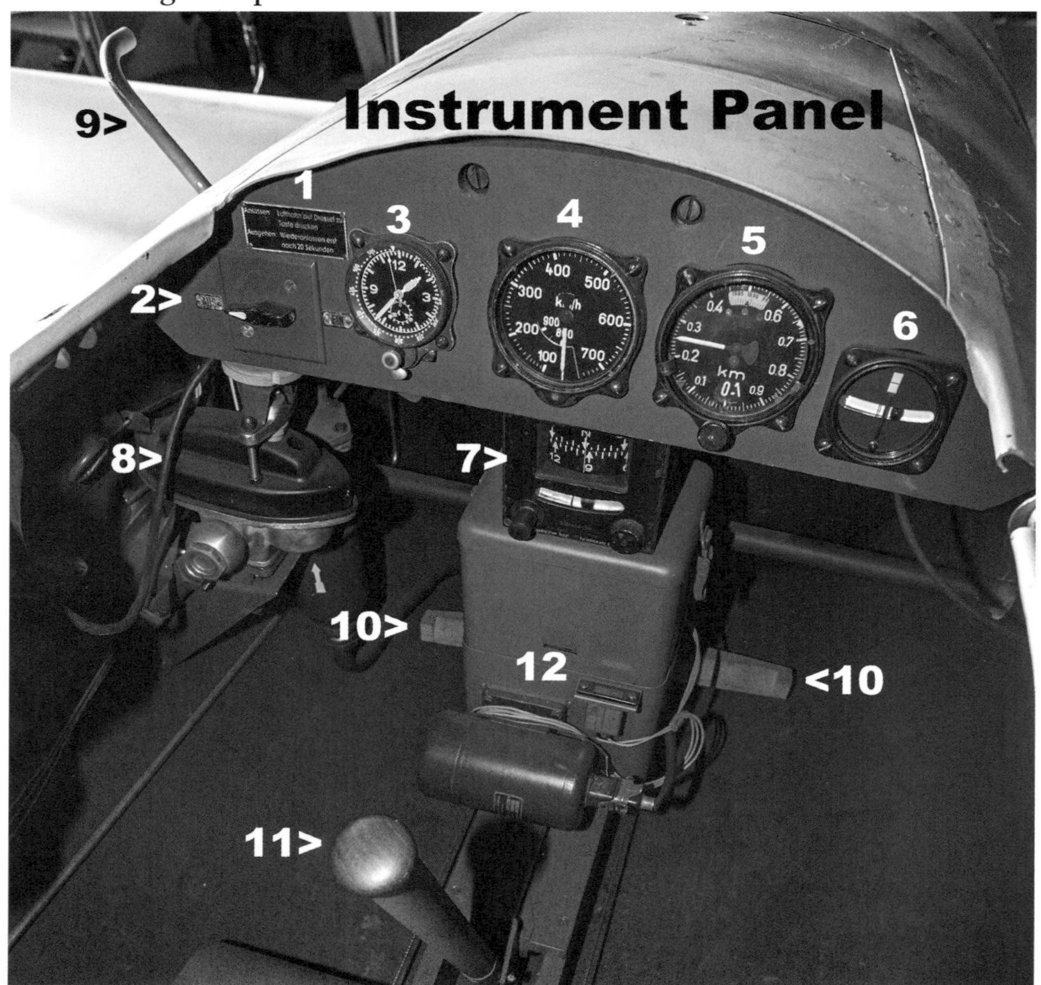

(*AFSHFC*)

13) The four training versions were equipped with a resilient curved plywood skid resting on rubber buffers at the rear for landing the pilot and aircraft for further use.

Reichenberg Trainer Instrumentation

The instrumentation of the different versions is not certain, but the training versions were completely instrumented. Although there are no documents available describing the instrumentation of the operational Reichenberg versions, photos of the cockpit of an R-4 indicate that this version was only equipped with a speedometer and altimeter, which seems plausible for a one-way attack. The complete trainer instrumentation was as seen in the photo on p.46:

Legend for previous photo

Cockpit Equipment, Instruments and Controls

1) Engine start-up and restart information board for the engine
2) Armament main switch (OFF>Left and ON>Right) operated by key wired to instrument panel
3) Clock
4) Airspeed indicator: 100–700kmph (63–438mph)
5) Altimeter (0.1km graduations)
6) Combined inclinometer and turn indicator
7) Gyro compass mounted in a shock mounted bracket
8) The special fuel regulator was relocated to the front next to the pilot.
9) Pitot tube
10) Right and left rudder pedals
11) Flight controls: Conventional stick and pivoted cross bar rudder control
12) 24-volt wet battery and 3-phase inverter

Personal equipment consisted of the following:

1) Parachute
2) Life-preserver
3) Leather helmet with headphones
4) Communication between the 'mother' aircraft and the Reichenberg would be essential, and with no conventional on-board radio, a rudimentary intercom wire contact was enabled with simple headphones and a microphone.
5) Plywood bucket seat
6) Padded headrest at the top of seat back
7) Safety belt
8) Shoulder straps
9) Crash-pad above instrument panel
10) Goggles
11) Flares

Manned V-1 Fi 103R-1 to 4

The conventional unmanned Fi 103 V-1 was converted into the first manned Fi 103R-1 V-1 variant within several days in an underground workshop under the direction of Gerhard Fieseler of the Gerhard Fieseler Werke (GFW). The modification project was so secret that even the engineers directly concerned were led to believe that the piloted V-1 was intended to be flight tested to resolve problems experienced in the aerodynamic performance of the conventional V-1 flying bomb. After only fourteen days, four conventional Fi 103s were converted into piloted versions, three of them being training versions, identified by the designations R-1, R-2, and R-3:

Reichenberg-1 (R-1): a single-seat glider trainer version converted from the conventional FZG 76, but without the Argus As 014 pulsejet engine installed. It was equipped with a one-piece cockpit canopy, water ballast in the nose area equal to the weight of the 1,874lb warhead, wooden landing skid, aileron, and flaps.

Reichenberg-2 (R-2): a dual-cockpit trainer version of the Reichenberg-1 converted from the conventional FZG 76, but without the Argus As 014 pulsejet engine installed. The second cockpit was located in the warhead's standard location in the FZG 76. It was equipped with ailerons, had no water ballast, while the tail fin and rudder area were enlarged over that of the Reichenberg-1.

Reichenberg-3 (R-3): a single-seat trainer version converted from the conventional FZG 76 but equipped with a fully operational Argus As 014 pulsejet engine. Its cockpit canopy was located directly in front of the air intake. Water was used as ballast to simulate the weight of a warhead. It was equipped with ailerons, wooden landing skid, and flaps.

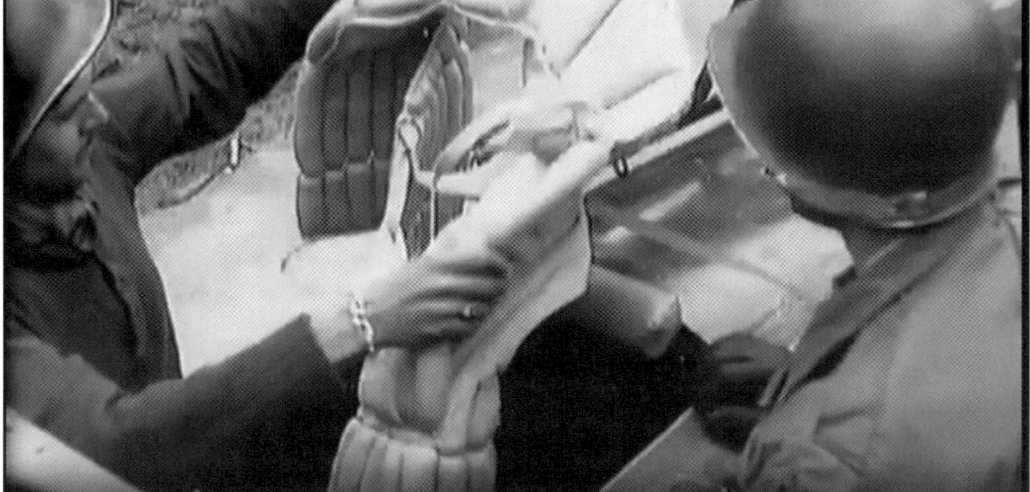

This photo from an US Army movie still shows two GIs removing a life vest from the cockpit of a captured Reichenberg. (*USAGF*)

Reichenberg-4 (R-4): the powered operational version converted from the conventional FZG 76. It would have been the operational version carried to the vicinity of its target under the wing of a Heinkel He 111H-22 in a similar manner to the way the unmanned Fi 103s were launched against England by Kampfgeschwader 53. A foresight was installed to assist in aiming towards the target. The bow section was designed somewhat differently, according to the intended type of use against land, sea targets, or for ramming operations. It had no landing flaps or landing skid as it was to be the one-way suicide version.

Reichenberg-5 (R-5): a proposed powered single-seat training version with landing skid, to be used as training type for the He 162 pulsejet fighter. The R-5 had a greatly shortened bow area with correspondingly protruding ballast weights.

Specifications: Fi 103R Reichenberg-4

Fuselage, Length: 24ft 3in (7.4m)
Fuselage, Diameter: 2ft 9in (0.84m)
Length, Overall: 26ft 3in (8m)
Length from Nose to Cockpit Seat Headrest: 14ft (4.3m)
Wingspan: 18ft 9in (5.7m)
Wing, Length (each): 8ft ⅓in (2.7m)
Wing, Width (with Aileron): 3ft 6in (1.1m)
Wing to Nose, Length: 7ft 1in (2.2m)
Aileron, Width: 9.75in (3m)
Aileron, Length: 7ft 8in (2.3m) (occupying entire trailing edge of the wing)
Wing Spar, Length: 14ft 4in (4.4m)
Wing Spar, Diameter: 4.36in (11cm)
Horizontal Stabiliser (with Elevator): 6ft 9in × 2ft 1in (2.1 × 0.64m)
Horizontal Stabiliser Elevator Control Surface (each): 2ft 10in × 9in (0.86 × 0.23m)
Vertical Stabiliser (with control surface): 3ft 2in × 1ft 9in (0.97 × 0.53m)
Vertical Stabiliser Control Surface: 1ft 4in × 1ft 9in (0.41 × 0.53m)
Cockpit (opening length): 1ft 9in (0.5m)
Cockpit (opening width): 1ft 5in (0.43m)
Seat to Top of Canopy: 3ft 1in (0.84m)
Windshield: Length: 11in. **Width** (at top): 6in/(at bottom): 5in (0.78 × 0.15 × 0.13m)

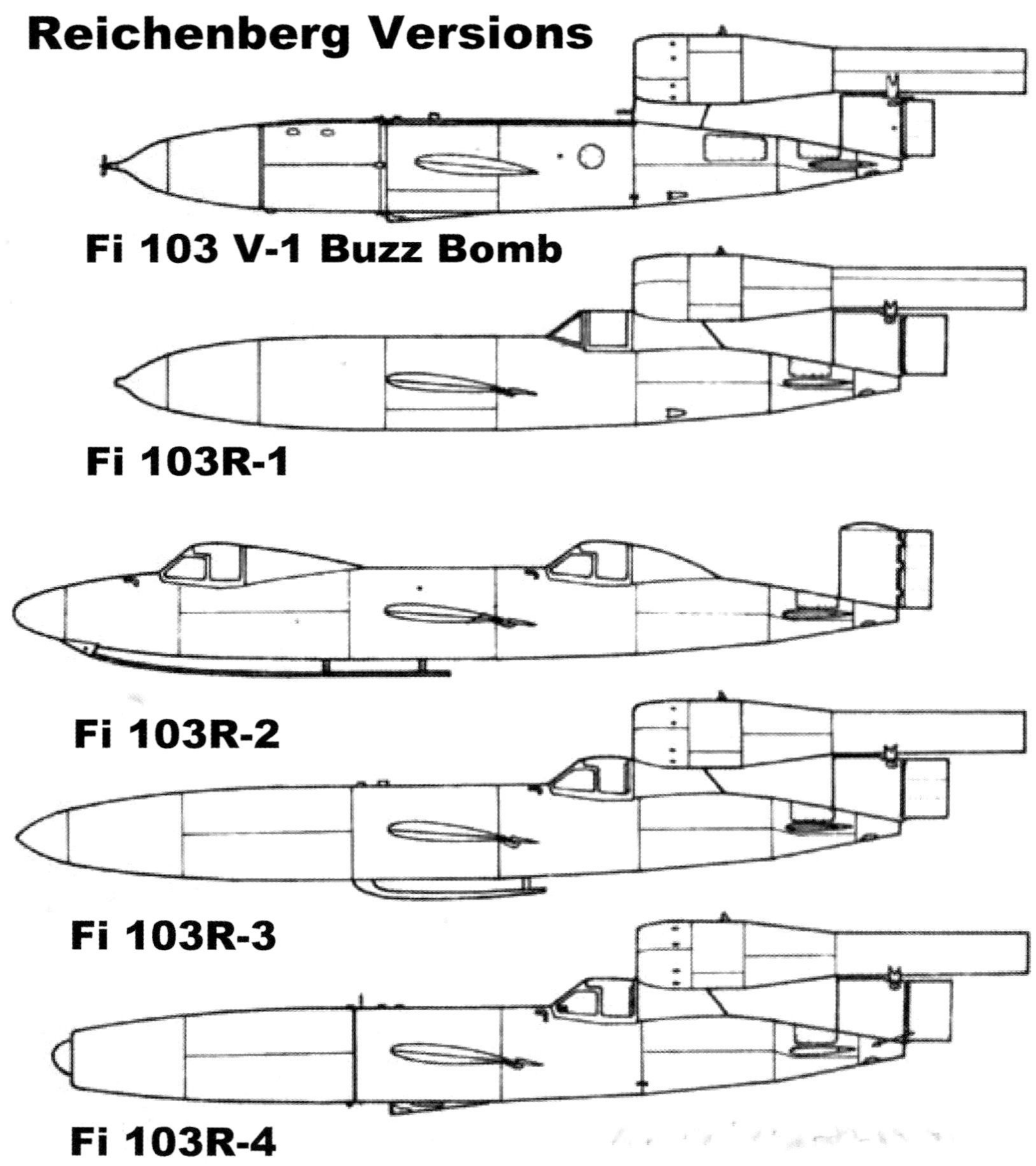

Camouflage and Markings

Since the piloted Reichenberg V-1s were modified from early 1944 onward from existing conventional V-1 airframes they probably, as seen in photos, were painted with the standard dark green upper surfaces separated by a wavy demarcation with a light blue lower body. However, several photos show the lighter blue fuselage surfaces covered by squiggly green mottles or large roundish green mottles. The warhead capsule could be a solid green. During mid-August 1944, late-war upper surface colours were instituted to accommodate night launches and modified for overland and overwater operations. The Swastika or the Balkenkreuz (straight-armed cross) were not used on the conventional V-1 or Reichenberg

Camouflage Scheme One: Standard dark green upper surfaces separated by wavy demarcation with a light blue lower body. (*AFSHRC*)

Camouflage Scheme Two: The lighter blue fuselage surfaces covered by squiggly green mottles or large roundish green mottles, as shown Fi 103R-4 Reichenberg at Farnborough in November 1945. (*NMUSAF*)

(none were seen on the captured examples), although a few post-war museums' restored models and fanciful drawings have these Nazi national markings. Captured Reichenberg aircraft did show an occasional aircraft test number but there could be many black and white stencilled transport, mounting and assembly instructions on various parts of the aircraft, left over from their previous unmanned bomb application.

Warhead

The 6ft (1.8m) warhead consisted of 1,874lb (850kg) of Amatol (a mixture of TNT and ammonium nitrate), a high-grade, blast-effective explosive. There were three fuses; one was an electrical fuse that could be triggered by a nose or belly impact; another was a slow-acting mechanical fuse allowing deeper penetration into the ground, regardless of the altitude; while the third was a time-delayed fuse, set to detonate two hours after launch. The purpose of this third version was to avoid having the British examine this secret V-weapon, if a soft landing had not triggered the impact fuses. The V-1 fusing systems were very reliable, with virtually no dud V-1s being recovered. There are photos showing the warhead with a protective covering when being transported to the He 111.

A very large, 15in (38cm), warship gun shell was developed at Schönefeld as a warhead to equip the operational Reichenberg. Dipl. Ing. Herbert Wagner, the creator of the successful Henschel Hs 293 anti-ship guided missile, headed the Henschel Underwater Warhead Project. These shells, fired by the Kriegsmarine battleship *Bismarck*, pierced and sank the Royal Navy battlecruiser HMS *Hood*. One of these shells was to be attached to the front of the Reichenberg fuselage in a wooden panel. It was carried very near the targeted ship and detached from the Reichenberg just as it entered the water, with the warhead's inertia carrying it submerged to explode below the target's waterline.

A tapered 6ft warhead consisted of 1,874lb (850kg) of Amatol, with two fuse cells and a plywood cover that replaced the standard olive-shaped warhead of the conventional V-1. (*AFSHRC*)

Transport Dolly TW 76A

A transport dolly TW 76A was a welded rectangular frame of tubular steel with four swivel steel wheels mounted on each corner and a long swivel hitch tube attached to the front wheels that swivelled on the fork. On the top of the pulse tube a wooden box was mounted to carry the removed horizontal stabiliser and assorted parts. At the very rear

US Army captors readying a Reichenberg for removal from the Tramm factory on a 76A transport dolly before the British arrived in their Occupation Zone. (*USAGF*)

of the dolly was the holder for the wings and the nose guard. On each side of the dolly there was a mount for the wing tube spars. A removable gantry or workshop crane could be attached to be used later. Dimensions: 10ft 4in long × 4ft 9in wide × 1ft 8in high (315 × 145 × 52cm).

Test Flights

A manned prototype Reichenberg was ready for testing within days and an assembly line was established west of the village of Tramm, near Dannenberg, in eastern Germany, near the Elbe River, about 70 miles south-east of Hamburg. The factory was a secret complex camouflaged as a mock village of circular (Rundling) construction named Tramm. It was built in 1939 as a barracks with an ammunition plant consisting of seven half-timbered houses arranged in a circle, which were clearly visible from the air, but the design served as camouflage against aerial reconnaissance. This was effective because the complex was not identified by the Allies and it was not until mid-April 1945 that advancing American troops discovered the facility by chance.

The complex was initially operated as a Wehrmacht ammunition plant and later as a Luftwaffe one. During 1943 the complex was expanded using Russian and Italian 'conscripts' and a railway connection to the main line at Karwitz was completed to transport the basic unmanned Fi 103 V-1 bodies for manned conversion. Three workshops and a main assembly building were used to rebuild and assemble the manned Reichenbergs by

The Tramm Reichenberg workshop shown just after the Americans left and the occupying British took possession to utilise it as a garage for small vehicle maintenance. (*USAGF*)

Manned Reichenberg IV (no skids) being assembled in the Tramm workshop when captured by the American Army. (*USAGF*)

fifteen Wehrmacht officers and soldiers, and 50 Henschel labourers during March 1944. Specific components for the Reichenberg were manufactured by Henschel Flugzeugwerke but probably the production of some parts was also outsourced.

There were four piloted Reichenberg versions, with three training variants: the Reichenberg R-1 single-seater with landing skid and flaps; the Reichenberg R-2 with a second cockpit in the position normally occupied by the warhead in the operational version, and the Reichenberg R-3 single-seater with a similar arrangement of landing skid and flaps but with the Argus As 109-014 pulsejet installed with a ballast compensating for the weight of the warhead. The operational model was the Reichenberg R-4.

The conventional unmanned Fi 103R V-1 was converted into a manned Fi 103R-1 V-1 variant within several days as a single-seat glider trainer version converted without the Argus As 014 pulsejet engine installed. The single-seat Fi 103 (Reichenberg R-1 was transported from Berlin Schönefeld during September 1943 for testing at the Larz airfield at the Luftwaffe's main testing ground for new combat aircraft prototypes, Erprobungsstelle (Test Unit) at Rechlin.

A catapult could not be used for take-off because of the high g-forces produced, which necessitated the Reichenberg being towed into the air by a two-seat, high-wing Henschel Hs 126, but all the remaining, R-2s, -3s, and -4s were to be air launched under wing from the Heinkel He 111H-22. Willy Fiedler, an accomplished test and glider pilot, was at the controls for the first flight, which was to test the aircraft's control's response and stability around its three axes, before installing the Argus As pulsejet engines. After its release at about 12,000ft, Fiedler performed the assigned tests by circling over the airfield and then landed smoothly after a six-minute flight on the shaped plywood belly skid. The final velocity was extremely high as the heavy Reichenberg with small wings was not designed as a glider.

Further tests were flown and led by former glider champion, Me 163 rocket fighter test pilot and renowned aviatrix Hanna Reitsch, and six other pilots who volunteered to join in these tests. However, the Erprobungsstelle Rechlin experimental station insisted on using their own pilots, which ended in crashes. The next Rechlin R-1 test flights were performed in early September 1944, with the Reichenberg being dropped from an He 111H, but after several moments in free flight, the pilot lost control as he had mistakenly actuated the cockpit canopy lock, causing it to unfasten at 9,000ft. Incredibly, the pilot was able to land his aircraft but violently and suffered serious injuries. The second R-1 flight also ended in a crash, as the pilot was not experienced as a glider pilot in making spot landings without an engine and touched down before the airfield, crashing the R-1 and suffering severe spinal injuries. Reitsch and Otto Skorzeny flew as observers in a nearby aircraft and Reitsch described the first test:

> On a warm summer's day, Otto Skorzeny and I attended the first test at Larz. On arriving, we found the plane ready to start. The V-1 was hanging under the right wing of the Heinkel He 111 bomber. Since the Allies had captured the launching sites in the Pas-de-Calais area, the pilotless V-1s had no longer been launched by catapult as their radius of action was insufficient to carry them to their objective from platforms inside Germany. They were now carried by an He 111 and launched from the mother-plane from a point nearer their target. A catapult start was also out of the question for the piloted V-1 on account of its high acceleration (about 17Gs) and it was therefore to be launched in the same way.

> Fascinated, we followed the Heinkel as it took-off with its burden and climbed higher and higher. Then the moment came when we saw the test pilot detach his plane from the bomber and drop away in the V-1 like some small, swift bird.
>
> The pilot flew in tight turns until, on a dead-straight course, he began to lose height, gliding at an ever-steeper angle towards the earth. It did not take us long to realise that this behaviour of the machine was in no way intended by the pilot. The machine disappeared from sight and shortly after we heard an explosion in the distance and saw a column of black smoke rising in the summer air. For half an hour we waited, fearing to hear the news, until at last the report came through that the pilot was severely injured but still alive.
>
> It transpired that the crash had been caused, not by some structural defect in the aircraft, but through the pilot's own inadvertence. He had unintentionally pressed the catch to the sliding hood of the cockpit and, half stunned by the force of the air current, had lost control over the plane.
>
> From Reitsch memoir, *The Sky My Kingdom*

Erprobungsstelle Rechlin wanted to end the tests, but the steadfast Reitsch used her enormous influence on Hitler to have them continued, and subsequent flights were carried out by herself and fellow test pilot and Me 328 and Reichenberg devotee Heinz Kensche. On 20 September 1944, Kensche made the first flight and successfully landed an unpowered tandem R-2 trainer with a sandbag replacing the front-seat pilot. Reitsch flew ten test flights in the Reichenberg-3 equipped with a fully operational Argus As 014 pulsejet engine with water used as ballast to simulate the weight of the warhead.

During her first flight she found the glide angle to be 'very bad' and that it was especially difficult to control the ailerons as they were 'much too sensitive', with even a small aileron motion causing a roll and making landing on a skid difficult at the high landing speed of about 120mph (193kmph). After the ailerons were modified, Reitsch stated that 'the manned V-1 could easily be controlled, it fulfilled the normal flight requirements, and could have been flown [not landed, as would be seen – author] by any average pilot'. Landing on a wooden skid only supported by three rubber cushions would prove to be a major challenge for future student pilots. To sum up her experiences flying the R-3, Reitsch reported that 'landing was at all times an extremely difficult and dangerous operation and, even when specially trained, pilots of average ability could never be certain of surviving the attempt … and to land it called for exceptional skill'. After she had a few more hair-raising close calls, she reported that it was 'not exactly enjoyable to fly the manned V-1, but by far not so adventurous [for her] as it looked to the observer'.

To train additional pilot candidates, three or four of the best pilots were selected to be trained as flight instructors in the R-3 two-seat trainer. The 'kamikaze' aspirants were to be trained just sufficiently to be able to steer their Reichenbergs in the specified one-way suicide attack flight plan. After the instructors finished a training session they had

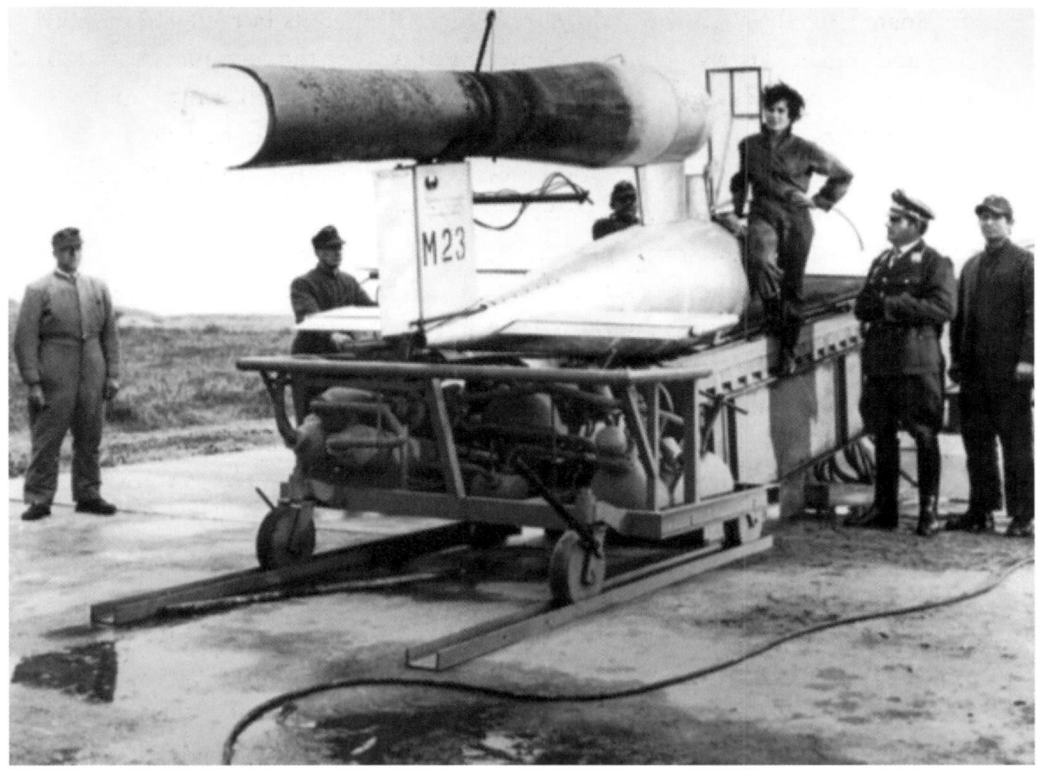

Hanna Reitsch posing on the Reichenberg test stand while the Argus pulsejet was being tested. (*AFSHRC*)

to return their students to base and perform the perilous skid landings themselves as the one-way students had no need to be able to land!

Most of the test flights were made in unpowered versions and very few with the Argus engine operating. Testing the Reichenberg was costly, with two fatalities and four injured, mainly with the engine operating. On 5 November 1943, during the second test flight of the R-3, flown by Heinz Kensche, the constantly repeated hammering detonations of the pulsejet loosened the glue of the wing's plywood skin and caused a wing to fall off. The experienced Kensche miraculously managed to parachute to safety from the cramped cockpit but only following the shutdown of the overhead Argus intake.

Reitsch made two successful flights under pulsejet power and eight unpowered glide flights but not without experiencing several what she referred to as 'moments' during her ten flights. During a release, the He 111H hit the rear of Reitsch's Reichenberg, bending the rudder and elevator and giving her 'great difficulty' in maintaining control. However, her vast flying experience allowed her to make a safe landing. She describes the incident:

> On one occasion, for example, the pilot of the He 111 had just released me from beneath the bomber's wing, when his plane grazed the rear of the V-1. There was a loud rending noise, as if the tail of my plane had been broken right off. Though

> only just able to continue to control the plane, I managed to make a smooth landing, finding, when I inspected it, that the tail had been crumpled and twisted to the right through an angle of almost thirty degrees. It seemed a miracle that it had not come right off.
>
> From Reitsch memoir, *The Sky My Kingdom*

During another test flight, Reitsch's R-3 made a very hard landing, but she escaped the spinal injuries that a heavier pilot would have sustained. She describes the harrowing flight:

> On another occasion I was testing the behaviour of the two-seater model of the V-1 at a wide range of speed along an inclined flightpath, flying at speeds up to 530mph. During the test, a sack of sand, which had been wedged in the front seat on my instruction to supply extra weight, somehow broke loose and shifted position. In blissful ignorance, I tried to flatten out at speed and suddenly found out that I could not move the elevator. I had not enough height, or time, to be able to bail out by parachute and had to risk all on a last, faint chance of saving myself and the plane. Just before the machine reached the ground, I pushed her nose down, and then, with all the response I could get from the elevator, quickly pulled out again. This manoeuvre checked the plane just enough for me to be able to make a landing, though an extremely hard one which splintered the skids and the hull. I emerged without a scratch.
>
> From Reitsch memoir, *The Sky My Kingdom*

While the many Reichenberg limitations were being resolved, the Allied D-Day invasion that the Reichenberg suicide squadron had been formed to devastate had long passed. Nonetheless, the Reichenberg programme continued as Skorzeny used Reitsch's participation and reputation to receive approval from Feldmarschall Erhard Milch to build five more prototypes and train his personal Kommandos. During the autumn of 1944, Skorzeny's suicide programme became seriously slowed when only a small quota of the fuel he requisitioned was delivered and he was able to only train a dozen pilots. In the spring, Lt Walter Starbati arrived as a Reichenberg test pilot. Previously he was chief pilot at Luftschiffbau Zeppelin-Werke in Friedrichshafen, where, among other

Veteran test pilot Walter Starbati lost his life during a March 1945 flight test when the stressed wings of his Reichenberg detached. (*AFSHRC*)

projects he was involved in was the development of the giant Messerschmitt Me 323 Gigant transport, which was derived from a glider. On 5 March 1945, Starbati took-off in a Fi 103R prototype (Re 3, factory number 10), modified with lengthened wings, which he had flown several times previously without a problem during a time when problems had become common. However, after initiating a slight port turn in level flight at about 9,000ft (2,800m), both wings unexpectedly broke away, causing his aircraft with its engine running to plunge uncontrollably into an almost vertical crash into the Nebelsee, close to the airfield. It was speculated that the cause was a fatigue fracture of the spar instigated by engine vibrations as the multiple usage of the manned V-1 was not planned when the wing spar was designed. Also, the wings of the manned flying bomb had been lengthened from a 17ft 6in span (5.3m) to 18ft 9in (5.7m) while the length of the spars remained the same, increasing the stress on the spars. The official cause of the crash was given as 'crash after the wing panelling was detached'. Starbati's body is interred nearby and marked with a small memorial.

Fi 103R-4 In Its Intended Combat Role

Two Reichenberg R-4 combat versions were developed: maritime and land. Externally, the two differed from each other by the shape of their forward ends. The maritime version was blunt and rounded (acting like a faired torpedo with a fuse), while the land target version was pointed. Both versions were controlled and directed by the pilot using an accurate magnetic compass. The original focus was on the maritime option, as the version of the project involved the use of the R-4 against Allied shipping during the anticipated invasion of the Continent.

There is an unverified report of an experimental version of a Reichenberg model that was examined in test tank of the Henschel factory, under the direction of Herbert Wagner, the developer of the effective Henschel Hs 293 guided missile. During a maritime combat attack, after preliminary reconnaissance of the attack area and target by the mothership, the Reichenberg, armed with a specially developed torpedo or armour-piercing bomb warhead, was to be released by the He 111 toward the side of the selected targeted ship, flying in a slight dive at a speed of about 500mph (800kmph). Once very close to the target, the suicide pilot was to jettison the Reichenberg's wings and dive into the water, hitting the enemy ship below the waterline at its most vulnerable point.

After the delivery of the Reichenbergs were much delayed, land targets in Great Britain were to be selected, such as vital power plants, reservoirs, industrial sites, and transportation centres. Despite speculation, no records exist indicating the possibility of R-4s being used for aerial ramming.

In a letter from Albert Speer to Hitler on 28 July 1944, the Reich Minister of Armaments and War Production, protested the waste of men and machines against the Allies in France, suggesting that it would be better to use them against power stations in the USSR.

Heinkel/Manned Fi 103R Air Launch Procedure

For air launch the Reichenberg was to be loaded on the He 111H-22 by the same method as the conventional V-1. A Scheuch-Schlepper (tractor) on a specialised tricycle trolley equipped with a hand-pumped hydraulic lifting device was to load the Reichenberg under the left wing. The Scheuch company of Erfurt originally developed this loading system in close co-operation with the auto maker Auto-Union to haul the skid-equipped Me 163B for take-off and after landing as it lacked the capability to taxi.

The Reichenberg arrived at the parked Heinkel with its wings and wing spars removed so that it could be backed into position under its carrying pylon located under the bomber's wing. The Heinkel's landing gear and propellers would block a winged version from being backed and attached. The hydraulic arms of the Scheuch-Schlepper on which the Reichenberg rested were pumped upwards until the T-shaped lug on top of the R-4 engaged with the suspension point under the mothership's bomb-carrying pylon.

The Reichenberg was held in place by a standard bomb shackle that attached to the T-shaped lifting lug on the top of the Reichenberg fuselage. The suspension point on the Heinkel carrier was located about 2.8ft (0.85m) behind its rear spar and the weight of the Reichenberg was distributed between the front and rear spars by a connecting structure. The area under the bomber, where the bomb doors were located, were faired over with metal plating, which did not fit flush with the surrounding surfaces but projected slightly on the front and sides. If the internal bomb racks had originally been installed, they were removed to save weight. A wide and shallow streamlined fairing covered the pylon, being only 4in (10.2cm) deep at one point, and 1.7ft (0.52m) wide at the widest point.

During the captive portion of the flight, the Reichenberg was steadied by two telescoping adjustable rods that projected from the Heinkel's under-wing surface and were fixed 5ft (1.5m) forward of the trailing edge. The two rods terminated into two flat disks, approximately 7in (17.8cm) in diameter, separated at their fixing points by 2.4ft (0.73m) and inclined forwards and inwards clasping the upper portion of the Reichenberg just forward of the warhead. Communication between the launching bomber and the Reichenberg pilot was carried out via a four-channel connector at the top of the fuselage in front of the canopy.

For the optimum launch procedure, the Heinkel was to climb to approximately 2,000ft (610m), before entering a shallow dive to achieve a launch speed of 150mph (241kmph), which was required for the pulsejet to sustain flight. The pilot initiated preliminary heating of the combustion chamber before igniting the spark plug to start the pulsejet once this speed was reached. After the pulsejet engine was started and allowed to run for a few seconds, the Reichenberg was released, with the He 111 mothership slowing to avoid damaging its fuselage and tail surfaces with the dangerous hot gases escaping from the pulsejet nozzle at the time of separation as well as to ensure a clean airflow for the Argus' intake. There were instances of the premature detonation of the conventional V-1's warhead after the He 111 left the runway. After separation the Heinkel would continue at wave-top level for the return flight back to base.

To minimise the associated risks of radar and fighter detection, the Heinkel aircrews developed a tactic called 'Low-High-Low' during which the He 111 motherships would, upon leaving their airbases and crossing the coast, descend to an exceptionally low altitude over the North Sea. When the launch point was neared, the bombers would ascend swiftly, launch their V-1s, and then descend rapidly again to the previous wave-top level for the return flight.

The Reichenberg pilot then had to guide his aircraft with the elevators and rudder, which were not overly responsive, toward the target, coping with wind direction and the extremely loud and uneven performance of the pulsejet engine just behind his head. The aircraft accelerated to 400mph (640kmph) as its 150 gallons (570 litres) of fuel burned off. If the Reichenberg was attacked by enemy fighters, the pilot's only option was the advantage of its high diving speed to successfully crash into its target as any escaping manoeuvre, even if successful, would be useless as the aircraft had no landing skid.

Detailed plans for an attack on warships were made during trials with a mock-up indicated by smoke bombs. An inventive celluloid aiming device enabled the pilot to compute how far from the target he would have to crash into the water to allow a time-fused torpedo warhead to explode beneath the keel. The pilot would also be able to immediately adjust his angle of attack to an extent that a ship's anti-aircraft defences would be useless, the aircraft travelling at more than 500mph (800kmph).

Although the Reichenberg pilots were to be equipped with psychologically comforting parachutes (unlike Japanese kamikaze pilots), there was a slim to non-existent possibility of successfully bailing out of the aircraft. An obstacle to leaving the cockpit was the complicated canopy release mechanism. The pilot would have to remove the canopy, which was mounted just below the Argus' engine's intake. The canopy was held in place by two curved prongs, that hinged into sockets on the right of the cockpit, while two eyelets and sliding pins held the left side of the canopy. The canopy was released by operating a lever on the left side of the cockpit, which undid the sliding pins from their eyelets. The pilot then slid the canopy about 45 degrees before the front prong on the right side released. Once this canopy release mechanism was undone, the pilot not only needed to raise it against the powerful slipstream but could find that the rear of the canopy was obstructed by the pulsejet's cowling.

There is the misconception that the escaping Reichenberg pilot could be ingested into the pulsejet's intake. Unlike a turbine jet engine, a pulsejet had no sucking intake, as combustion was sustained by ram air operating a set of spring-loaded shutters that rapidly opened and closed from air impacting them. However, a jet engine's compressor produces a huge suction as it draws in increasing amounts of air to sustain combustion. Since hot, expanding gases exited the pulsejet intake before the shutters or valves could close, an escaping non-suicidal pilot, not wanting to confront that overhead inferno, the wing, and roaring slipstream, would opt for the 'simpler' solution of shutting the engine down and executing the rollover and then moving the canopy rearward and up to the right. He was to then roll over the left side of the cockpit, pushing downward and out into the slipstream, waiting to clear the aircraft before opening his parachute. This was all the while approaching close enough to the target to ensure a hit at 500mph (800kmph) under enemy AA fire somewhere over an enemy fleet that would not rescue him.

The Need for the Pilot to Escape Suicide

After Feldmarschall Erhard Milch learned of the Reichenberg's pilot's poor survival expectations, he commanded that the pilots be saved by introducing an ejection seat. If an attack occurred from underneath, then the pilot's seat had to be ejected downwards and if it came from above then only an upwards separation of the pilot's seat could save him. On 13 January 1942, Helmut Schenck became the first pilot known to have used an ejection seat to successfully exit his aircraft in an emergency situation. Schenck's Me 280 jet fighter was being used in tests of the Argus As 014 pulsejets for Fieseler Fi 103 development. Its usual Heinkel HeS 8A turbojets had been removed and replaced with the Argus pulsejet to be tested. It was towed aloft from the Luftwaffe's Erprobungsstelle Rechlin central test facility by a pair of Messerschmitt Bf 110C tugs in a heavy snow shower. Schenck's aircraft's control surfaces iced up, and he ejected safely in his *Schleudersitzapparat*, 'seat catapult device'. The Germans experimented with seats ejected by compressed gas, a spring-operated mechanism, or a propellant charge. The first operational aircraft built anywhere to provide ejection seats for the crew was the Heinkel He 219 Uhu night fighter in 1942. The first operational military jet to feature one was the lightweight Heinkel He 162A Spatz, in late 1944. Its new type of ejection seat was fired by an explosive cartridge. During the war approximately sixty Luftwaffe pilots ejected from their aircraft. However, the demand for the Reichenberg ejection seat was a moot one considering that at the time it was only in its initial design/test phase and if available the aircraft's cockpit space would be far too small and narrow to house a catapulted seat mechanism.

Reichenberg Suicide Epilogue

After the Allied D-Day armada appeared off the Normandy coast, neither the Me 328 nor the piloted V-1 Reichenberg were ready to be used as intended, to decimate offshore Allied shipping, and the decisive moment had been squandered. Hanna Reitsch stated:

> And now that it was too late, we realised, too, that, from the very start the obstacles that were put in our way were greater than our will to carry the plan through. Among these were the misunderstandings and the clash of personalities among the very people who were working hardest for its success. A yet more formidable difficulty was the total failure on the part of higher authority to appreciate that the Suicide Group was no stunt, but a collection of brave, clear-headed and intelligent Germans who seriously believed, after careful thought and calculation, that by sacrificing their own lives they might save many times that number of their fellow-countrymen and ensure some kind of future for their children.

But this conception was too cold to kindle the imaginations of Himmler and Goebbels. Himmler suggested that the suicide-pilots should be recruited among the incurably diseased, the neurotics and the criminals so that through a voluntary death they might redeem their 'honour.' Goebbels hastened to exploit the Group for propaganda purposes by summoning its members to his Ministry and reciting to them a premature panegyric on the theme of heroism. Is it surprising that when the suicide-pilots were finally ready to go into action, it was already too late?

[From Reitsch's memoir, *The Sky My Kingdom*]

Nearly six months after D-Day, in October 1944, about 175 Fi 103R Reichenberg R-4s were available for combat with about sixty Luftwaffe pilots and thirty from Skorzeny's Kommando unit, who had joined *Leonidas* Staffel, were ready to fly these aircraft into combat. However, the slow disfavour and dissolution of Otto Skorzeny and Hanna Reitsch's Selbstopfermanner (Suicide Men) Squadron appears to have begun about October 1944 when Oberstleutnant (Lt Col) Werner Baumbach became the new Geschwader Kommodore of KG 200. Baumbach postponed and downgraded the Selbstopfermanner due to a number of factors. The basic one was a reluctance to continue the implausible experimental suicidal weapon in favour of the more promising and non-suicidal Mistel

Once Oberstleutnant Werner Baumbach, shown in an official 'Aryan' pose, became Kommodore of KG 200 he postponed and downgraded the Selbstopfermanner Reichenberg in favour of the more promising and non-suicidal Mistel concept. (*Author's collection*)

Baumbach and Albert Speer (shown), Reich's Minister of Armaments and Production, a declared critic of the Reichenberg project, met with Hitler and persuaded him that suicide missions were not 'part of the German warrior tradition'. (*NARA*)

concept of a manned fighter (Fw 190) attached to and directing an unmanned powered bomber (Ju 88) carrying high explosives toward a target.

However, by the beginning of 1945 the reduced Reichenberg programme floundered. A cadre of Reichenberg pilots had completed their training and had several Reichenbergs available, but their planned self-sacrificial deployment was no longer feasible. The production of the He 111 had ceased and Kampfgeschwader 53 had lost almost all of its carrier aircraft. The He 111 carriers and their Reichenbergs were easy targets for Allied day and night fighters. Previously, almost half of the conventional air-dropped unmanned Fi 103s were lost soon after release. This factor, the Reichenberg's limited speed and range and the insufficient warhead for important targets was deemed not worthy of sacrificing a human life.

It would not be until 15 March 1945 that Baumbach and Albert Speer, Reich's Minister of Armaments and Production and an avowed critic of the project, met Hitler and succeeded in convincing him that suicide missions were not 'part of the German warrior tradition'. Later that day Baumbach ordered the Reichenberg unit be disbanded.

If Hitler, Göring, and the Nazi High Command had recognised the potential of Skorzeny's and Reitsch's suicidal volunteers and their piloted flying bomb, it remains highly unlikely that their limited numbers could have thwarted the invasion of several hundred thousand men and 5,000 ships, even if exploited on the scale later employed by the Japanese.

Nazi suicidal notions did not end with the dissolution of the suicidal *Leonidas* squadron. At the end of the war Oberst (Colonel) Hans-Joachim, 'Hajo' Herrmann formed the *Sonderkommando Elbe*, a 'Special Unit' of young, impassioned Luftwaffe pilots who were expected to bail out either just before or after they had rammed their fighters into American bomber targets. Although 'self-sacrifice' had not been evoked during recruitment, bailing out after a successful ramming attack was still a rather suicidal expectation. Herrmann's objective was to assemble an overwhelming number of these fighters for a massive one-time attack on the large USAAF bomber formations devastating Fatherland cities. The expectation was to cause such heavy losses as to limit the bombing offensive for several months. However, aircraft, pilot, and fuel shortages prevented employment of the large numbers necessary for success for the group's only mission on 7 April 1945. The unit's force of 120 fighters managed to ram 15 Allied bombers, downing 8 of them, but suffered such prohibitive losses to the bomber formation's fighter escorts that only 15 returned. The *Sonderkommando Elbe* was disbanded on 17 April and the remaining pilots were transferred to Berlin to fight as infantrymen against the Red Army in the Battle of Berlin, another suicide mission.

Oberst Hans-Joachim 'Hajo' Herrmann formed the *Sonderkommando Elbe*. (*Author's collection*)

Post-War Fi 103R Reichenberg Gallery

Tramm was quickly liberated by the US Army's 5th Armoured Division on 23 April 1945, when its German commander, Major Hahn (wearing cap, photo centre), surrendered the camp without a fight. (*USAGF*)

New R-2s, the two-seat training versions, were stored at the Pulverhof assembly plant. (*USAGF*)

Tramm was in the designated British Occupation Zone, but the Americans had removed most of the Reichenbergs before the occupying British troops arrived. (*AFSHRC*)

A captured Reichenberg sits on display outside the Continental Hotel, Antwerp, Belgium, after the city had been bombarded by more than 4,000 V-1s and more than 1,700 V-2s over a 6-month period, killing more than 3,700 civilians and injuring some 6,000 others. (*USAGF*)

An American Intelligence Unit removes two Reichenbergs from Tramm before the British claim the area as part of their Occupation Zone. (*USAGF*)

A Reichenberg was among the captured Luftwaffe aircraft and many British prototypes undergoing late-war evaluation on public display at Farnborough October/November 1945. A sad footnote is that many of the aircraft displayed were later scrapped. (*AFSHRC*)

Post-war testing the Reichenberg's Argus pulsejet engine. Note that a Swastika and Balkenkreuz have been added to the captured aircraft. (*USAGF*)

Post-War Reichenberg Capture by the Allies

It is probable that most of the Reichenbergs were assembled at Dannenberg and brought to a nearby rail head as 'many' were captured and then quickly liberated by the US Army's 5th Armoured Division on 23 April 1945 when Commander Major Hahn (see photo) surrendered the camp without a fight. There are conflicting figures on the number of converted manned Fi 103Rs assembled but over 300 seems to be likely based on an American report. This report stated about 175 newly converted Fi 103R-4s were discovered at the Dannenberg assembly plant, while another 125 were found in storage buildings at the assembly plant's rail head ready to be loaded on to railroad cars. At Pulverhof, 25miles (62km) north, 'many' new R-2s, the two-seat training versions, were stored at an assembly plant. Except for the early prototypes and test models, no other operational Fi 103R-4s were found loaded on any railway cars or had been shipped.

Like all unconventional weapon developments of the Nazi regime, manned buzz bombs naturally stirred Allied interest at the end of the war. The Americans removed most of the Reichenbergs before the advancing British troops arrived in Tramm as it had been designated to became part of the British Occupation Zone. However, some remained in the British zone and were sent to England and Canada for study.

Fi 103R Reichenberg on Display

Flying Heritage Collection, Everett, Washington (restored No. 29)
Lashenden Air Warfare Museum, Headcorn, Kent (restored No. 85)
La Coupole, Saint-Omer, France (restored No. 126 or 123)
Schweizerisches Militärmuseum Full, Full-Reuenthal, Switzerland (restored No. 27)

The Reichenberg (No. 27) on display, shown with a V-1, at the Swiss Military Museum at Full-Reuenthal, is one of only four fully restored Reichenbergs. (*Schweizerisches Militärmuseum*)

Canadian War Museum, Ottawa (No. 135 in restoration)
National Military Museum (Soesterberg), Netherlands (partially restored No. 24)
Olympic Flight Museum, Olympia, Washington (Replica)
Texas Air Museum, Stinson Airfield, San Antonio, Texas (Replica)
Rechlin Aviation Technology Museum, Germany (Replica)

Hanna Reitsch Epilogue

Hanna Reitsch is considered the leading female German pilot of the twentieth century. Reitsch originally trained as a doctor but became interested in flying gliders and in 1935 she became a glider instructor and test pilot at the Deutsche Forschungsanstalt für Segelflug (DFS), which was the German Institute for Glider Research. During the next few years she set numerous gliding records and became an accomplished powered aircraft pilot. In 1937, she was appointed as a civilian test pilot of the Luftwaffe by Ernst Udet, a position she held until the end of the Second World War. Her fame as a pilot and her blue eyes and blonde hair gave her the favoured Aryan appearance and made her an ideal candidate for Nazi propaganda during the late 1930s and early 1940s. In 1938, Udet asked her to demonstrate that one could fully control a helicopter by flying one inside a building, which received international exposure.

During the war Reitsch tested many of Germany's latest designs including the Junkers Ju 87 Stuka and the Dornier Do 17. In 1942, she tested the dangerous rocket-propelled

After her fifteen-month post-war captivity, Hanna Reitsch settled in Germany and returned to gliding, winning championships and setting several records in the 1950s. She is shown here with pre-war glider and Me 328 colleague Heinz Kensche during the training for the 1954 Glider World Cup in England. (*NARA*)

Messerschmitt Me 163 but on her fifth test flight the take-off undercarriage did not fall away as designed. On landing the aircraft crashed and she suffered severe injuries, including a fractured skull and broken jaw, which hospitalised her for five months. During February 1944 she promoted the modified manned/piloted V-1, Fi 103R, to be flown by volunteers who would sacrifice their lives by crashing into the anticipated Allied invasion fleet. After this proposal was dismissed, she was severely injured during a late 1944 Allied air raid on Berlin. After her recovery, in late April 1945, with Soviet troops surrounding Berlin, she landed a small aircraft near the Führer Bunker, spending three days there before Hitler ordered her to leave. After the war she was arrested and held in an American POW camp for fifteen months. After her release Reitsch settled in Germany and returned to gliding, winning championships, and setting several records in the 1950s. From 1962 to 1966 she helped organise the West African country of Ghana's air force and then returned to West Germany, where the government retained her as a technical adviser. Throughout the 1970s, Reitsch continued breaking gliding records in many categories. She wrote her autobiography, *Flying My Life*, in 1951 and her memoirs, *The Sky My Kingdom*, in 1955. Reitsch never married but in 2015 DNA identified her as the mother of Alicia Webber, who was secretly fathered by famous rocket scientist Wernher von Braun in 1932. Reitsch died on 24 August 1979 of a heart attack in Frankfurt at 67.

During the post-war Reitsch She wrote her autobiography, *Flying My Life*, in 1951 and her memoirs, *The Sky My Kingdom*, in 1955. (*Author's Library*)

It seems, Reitsch believed zealously that once the successes of the first cadre of trained suicide men were achieved, a comprehensive Reichenberg deployment would have been initiated. But even when a training programme was completed, the decisive D-Day moment for which the Reichenberg existed had been missed. Thus, the indifference and delay of those responsible to approve a suicide aircraft and its pilots meant that there was no longer any time left to make a difference. Three weeks after D-Day the Allies had landed nearly a million men ashore and the opportunity to keep them from landing was long past.

Reitsch blamed the total failure of her suicide squadron on Hitler, Göring, and Milch, who considered the Selbstopfermanner as just another unconventional tactical venture when mass suicide was against the German psyche, yet she persisted:

> And so did an idea that was born of fervent and holy idealism, only to be misused and mismanaged at every turn by people who never understood how men and women could offer their lives simply for an idea they believed.

Otto Skorzeny Epilogue

At 6ft 4in tall, the imposing Otto Skorzeny was another Nazi Ubermensch 'Superman' legend connected with the Fi 103 project. As a university student he fought fifteen ritual sabre duels, during which he received a slash to the face that left him with a distinctive, macho scar. Skorzeny joined the Austrian Nazi Party in 1930 and was appointed as one of Hitler's personal bodyguards. He distinguished himself fighting with the SS on the Western Front (1940) and then in the Balkans. During September 1943, under Hitler's personal patronage, he organised the successful rescue of Benito Mussolini, who was imprisoned high in the Abruzzi Apennine Mountains. Skorzeny was subsequently promoted to Oberstleutnant (Lieutenant Colonel) and assigned the operational control of Hitler's SS Kommando, after which he became known for his swashbuckling appearance and exploits. As part of his Kommando Special Forces he formed a new unit, the *Leonidas* squadron, which was a suicide unit that became part of KG 200. After he and Reitsch left the Reichenberg project, his exploits continued, including the successful kidnapping of Miklós Horthy, the Regent of Hungary, who wanted to surrender Hungary to the advancing Red Army in October 1944. After being acquitted of war crimes in September 1947, Skorzeny relished his reputation as 'Europe's Most Dangerous Man'. He became an advisor to various governments, spending time in Argentina, where he acted as an advisor to President Juan Perón and as a bodyguard for Eva Perón. In 1962 he worked for Egypt's President Nasser, where he recruited former SS and Wehrmacht officers to train the army. After the Israelis threatened to assassinate him, he switched sides and worked with the Israeli Mossad against his former Nazi comrades in Egypt. In 1975 Skorzeny published his memoir: *My Commando Missions: Hitler's Most Daring Commando*, and updated his daring deeds with *Skorzeny's Special Missions: The Memoirs of the Most Dangerous Man in Europe*. Skorzeny died of lung cancer on 5 July 1975 in Madrid at the age of 67.

In the post-war Skorzeny continued his daring exploits, which he chronicled in his book, *Skorzeny's Special Missions: The Memoirs of the Most Dangerous Man in Europe*. (*Author's Library*)

Chapter Three

Nazi Drawing Board Suicide Parasite Proposals

Section One: Arado Ar E.377 Parasite/Ar 234 or He 162 Composite Design

Among the final glide bomb developments proposed to the RLM before the end of the Second World War, Arado, in cooperation with Rheinmetall-Borsig, Hitler's second largest arms supplier of all varieties, designed a rudimentary glide bomb as the Mistel 5 Project. Designated as the Arado Ar E.377, it was designed in an unpowered (Version A) or powered Version B (two BMW 109-003 turbojet engines) that could be air or ground launched. Except in length, due to the type of warhead, the E.377B was almost identical in all other regards to the unpowered glide E.377A. The air-launched E.377 was a planned manned suicide or unmanned flying bomb design to be carried under the Arado Ar 234 Blitz twin-jet engine bomber. The combination could be ground-launched using a special trolley as an unmanned flying bomb, which was to be guided by a radio controlled or target guidance system that made changes in the control and rudder movements from the Arado mother aircraft after launch, or the E.377 could simply be set to glide straight after separation. The E.377 was to attack targets such as ships or large fixed objectives such as factories, large utility structures, or fortifications. Keeping with Germany's use of non-essential war materials toward the end of the war, the entire sleek, rocket-shaped E.377 was constructed of wood with plywood cladding. Its two BMW 109-003 turbojet engines would allow the E.377 to make an approach to the target at a speed of 466mph (750kmph). The only production aircraft to be powered by the BMW 003 would be the Heinkel He 162 and the later C-series, four-engined versions of the Arado Ar 234.

Explosive Armament

The nose section housed 4,408lb (2,000kg) of Trialen 105, which was an enhanced blast explosive, the German equivalent of the British explosive Torpex, that was especially useful for attacking shipping. It was composed of a mixture of TNT, hexogen (RDX), and aluminium powder in varying proportions for each of three versions. The explosive's production was hindered by a shortage of the aluminium powder that was added to increase its explosive power. A standard SC 1800 bomb could also be mounted in the forward fuselage in place of the Trialen. The rear fuselage housed 1,200lb (500kg) of an incendiary liquid that also acted as ballast to counterbalance the forward warhead.

Ground Launch

To achieve take-off of the wheelless E.377/He 162 or Ar 234 combination, a releasable five-wheeled trolley, like one that Rheinmetall-Borsig had previously designed for the Arado 234A take-off, was used, sometimes with an additional set of wheels. To position the Ar 234 or He 162 mothership, which attached Mistel *Huckepack* (Piggyback) style to the lower unmanned (manned in the suicide version) E.377 aircraft on to the top of the trolley, a trestle and frame apparatus was specifically developed. Once the combination attained take-off speed, the reusable trolley was released and slowed and manoeuvred on to the ground by a combination of parachutes. When necessary, the two rocket engines of the E.377 were additionally boosted into the air by two Walter HWK 109-500 accelerator rockets on the trolley. Once airborne, the single turbojet engine of the carrying He 162 would not have been powerful enough to transport the heavy E.377, so this E.377 Version B was to be powered by two BMW turbojet engines mounted under its wings.

Air Launch of the Manned E.377 Version

The manned parasite version had its pilot laying prone manually controlling the E.377 toward the target. Upon arrival at the target, the E.377 was released from the mother aircraft by explosive bolts and was then manoeuvred toward its target. There is virtually no information regarding the manned E.377 as it probably was no more than drawing board conjecture. Neither Version A nor Version B of the Arado E.377 ever reached the prototype stage but remained as preliminary designs as the war ended.

As a 'Flying Fuel Station'

The circular, tapered fuselage held tapered, shoulder-mounted wings that acted as auxiliary fuel tanks supplying 9,918lb (4,500kg) of fuel for the Ar 234 carrying aircraft. In this role the E.377 acted as a disposable 'flying fuel station', supplying the Ar 234 with additional fuel to extend its bombing or reconnaissance range over the UK. Fuel was drawn from the E.377's tanks by jet pressure, which drove a compressor in the powerplant of the carrying aircraft. The cruciform tail unit was symmetrical on top and bottom with a horizontal tail mounted on the upper half of the fin.

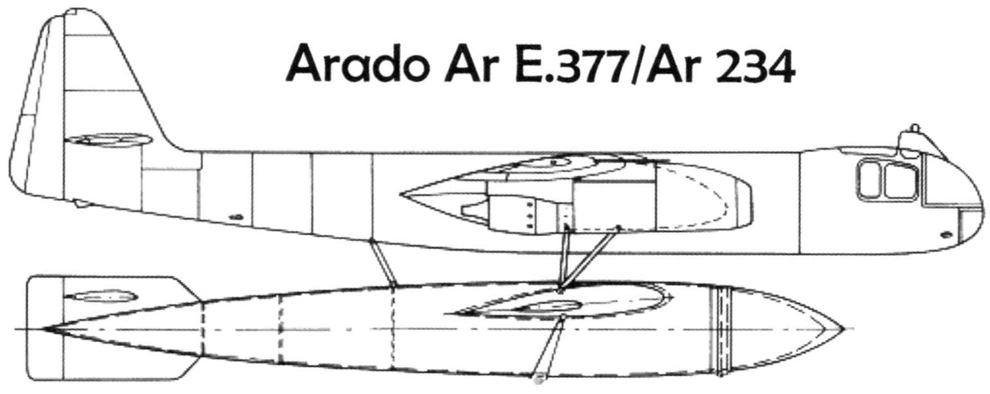

Arado Ar E.377/Ar 234. (*Author's collection*)

Specifications: Arado Ar E.377
Length: Version A: 34ft 8.5in (10.6m)
Version B: 33ft 1.75in (10.7m)
Height: 4ft 5.5in (1.368m)
Wingspan: 37ft 8.5in (11.50m)
Wing Area: 291 sq ft (27 sq m)
Engine: BMW 003 jet-powered version
Launch Weight: 22,040lb (10,000kg) without trolley
Launch Height: 34,450ft (10,500m)
Gliding Range: 130 miles (209km)

Section Two: Zeppelin Rammjager (Rammer Fighter)

Zeppelin Abteilung Flugzeugbau GmbH at Friedrichshafen lost much favour with the Nazi Party following the high-profile *Hindenburg* airship disaster in 1937, which forced the company to terminate its airship manufacturing in 1938. All existing Zeppelin airship operations ceased by 1940, with the *Graf Zeppelin* and *Graf Zeppelin II* airframes subsequently being scrapped for their materials, which were used to manufacture Luftwaffe fixed-wing military aircraft. During the autumn of 1941, the company accepted contracts to produce components of the V-2 rocket but in August 1943 Allied bombing during Operation Bellicose severely damaged the Zeppelin V-2 facility, leading to production being subsequently relocated to the underground Mittelwerk facility. Mittelwerk was infamous for using slave labour to produce V-2 and V-1 flying bombs and other weapons. Meanwhile, the Zeppelin company struggled to remain viable and answered the RLM's Miniature Fighter request by developing its Rammjager (Rammer Fighter) project, completing a proposal during November 1944.

Described

The once proud builders of huge, majestic Zeppelin airships had devolved into presenting the RLM with plans for a miniscule rocket fighter. It was to be 16ft 1in (4.9m) long, 3ft 1.25in (1.2m) high and weighed only 390lb (860kg) without its pilot. It was to have a steel-clad fuselage sprouting straight, 16.4ft (5m) constant-chord wings containing three steel tubular spars covered by 0.8–1.2in (20–30mm) of hardened steel that reinforced its leading edges for ramming. The pilot was protected by a heavily armoured cockpit frontal armour of 1.1in (28mm) and dorsal armour of 0.8in (20mm), and a 3.2in (80mm) glass plate windscreen with 1.6in (40mm) glass side panels. The RLM issued a contract for sixteen Rammer prototypes in January 1945. The name Rammjager and its fanciful concept was probably Zeppelin company propaganda, possibly meant to keep the company afloat and to prevent the company's engineers from being conscripted as common soldiers. This ploy had the surreptitious intention of most of these type of projects during the last months of the war, many of which never progressed beyond the drawing board or model stage.

In Combat

The Rammer was to be towed aloft by another fighter (a Bf 109 or Bf 110?) or carried aloft by a bomber (Ju 88?) Mistel-style and then released at combat altitude at nearby enemy bombers, using its tiny size and high speed to make it a difficult target. Once released, the pilot, flying from his prone position, was to ignite the Schmidding 533 solid-fuel rocket, which yielded 2,205lb (1,000kg) thrust, to hypothetically accelerate the aircraft to 600mph (970kmph) during a total on-off burn time of forty-five to sixty seconds. The pilot would manoeuvre his fighter toward the clustered bombers below and launch fourteen R4M rockets at the target from a long proboscis-like plastic nose pod that was a cylinder with a cap containing the rockets. The R4M, (Rakete, 4kg, Minenkopf) was a 9lb (4kg), 2.17in (55mm) calibre folding-fin, air-to-air, solid fuel rocket. Its warhead contained 1.15lb (0.52g) HTA 4 (torpex) having a maximum range of 4,900ft (1,494m) but an effective range of about 1,800ft (550m). Since the R4M missiles had a similar trajectory as 30mm MK 108 cannon rounds in flight, the standard Revi 16B gunsight could be utilised to aim the rocket barrage. After firing its rockets, the pilot was to make a second pass, this time making a ramming attack with its reinforced wings that at the high attack speed were to theoretically cut cleanly through the tail section of a B-17 and continue without the great loss of speed or stability. Then, improbably, once the Rammer's rocket engine's solid fuel was consumed, its R4M rockets fired, the nose rocket pod released, then the Rammer's centre of gravity was restored, keeping it flyable during its gliding descent and landing on a retractable skid. Realistically, the aircraft and its pilot would not survive what was truly a kamikaze attack that had been forbidden by the Reich Air Ministry.

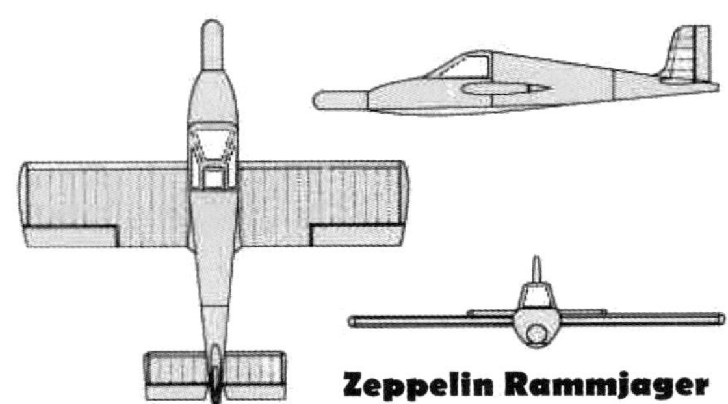

Zeppelin Rammjager. (*Author's collection*)

After launching its fourteen R4M rockets on a USAAF B-17 formation that was devastating German cities, a rocket-powered Rammjager slices through the empennage of a bomber using its reinforced wing. (*Author's collection*)

Rammer Epilogue

After towed glide flights were conducted during January 1945, an order for sixteen pre-production prototypes was placed, however, US bombers destroyed the Zeppelin factory before their manufacture could begin. Nearly fifty years since Count Ferdinand von Zeppelin had founded the Zeppelin company in 1896, Luftschiffbau

Zeppelin effectively ceased to exist after the Second World War. Then, almost forty years following its disappearance, Zeppelin was resurrected using its residual assets and during 1993 the parent group company of the current Zeppelin maker was re-established, while the operating company currently building Zeppelins was created in 2001.

Zeppelin Rammjager: Specifications

Crew: 1
Length: 16ft 1in long (4.9m)
Height: 3ft 1.25in (1.2m)
Wingspan: 16ft 5in (5m)
Gross weight: 390lb (860kg) without its pilot

Performance
Engine: 1 Schmidding 109-533 rocket engine
Maximum speed: 530mph (850kmph)

Armament: 14 R4M rockets

Section Three: Focke-Wulf Kamikaze Project

During the early 1940s, Focke-Wulf designers submitted a Selbstopfer/self-sacrifice combination to the Reichsluftfahrtministerium (RLM) consisting of five lightweight underwing parasites powered by a single turbojet that would be carried to the vicinity of the target by a very large, multi-engined, high-thrust, turboprop-powered mothership. The high speed of the turbojet composite and the surprise of its approach was thought to give the mission safety from enemy interception.

Focke-Wulf Selbstopfer/Self-Sacrifice Parasite

The Focke-Wulf parasite was to be powered by a single He S 001 turbojet having 2,866lb (1,300kg) of thrust that was expected to achieve 576mph (927km/h) at 19,686ft (6km). The first engine ran in early 1944, with all the performance data met or exceeded by early 1945. It was flight tested under the fuselage of a Junkers Ju 88 test bed, but by the end of the war had never been flown under its own power and never went into production. The parasite was to be constructed from as much wood and other non-essential material as possible. It was to carry a large 5,000lb (2,268kg) explosive warhead, which was equipped with a stand-off probe with electrical crush fuses used to detonate a hollow explosive charge, powerful enough to sink an armoured warship hull or penetrate concrete fortifications. The pilot was to be provided with only a few essential instruments: a gyro compass, an altimeter, an air speed indicator, a clock, and a turn and bank indicator. Flight controls were to be the conventional stick and rudder foot pedal. The pilot sitting in a plywood bucket seat with a safety belt with shoulder straps was provided with a parachute, a life preserver, a helmet with headphones and throat microphones, and sunglasses.

The proposed operational 'plan' was to have the pilot dive his Selbstopfer parasite toward the target, bail out just before collision, and parachute to safety. That was the plan, however, considering the aircraft's anticipated high diving speed, it was improbable that the pilot could have escaped safely before crashing the target. A ramming Selbstopfer aircraft could only successfully destroy an enemy bomber by cutting through the empennage controls and flying safely afterward or by directly impacting it, with both becoming entangled in a fatal crash.

However, Gotha Company engineers sought to design a cone-shaped break-away armoured cockpit that could bore through the targeted aircraft. The fuselage of the attacking aircraft would remain caught in the target aircraft, while the armoured cockpit detached itself and, like a projectile, punched through the target for a very terrifying ride! With the cockpit in the front of the aircraft, it would have possible to keep the actual fuselage as basic as possible, by providing a very strong, easily built, and inexpensive aerodynamic cross-shaped airframe that acted both as a fuselage and wing. To provide the half-reclining and half-sitting pilot with the best view during normal flight, an adjustable seat was placed and at the moment of impact, the seat was to automatically recline to protect the plots from the impact and then eject him out of the cockpit to parachute to safety. More bizarrely, the rammer's nose could be fitted with an explosive device that, at the moment of impact, would burst a lethal hole in the target aircraft, for the detachable cockpit to shoot through. This explosive device could also be detonated on demand.

Specifications: Parasite

Crew: 1
Wingspan: 27.9ft (8.5m)
Wing Area: 161.2 sq ft (8.5m)
Length: 30.2ft (9.2m)
Height: 10.5ft (3.2m)
Weight, Empty: 3,968lb (1,800kg)
Weight, Take-off: 9,921lb (4,500kg)
Engine: 1 × Heinkel-Hirth He S 001 turbojet having 2,866lb (1,300kg) thrust
Speed, Cruise; NA
Speed Maximum: 576mph (927km/h) at 19,686ft (6km)
Service Ceiling: 34,450ft (10.5km)
Range: 1,068 miles (1,720km)
Armament: None
Bomb Load: 5,000lb

Focke-Wulf Mothership

The Focke-Wulf carrier was to be a huge (115ft long), high-mounted, gull-shaped wing monoplane, with long, slender twin tail booms, with two fins connected by a central high-mounted horizontal stabiliser. The 177ft (54m) span wing was to be moderately swept back, about 32.8ft (10m). The glazed-over cockpit at the very front of the fuselage contained the two-man crew. A tricycle landing gear was proposed, with each of the two main fixed landing gear assemblies having six tyres while the nose gear heel was to contain two tyres, with the gear retracting into the fuselage. Landing the massive parasite-conveying mothership was not believed to be problematic since the wing loading of the aircraft, having discharged its five parasites, would be much lighter. This large aircraft could also operate as a heavy lift or troop transport serving the front lines as its high-wing design permitted short field landings, while its sturdy landing gear allowed the use of rough strips. It was to be powered by six Daimler-Benz DB 603N, liquid-cooled, 12-cylinder inverted V12, 1,900hp engines, which were to propel the aircraft at an estimated maximum speed of 348mph (560kmph). This engine was the largest-displacement inverted V12 aviation engine to be produced and used in front-line Luftwaffe aircraft; powering several aircraft, including the Do 217, Do 335, He 219, Me 410, BV 155 and Ta 152C. Two engines, located ahead of each boom, protruded from the leading edge of the wing. Outboard of these engines would be two push-pull coupled engines contained in a long nacelle that protruded beyond both the wing's leading and tailing edges. As a parasite mothership, the aircraft's role was to carry these from their base through Luftwaffe-controlled airspace, to rendezvous with a long-range turbojet-powered reconnaissance aircraft such as an Arado Ar 234B. At the rendezvous the parasites would start their turbojets, be released from the mothership, and follow the reconnaissance aircraft to the planned target for a maximum two-hour flight duration over a range of 1,056 miles (1,700km). After releasing its parasites, the carrier would return to base.

Specifications: Mothership

Crew: 1
Wingspan: 177ft (54m)
Wing Area: 5,382 sq ft (500 sq m)
Length: 114.8ft (35m)
Height: 39.4ft (12m)
Weight, Empty: 113,095lb (51,300kg)
Weight, Take-off: 268,961lb (122,000kg)
Engines: 6 × Daimler-Benz DB 603N, 12-cylinder 1,900hp piston engines
Speed, Cruise: NA
Speed Maximum: 348mph (560kmph)
Range: 1,068 miles (1,720km)
Armament: None
Bomb Load: None

Neither mothership nor the parasite progressed beyond the Focke-Wulf drawing board and was one of the many fantastical Nazi designs.

Part II

Japanese Manned Suicide Composites

Chapter One

Japanese Ohka Parasite/G4M Betty Mothership Suicide Composite

The Origins of the Kamikaze

The Battle of the Philippine Sea on 19–20 June 1944 eliminated the Imperial Japanese Navy's ability to conduct large-scale carrier actions. During this pivotal sea battle the Japanese lost 3 irreplaceable carriers, more than 350 carrier aircraft, and approximately 200 land-based aircraft. The heavy losses that had been sustained by the G4M Betty bombers and other Japanese bombers during previous anti-shipping operations led Capt. Motoharu Okamura, in command of the Tateyama Base, Tokyo, and the 341st Air Group Home, to first propose the idea of a Special Attack Force on 15 June 1944, to V Adm. Takijirō Ōnishi, the commander of Japan's First Air Fleet:

> In our present situation, I firmly believe that the only way to swing the war in our favour is to resort to crash-dive attacks with our planes … Provide me with 300 planes and I will turn the tide of war. There is no other way.

Ōnishi had originally opposed the kamikaze concept but following the loss of the Mariana Islands and the devasting IJN air and sea losses during the Battle of the Philippine Sea, and now confronting orders to destroy the USN aircraft carrier fleet in advance of the enemy invasion of the Philippines, he changed his position.

Ōnishi and Okamura organised the first investigations and reports on the plausibility and designs for what they termed as 'premeditated body crash attacks'. Their investigations, however, were an opportune method to gain political favour and to give the growing number of proponents the influence they needed to get the programme under way despite its relative unpopularity.

Motoharu Ohkamura. (*Author/Lansdale*)

Motoharu Okamura

During the 1930s Okamura became a well-known test pilot and served as a flight leader in the navy's 12th Air Group's Fighter Squadron during 1938 in the China campaign, where he was recognised for developing new air tactics. At the beginning of the war, he instructed the Yokosuka Air Corps and later became the CO of Tokyo's Tateyama Base and the 341st Air Group Home.

Takijirō Ōnishi

Ōnishi graduated from the Imperial Japanese Navy Academy and served on various pre-First World War warships before being assigned to a seaplane tender, where he assisted in the development of the early Imperial Japanese Navy Air Service. During 1918 he was assigned duty in England and France to study the development of combat aircraft. After the war he served in naval air staff positions through the 1920s, being promoted to lieutenant commander and assigned to the aircraft carrier *Hōshō* in 1928 as commander of its carrier air wing. He became executive officer of the aircraft carrier *Kaga* in 1932. During November 1939, he was promoted to rear admiral and Chief of Staff of the Eleventh Air Fleet. He aided in the planning of the Pearl Harbor attack and his Eleventh Air Fleet played an important part in the early air operations in the Philippines. During May 1943, he was promoted to vice admiral, participating in staff duties until October 1944, when he became commander of the First Air Fleet in the northern Philippines.

Takijiro Onishi. (*Author/Lansdale*)

Kamikaze and Ohka Etymology

Admiral Takijirō Ōnishi is generally acknowledged for creating and organising the IJN Special Attack Force, the Shimpu Tokubetsu Kogekitai (Divine Wind Special Attack Unit), which first became operational in October 1944. Shimpu is an alternative pronunciation of the Japanese ideographs that also represent kamikaze: 'kami' means divine, 'kaze' means wind. Kamikaze originated in 1281 when Kublai Khan's Mongol hordes were on the brink of overwhelming the Japanese Home Islands when a destructive typhoon named kamikaze (Divine Wind) devastated the invasion fleet.

However, the Japanese never used the term 'kamikaze' in relation to the suicide attacks. US translators used the indigenous Japanese pronunciation for 'Shimpu', which uses the same kanji characters as 'kamikaze', giving the English language the word kamikaze. This phrase eventually gained worldwide acceptance, and after the war was reimported into Japan, where the attacks are now known as 'kamikaze tokubetsu kogeki tai (the abbreviated version is 'tokkotai' or 'tokko' for short)'.

The Ohka prototype aircraft was originally designated as the MXY7 and deceptively code-named Project Marudai (marudai: a frame used for making a type of Japanese braid). After prototype development, ten models were produced and the MXY7's successors were renamed the Ohka (Oka), meaning 'Cherry Blossom'. The word, a popular Japanese girl's name, aōsō has many kanji (a system of symbols that represent words or ideas, and that can have different meanings and pronunciations depending on their context) variations in meaning such as: To Fly (spread your wings and fly), and also refers to rebirth and the legendary bird, the phoenix, rising from the ashes. Ohka was also dubbed the 'Baka Bomb' by the Allies as Baka's Japanese translation is 'foolish' or 'idiotic', since the Japanese strategy of using them was, in the view of the Allies, foolhardy. Another Baka naming version was that fifteen Ohkas were captured by the US Marines on the first day of the invasion, 1 April 1945, April Fool's Day, and were dubbed 'Baka', Japanese for fool.

Condemnation of the Kamikaze Programme

The kamikaze programme was a divisive issue among the Japanese military hierarchy, many branding the idea as a waste of life and resources. Adm. Soemu Toyoda, as the Commander-in-Chief of the Combined Japanese Fleet, like R Adm. Ōnishi, initially did not approve of aerial suicide attack tactics. After his fleet's crushing defeats during the Battles of the Philippine Sea and Leyte Gulf, he was nonetheless promoted to being the Imperial Japanese Navy Chief of Staff who had no fleet to command except the super battleship *Yamato*, which he would sacrifice in a kamikaze operation. To counter the impending invasion of Okinawa, Toyoda's Operation Ten-Go was to concentrate Japanese naval air power based on Kyushu and Formosa for the air defence of the island. The Formosan Ohkas were those delivered by the *Ryuho* during January 1945. Ten-Go was scheduled to involve 4,500 naval aircraft, but by 6 April 1945 only 700 were available, about half of them kamikazes, leaving Toyoda with no option but to utilise them. Now that the kamikaze corps officially existed, the Ohka, a parallel suicide attack programme, could be established.

Adm. Soemu Toyoda, Commander-in-Chief of the Combined Japanese Fleet. (*NARA*)

From early November 1944, R Adm. Toshiyuki Yokoi was commander of the 25th Air Flotilla based on Kanoya Airbase in southern Kyushu, the southernmost large Japanese home island. Yokoi had participated in the Marianas campaign and was seriously wounded while in command of the carrier *Hiyō*. When the kamikazes were formed in late 1944, he was commander of the 25th Air Flotilla and then on 9 February 1945 he was appointed to be Chief of Staff to the Fifth Air Fleet to V Adm. Matome Ugaki, commander of Fifth Air Fleet, whose mission was to stop enemy carrier striking forces by concentrating on suicide air attacks. Yokoi claims to have requested permission to decline the position due to his opposition to such missions but was still 'requested' to take the post. Yokoi expressed his opinion when he heard about the order from general headquarters that suicide attacks would be adopted by the military:

> Imperial General Headquarters was so fully convinced that it issued an outrageous and unprecedented order to the effect that all armed forces should resort to suicide attacks. This proved that the high command, utterly confused by a succession of defeats, had lost all wisdom of cool judgment and had degenerated to the point of indulging in wild gambling. The order was nothing less than a national death sentence. Like every military order, it was issued in the name of the emperor and was, therefore, no matter how outrageous, not open to question or criticism. Obedience was imperative; there was no alternative. Critics of the kamikaze attacks should distinguish the completely volunteer flights of October 1944 from those made after this imperial order.
>
> *The Japanese Navy in World War II: In the Words of Former Japanese Naval Officers*, Naval Institute Press, 1986

G4M Betty Mothership Historical Background

A total of 2,446 Mitsubishi G4Ms were built in several versions between September 1939 and August 1945, proving to be excellent combat aircraft on all fronts. Code-named 'Betty' by the Allies, this twin-engine, long-range medium-bomber remained in service with the Japanese Navy from the first to the last day of the war, when two white-painted G4M1s, painted with green crosses, carried the Japanese surrender delegation on 19 August 1945 to its final destination with the Allies on the USS *Missouri* in Tokyo Bay.

Designed for long range and high speed at the time of its introduction, the G4M gained initial fame for its part in the long-range attack that sank the British warships HMS *Prince of Wales* and *Repulse* in December 1941, its outstanding range revolutionising operational bombing concepts in the Pacific. The Betty is probably best known for its involvement in the death on 18 April 1943 of Admiral Isoroku Yamamoto, IJN Commander-in-Chief and Pearl Harbor architect, when sixteen P-38 Lightnings of the 339th Fighter Squadron of the 347th Fighter Group, Thirteenth Air Force, shot down his G4M1. It was nicknamed the 'Flying Cigar' (*Hamaki*) on account of its shape, and the 'Flying Ronson' because its fuel tanks were unprotected and easily caught fire.

After their catastrophic losses during the Battle of Midway on 4–7 June of the previous year, during 1943 the Imperial Japanese Navy was steadily confronted by the US Navy in a war of attrition that it was incapable of significantly increasing its air and sea forces to counter. Causing the Japanese particular concern were the number of its main G4M2e Betty Navy Type 1 attack bombers available to combat units, as steady losses almost matched its manufacturer Mitsubishi's attempt to increase production during 1943.

With far superior manufacturing capabilities, the Allies increased their offensive during the first six months of 1944 with advances in northern New Guinea, in the Northern Solomons, and in the Central Pacific. Meanwhile, in these conflicted areas the IJN's bomber Kokutais (air groups) seldom engaged with more than a dozen Bettys for each mission, as the High Command, anticipating Allied operations against the Marianas and the Philippines, was endeavouring to retain as many as possible in reserve.

On 19 and 20 June 1944, during the Battle of the Philippine Sea, the IJN was engaged in another calamitous air-sea battle that took place off the Marianas. The USN carriers of Task Force 58 deployed 900 aircraft against the Imperial Japanese Navy's 450 carrier-based aircraft and 200 land-based aircraft, including the G4Ms of the 755th Kokutai based on Guam. During this battle, which became known as the 'Great Marianas Turkey Shoot', the 4 Japanese air strikes involved 373 carrier aircraft, of which 243 were lost, and while 130 managed to return to their carriers, many of them were subsequently lost when the carriers *Taiho* and *Shokaku* were sunk. After the second day of the battle, IJN losses totalled 3 carriers, more than 350 carrier aircraft, and approximately 200 land-based aircraft, including the 755th Kokutai that now only existed on paper.

In the Philippines, during the early autumn of 1944, the IJN only had the 761st Kokutai's G4Ms based at Davao, and these suffered heavy losses during MacArthur's October reconquest of the islands. Nonetheless, the 761st Kokutai, based at Clark Field, remained the only Betty unit available in the Philippines until December, when they were reinforced by the 762nd and 763rd Kokutais. Over the next months, these Betty units confronted crushing American air superiority, and were forced to increasingly resort to night sorties by small formations. However, US night fighters, P-61 Black Widows and F6F-5N Hellcats, stalked and destroyed them. Finally, by February 1945, with the 761st and 763rd Kokutais decimated, the remains of the 762nd Kokutai were returned to Kanoya, Japan, where the unit converted to much faster two-engined Yokosuka P1Y Ginga (Frances) bombers.

At this juncture in the war, it became obvious that the Betty had become obsolete, nevertheless, during the spring of 1945 and until the 15 August armistice, three Kokutais; the 706th, 752nd, and 765th, continued operating G4Ms in their conventional bombing role, while a few G4Ms were operationally tested by the Yokosuka Kokutai. In its final incarnation, the once premier G4M Navy Type 1 Attack Bomber would serve as a mother aircraft for the Navy Suicide Attacker Ohka (Oka) Model 11.

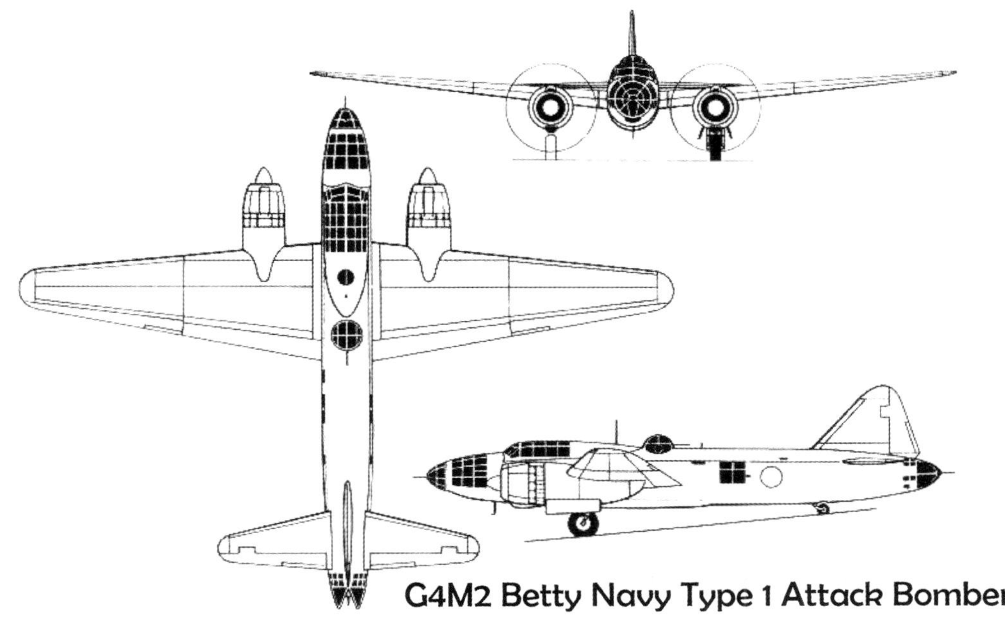

Serving from the first day to the last day of the war, the 2,446 Mitsubishi G4Ms built were the backbone of the Japanese Navy's bomber force but suffered heavy losses to Allied fighters. During the spring of 1945, it became obvious that the Betty had become obsolete, as Japanese bomber combat units converted to the much faster two-engined Yokosuka P1Y Ginga (Frances). The remaining Bettys were chosen as the mothership to carry the Ohka. (*Author's collection*)

General Characteristics G4M1 Model 11

Crew: 7 (pilot, co-pilot, navigator/bombardier/nose gunner, captain/top turret gunner, radio operator/waist gunner, engine mechanic/waist gunner, tail gunner)
Length: 65ft 6in (20m)
Wingspan: 81ft 8in (24.9m)
Wing area: 840.9 sq ft (78.1 sq m)
Height: 16ft 1in (4.9m) in rigging position
Empty weight: 14,861lb (6,741kg)
Gross weight: 20,944lb (9,500kg)
Max take-off weight: 28,351lb (12,860kg)
Powerplant: 2 × Mitsubishi MK4A Kasei 11 14-cylinder air-cooled radial piston engines, @1,530hp each for take-off/1,410hp 6,600ft at (2,000m)/1,340hp at 13,000ft (4,000m)
Propellers: 3-bladed Sumitomo (Hamilton Standard licensed) constant speed variable-pitch

Performance
Maximum speed: 266mph (428kmph) at 13,800ft (4,200m)
Cruise speed: 196mph (315kmph) at 9,800ft (3,000m)
Stall speed: 75mph (120kmph)
Range: 1,772 miles (2,852km)
Ferry range: 3,130 miles (5,040km)
Rate of climb: 1,805ft/minute (550m/min)

Armament
Guns: 1 × 20mm Type 99 cannon (tail turret), 4 × 7.7mm Type 92 machine gun (nose turret × 1, waist positions × 2, top turret ×1)
Bombs: 1 × 1,892lb (858kg) Type 91 Kai-3 (improved model 3) aerial torpedo or 1 × 1,764lb (800kg) bomb or 4 × 551lb (250kg) bombs or 1 × 2,645lb (1,200kg) Yokosuka MXY7 Ohka manned suicide rocket bomb

Designer: Kiro Honjo
Primary User: Imperial Japanese Navy Air Service
First Flight: 23 October 1939
Introduction: 2 April 1941
Number built: 2,435 (There are no complete or flyable Mitsubishi G4Ms remaining today, although three G4Ms survive as sections of preserved fuselage, and as the remains of several wrecks found on Pacific islands and in south-east Asia.)

Ohka Development

The kamikaze aircraft were a variety of Japanese Army and Navy types; existing models in poor condition, obsolete types, while others were trainers. Good-quality, front-line aircraft were reserved for more experienced pilots and conserved for the defence of the beleaguered homeland islands. However, the Japanese designed only one aircraft, the Ohka (Oka), solely as a dedicated suicide aircraft.

It was the relatively greater successes achieved by smaller and faster conventional aircraft during previous anti-shipping sorties that led Ensign Mitsuo Ohta, a former transport pilot flying with the 405th Kokutai, to propose a new dedicated suicide aircraft to the IJN during 1943. Ohta's proposal was for a piloted glide bomb powered by a battery of solid-propellant rockets and containing an internal load of explosives in its nose to be carried in the bomb bay of a specially modified G4M and then released within the vicinity of Allied naval vessel targets. After release, it would glide toward the target, then ignite its rocket boosters to accelerate its approach and terminal dive on to the target as quickly as possible to minimise the chances of interception by enemy aircraft and present a very fast-moving target to defending anti-aircraft gunners.

Professor Hidemasa Kimura also designed the Japanese Army Air Force long-range, twin-engine Ki-77, which set a world non-stop endurance record on 2 July 1944, flying fifty-seven hours nine minutes and covering 10,212 miles (16,435km) during nineteen circuits over Manchuria. (*Author/Lansdale*)

Not being an experienced aeronautical engineer, Ohta was unable to offer a definitive plan for his aircraft and his scheme was disregarded until the devastating Marianas 'Turkey Shoot' defeat in June 1944, when he was ordered back to Japan to update IJN officials at the Aeronautical Research Institute at the University of Tokyo on his glide/rocket suicide aircraft concept. At the university he received assistance from Professor Taichiro Ogawa, who directed the development of Ohta's concept, while Professor Hidemasa Kimura provided the basic design of the aircraft, constructing models that were wind tunnel tested. After only several weeks, Ogawa and Kimura had Ohta's proposed design drafted, drawings finished, and completed wind tunnel tests that supplied performance estimates.

Lt Cdr Tadanao Miki, Head of the First Naval Air Technical Arsenal. (*Author/Lansdale*)

These refined plans were presented to Lt Cdr Tadanao Miki, head of the *Dai-Ichi Kaigun Koku Gijit-susho* (First Naval Air Technical Arsenal) at Yokosuka, and Kugisho Chief Adm. Yushiro Wada. The two men and their staffs were initially reluctant on a personal basis to approve the Ohka's human guidance system and the defenceless Betty/Ohka combination's need for a considerable fighter escort, which themselves would also be vulnerable to US Navy defending combat air patrols (CAPs). But, by that time Japan's critical war situation prevailed over the sanctity of human life and the Shimpu programme was approved and ongoing. On 5 August 1944. Miki presented the design to Cdr Minoru Genda, who authorised the concept and advised Adm. Koshirō Oikawa to proceed with producing a prototype, designated as the MXY7 (M for special-purpose aircraft; X denoting experimental in conjunction with Y for Yokosuka Kugisho; and 7 for seventh in the series), at the Kaigun-Koku-Gijutsu-Sho (Naval Air Technical Arsenal) at Yokosuka.

Cdr Minoru Genda, Naval General Air Staff Officer, was a major Imperial Navy contributor to the planning of the Pearl Harbor attack and other major campaigns, and later the post-war Chief of Staff of the Japanese Air Self-Defense Force. (*Author/Lansdale*)

The Imperial Naval Air Headquarters proceeded promptly and allocated the secret code name *Mani-Dai* (*Mani* meaning circle, to indicate a code name, and *Dai* being the first Japanese character of Ensign Ohta's name) to Kugisho for Ohka development. Other than its design and engineering expertise for the IJN's advanced aircraft concepts, Kugisho included an aircraft manufacturing factory and the Yokosuka Air Wing, which served as the flight test unit. On 16 August 1944, Miki as chief designer assembled a team of three engineers led by Cdr Masao Yamana as project manager, and assisted by Tadanao Mitsugi and Rokuro Hattori, who began drafting and refining the design. To conserve war materials, the MXY7 was to be constructed using wood and other non-strategic materials, and critically limited aluminium only if necessary. Its construction had to be uncomplicated for quick mass production by semi-skilled and unskilled labour. Since its pilots would only have nominal flying skills, instrumentation was kept to a minimum, except on the training versions where altimeter, compass, attitude indicator (artificial horizon), airspeed indicator, and rocket temperature gauge were included. An arming handle for the fuses of the rocket motor ignition switches and a post and ring sight was mounted for aiding the pilot in aiming the Ohka at its target on the combat version. Despite its simplicity and short 20ft length and 16ft wingspan, the aircraft had to have good handling and manoeuvrability to ensure a successful shipping strike. The Ohka pilot controlled his aircraft by a conventional stick and rudder bar arrangement. The Ohka was not to take off on its own but be carried aloft to its target. It was anticipated that it would fly at maximum speeds of 400mph (630kmph) and all control surfaces were dynamically balanced to eliminate flutter at the high speeds at which the Ohka operated. Because the Ohka would have to fly through heavy anti-aircraft fire as it approached its target as well as possible interception by fighter cover, the pilot was protected by armour plate: a 0.75in (19mm) strip installed on the underside of the fuselage near the pilot's feet and a bucket seat with between 0.3 and 0.6in (8 and 15mm) of armour, mostly protecting his back. The one-way Ohka had no landing gear and had to be moved on a special dolly when on the ground. From the mid-August design stage, by September 1944 Miki and his team had completed ten MXY7s that were ready for testing.

Adm. Koshiro Oikawa was a forty-one-year Imperial Navy veteran who had served as a Naval Minister and Councillor and was newly named as the Chief of the Navy General Staff. (*Author/Lansdale*)

MXY7 Ohka 11 Specifications

Generally, the Ohka 11 was a cantilever low-wing monoplane with twin tails, of mixed construction. The wings and the tail were of wooden construction and the fuselage was monocoque, all-metal, divided into three sections: nose, centre, and tail. The nose section contained the warhead, the centre section included the cockpit, equipped with instruments, and the tail section housed the rocket propulsion unit.

On 28 August 1944, Cdr Minoru Genda, organised a meeting at IJN Headquarters at which the Ohka's performance, operation, and design requirements were specified:

1) Its simple design would contribute to easy manufacturing in one tenth the time required for a conventional fighter (1,500 man hours)
2) It would be manufactured from easily obtainable, non-strategic materials
3) It was to be exceptionally small for ease of assembly and storage in narrow underground bunkers
4) Its armour piercing warhead would occupy 80 per cent of the payload
5) It would be of extremely high-speed design to penetrate enemy fighter cover. The specifications also projected a jet-powered model, with fuel capacity for one-way travel

MXY7 Ohka 11: Specifications

Crew: 1
Length: 19ft 11in (6.07m)
Height: 3ft 10in (1.16m)
Wingspan: 16ft 10in (5.12m)
Wing area: 65 sq ft (6 sq m)
Wing loading: 73.1lb/sq ft (356.7kg/sq m)
Empty weight: 970lb (440kg)
Gross weight: 4,718lb (2,140kg)

Performance

Maximum speed: 403mph (648kmph) at 11,483ft (3,500m)
Range: 23 miles (37km)

Armament

The 2,640lb (1,200kg) Ammonal (ammonium nitrate and aluminium powder) warhead had been designed for the destruction of major warships with its hardened steel casing able to pierce any armoured deck and the wooden decks of US Navy carriers. It had a length of 5.9ft (1.80m) without the nose priming plug and a diameter of 2ft (60cm) including the three rear bolts. A post and ring sight was mounted on the Ohka's fuselage forward of the canopy windscreen for aiding the pilot in aiming his kamikaze at its target. It had a wind air-armed fuse in the nosecone that automatically unblocked itself when the Ohka was released by the mothership. Five fuses were installed, one in the nose and the remaining four on the rear plate charge. The nose fuse was straight impact and vane armed. Two of the base fuses were straight impact and the other two were of the all-way type. All fuses were armed manually by a T-handle located to the front right of the cockpit and were to explode on impact, or the detonation could be delayed by up to 1.5 seconds to allow the

The 2,640lb Ammonal warhead had been designed for the destruction of major warships with its hardened steel warhead able to pierce any armoured deck using five fuses. (*USAGF*)

Ohka to penetrate the target (such as the ship's hull) and explode inside. (Note: The Ohka 22 had half the size of warhead, with 1,323lb (600kg) Trinitroanisol).

Ohka Toku-Ro.1 Type 4 Mark 1 Model 20 Solid-Propellant Rocket Motors

The original plan was to power the MXY7 using a Toku-Ro.2 (KR-10) liquid-fuel rocket motor that was being adapted from the German Walter HWK 109-509 rocket motor by Mitsubishi's Nagasaki plant in conjunction with the Yokosuka Naval Aeronautical Engineering Arsenal for Japanese production. The Walter HWK 109-509 was a German liquid-fuel, bi-propellant rocket engine that powered the Messerschmitt Me 163 Komet and Bachem Ba 349 Natter. During July 1944 the Germans had provided the plans for the Me 163 and its rocket motor to the Japanese, from which they began development of their Mitsubishi J8M Shusui copy that was powered by the Walter HWK 109-509 rocket motor. The Japanese Walter HWK 109-509 version was designated by the Japanese as the Toku Ro. 2 (KR-10), which was not delivered until early June 1945. This German bi-propellant motor used hydrazine hydrate and methanol, designated C-Stoff, that burned with the oxygen-rich exhaust from the T-Stoff, which was used as the oxidiser for added thrust. However, this two-component liquid fuel posed a critical technical problem for the Japanese chemical industry, which was considered as unable to maintain regular supply of the two-fuel component. Due to the long delay in the HWK 109-509's development and

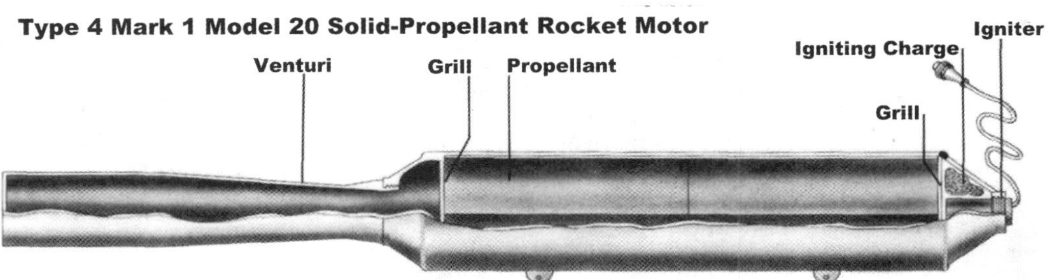

its cost and complexity, MXY7 engineers changed to using the less costly, less complex and available set of five Toku-Ro.1 Type 4 Mark 1 Model 20 solid fuel rocket engines, three installed in the rear section and one under each wing. However, the wing-mounted rockets were abandoned after the 31 October test flights and a second static ground test on 19 November when it was determined that they produced steering problems due to their uneven burn rates; resulting in asymmetric thrust. Uneven burn rate was not a problem on the three fuselage rockets since they were positioned so close to the centreline. However, the first Ohkas, such as those deployed to Okinawa, were issued with all five. Each rocket could produce up to 588lb (267kg) of thrust for a total of 1,764lb (801kg). The MXY7 would be carried into combat by a larger bomber and released to begin its dive, with this propulsion system intended to be ignited only to significantly accelerate the aircraft during its final dive.

The decision to use the shorter-range Toku-Ro.1 rockets was to prove detrimental, as this propulsion system gave the Ohka only a limited operational range and was responsible for limiting its future success during operations. The pilot could activate the rockets as he decided and could fire them one by one or all three at once, with total burn time for each rocket being eight to ten seconds.

Specifications

Three Toku-Ro.1 Type 4 Mark 1 Model 20 solid-propellant rocket motors were contained in the after portion of the Ohka and served as the main propulsion units. The motors were ignited by electrically fired squibs fitted into the nose portion of the motor. The firing circuit was controlled by a selector switch in the cockpit.

Motor (One of Three)
Overall Length: 78in (198.1cm)
Maximum Diameter: 10.1in (25.7cm)
Weight: 206lb (93.4kg)

Propellant
Ignition Charge Weight: 4.29oz (120g)
Propellant Weight: 97.8lb (44.5kg)
Length of Propellant Stick: 19.4in (49.3cm)
Depth of Propellant Stick: 4.4in (11.2cm)

Propellant components
6 sticks of 500 special DT (code designation) comprised of:
59.9% nitrocellulose
26.9% nitroglycerine
6.1% mononitronaphthalene
2.9% ethyl centralite
1.3% volatiles

Toku-Ro.1 Type 4 Mark 1 Model 20 Solid-Propellant Rocket Motor Gallery

Rear view of three Toku-Ro.1 Type 4 Mark 1 rocket motors. (*USAGF*)

Rear view of rocket compartment where three nozzles are attached to three rocket motors. (*USAGF*)

Three nozzles attached to rocket motors. (*USAGF*)

Close-up of rocket nozzles. (*USAGF*)

Attaching empennage unit. (*USAGF movie still*)

Some of the last Model 11 series carried two Toku-Ro.1 Type 4 Mark 1 rockets under the wing roots that generated 660lb (300kg) thrust for ten seconds to increase speed and range.

Cockpit

The Ohka cockpit was quite rudimentary, with a three-section windscreen, forward/rear sliding jettisonable Plexiglas canopy with two metal side-to-side dividers with a small wooden block handle above the pilot's head and a stationary third rear rounded Plexiglas section. Directly ahead of the windscreen was a simple metal fixed ring-and-bead-type aiming sight, ahead of which was the suspension lug, and then a rod bead that acted as the forward part of the sight. The pilot was protected by armour plate: a 0.75in (19mm) strip of plating installed on the underside of the fuselage near the pilot's feet and a bucket seat with between 0.3 and 0.6in (8 and 15mm) of armour, mostly protecting his back. The metal bucket seat was equipped with a shoulder and seat belts. There was a vertical pilot bracing handle forward of the portside instrument panel. The junction box (forward) and oxygen cylinder (aft) were located on the port side of the cockpit floor next to the pilot's seat.

Ohka Canopy and Cockpit

(USAGF)

(USAGF)

Pilot Controls and Control Surfaces

The rudder controls were not pedals but a pivoting bar located in front of the control column that would actuate sensors in the two full-length rudders in the horizontal stabiliser to control yaw. The control column was a joystick that moved forward and backwards to control the full-length elevators in pitch to lift the wing and left and right to control the 40 per cent wing length to wing tip ailerons in pitch and roll. The control surfaces had no trim tabs.

The wing and empennage control surfaces are readily seen on the posterior view of a captured Ohka. (*USAGF*)

Ohka Model 11 External and Cockpit Colours and Markings

For decades the actual colour of operational Ohkas has been a matter of debate, especially among modellers, as while several survived the Second World War, they were quickly repainted in rather spurious colours post-war for exhibition. The Ohka's exterior colour appears not to be found on other Japanese aircraft but is unique to the Yokosuka Aviation Technical Arsenal that produced it. Some colour photographs and movie film survive but also because of their age the colours have faded and changed, although the main scheme is often depicted as a whiteish grey or sometimes a light greenish grey. Modellers have noted that there seems to be colour differences between the metal fuselage and the fabric-covered and plywood control surfaces. The metal surfaces were amber light grey or yellow light grey, while the fabric-covered surfaces were more blue-green light grey to blue light grey. The K1 trainer had a distinctive orange upper fuselage over grey underside scheme, while the Ohka Model 22 was a light greyish green.

The Ohka had the distinctive Cherry Blossom logo painted just anterior to the wing root on the starboard side of the aircraft and the I-00 aircraft number on the portside, but there were exceptions with both being seen in photographs on the port side on captured

Ohkas on Okinawa. Many Ohkas displayed in museums are painted with the Hinomaru (rising sun/'meatball') but none are seen on Ohkas captured on Okinawa, although there are a few photos of the K1 trainer with large Hinomaru on their fuselage between the wing and empennage.

Ohka Mothership Proposals

The main Ohka carrier was the Mitsubishi G4M2a (Models 24B and C) bombers that were modified by having their bomb bay doors removed to be replaced by shackles. These modified Bettys were redesignated G4M2e (Model 24J). Since the Ohka's weight of 4,718lb (2,140kg) far exceeded the bomber's standard bomb load of 2,200lb (1,000kg), the G4M2e demonstrated poor handling and performance. Since the Ohka had a very limited range – the maximum practical horizontal range after release from 17,000ft (5,182m) was from 20 to 25 miles (32.2 to 40.2km) – it had to be carried toward the target by a Betty mothership, although other types were capable of the task but rarely used. Carrying the Ohka reduced the range of the mothership and its speed and manoeuvrability significantly. The Betty's range was normally about 2,000 miles (3,219km) but while transporting the Ohka it would be about a quarter of that, and the Betty's maximum speed declined from 265 to 160mph (425 to 260kmph). US Navy reports indicated that as soon as a mother Betty bomber came under attack, often the first thing it did was to jettison its rocket-powered charge far from the target area in order to save itself.

Cockpit Exterior Area and Instrument Panel

1) Battery Compartment Cover
2) Suspension Lug
3) Ring and Bead Aircraft Aiming Sight

Instrument Panel

4) Rocket Motor Selector Dial
5) Intercom Switch to Betty Mothership using Morse Code
6) Warhead Fuse Arming Handle to set four of the five fuses
7) Altimeter
8) Airspeed Indicator
9) Inclinometer
10) Pilot Good Luck Amulet
11) Compass

Legend (Photo on next page)

Cockpit Surface Controls and Safety Equipment

12) Rudder Bars
13) Joystick
14) Metal Joystick Release Safety Rod
15) Metal Joystick Movement Safety Rod

Miscellaneous

16) Rocket Selector Button
17) Electrical Plug

Pilot's Seat

18) Metal Pilot's Seat containing seat belt and shoulder harness
19) Pilot's Armoured Seatback

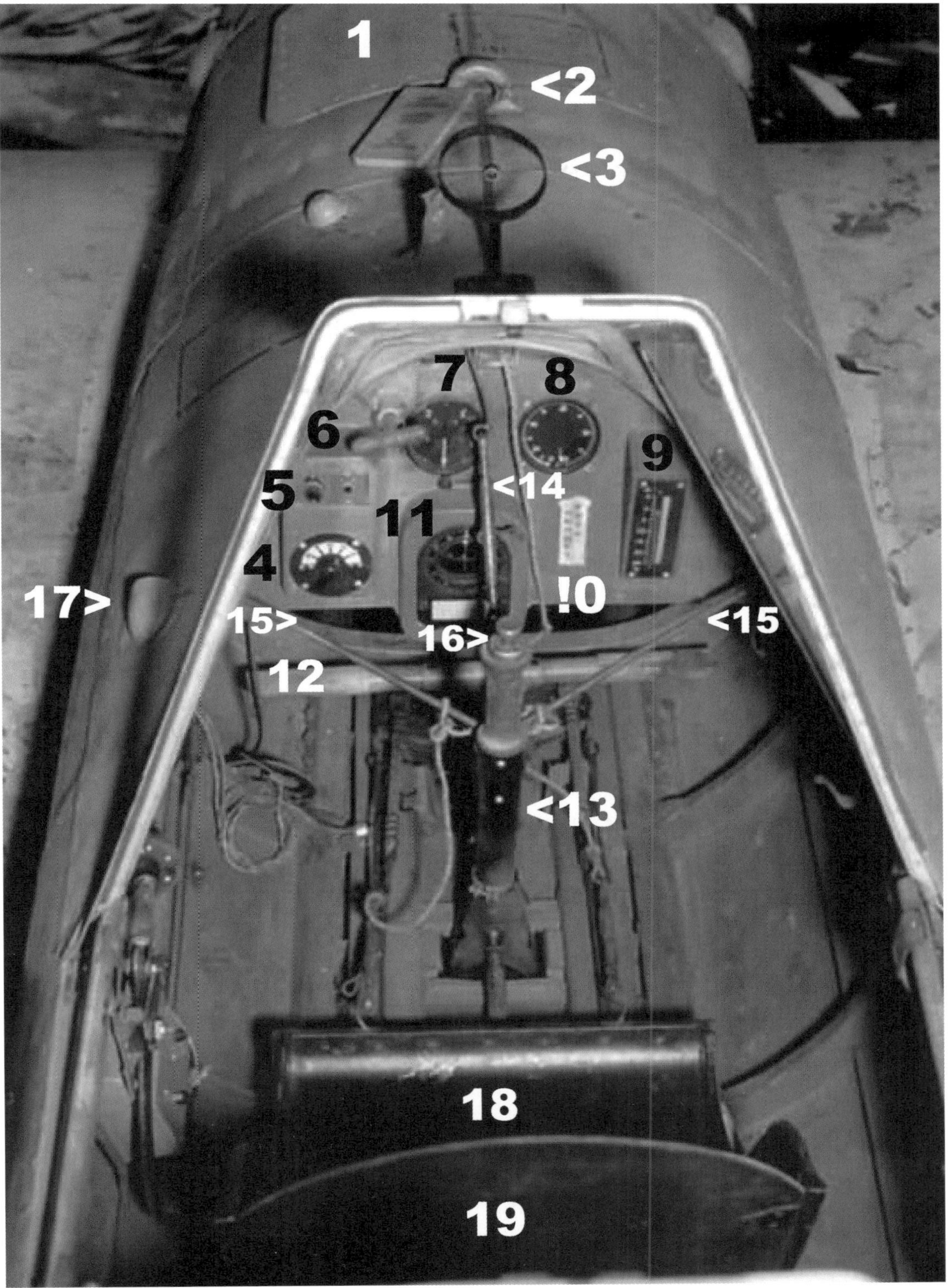

(*Author's collection*)

Cherry Blossom logo was painted just anterior to the wing root on the starboard side of the aircraft. (*Author/Lansdale*)

A few K-1 trainers built in Japan had large Hinomaru Rising Suns on both sides of their fuselage between the wing and empennage. (*USAGF*)

An Ohka captured on Okinawa showing the aircraft number and Cherry Blossom logo. Note that there are no Hinomarus on these Okinawa aircraft. (*USAGF*)

While the majority of USN after-action reports involving Ohka encounters indicated that it was carried by Bettys, Allied intelligence reports at the beginning of the Okinawa campaign had indicated that any of the twin-engine Japanese medium bombers could 'probably' be capable of launching the Ohka or could be adapted for launch without major modifications: Frances: IJN Yokosuka P1Y (twin engines); Peggy: IJA Mitsubishi Ki-67 Hiryu (twin engines); Helen: IJA Nakajima Ki-49 Donryu (twin engines); Sally: IJA Mitsubishi Ki-21 (twin engines); Rita: IJN Nakajima G8N Renzan prototype (four engines); Taizan: IJA Mitsubishi G7M planned long range (twin engines). Early in the Okinawa campaign, during an early morning 16 April 1945 CAP, 1Lt Dewey Durnford, of Marine Corps VMF-323, encountered a twin-engine bomber carrying an Ohka flying 30 miles north of Ie Shima. Durnford's indistinct gun camera film verified his aerial victory over the alleged Helen mothership. There were several other Helens misreported as Ohka mothers and on 4 May 1945 pilots of VC-90 reported an Ohka carried by a Mitsubishi K-46 Dinah near Radar Picket Station No. 12. However, the Dinah was too small to carry an Ohka and the VC-90 pilots had obviously misidentified the mothership.

Yokosuka P1Y Ginga/Frances as an Ohka Mothership

A Japanese report intercepted on 17 July 1945 stated that the Japanese Air Group 762 was planning to use the twin-engine bomber IJN Yokosuka Frances as an Ohka-carrying aircraft. Combat had shown that the G4M2e Betty carrier bomber was clearly too slow and an easy target for USN F6F Hellcats and USMC F4U Corsairs without heavy fighter escort. Consequently, Kugisho decided to use a specially modified version of the superior Yokosuka P1Y Ginga as the carrier aircraft.

The Yokosuka P1Y Ginga (Japanese: Milky Way/Allied: Frances) was an elegant twin-engine, land-based bomber developed for the IJN as the successor to the obsolete G4M Betty. The streamlined design is attributed to Tadanao Miki of the Yokosuka Naval Air Technical Arsenal, an engineer who after the Second World War went on to create a similar aerodynamic design for Japan's earliest bullet trains (Shinkansen). The Ginga was designed to the n avy specification 15-Shi, which called for a fast bomber with speed matching the Zero, range matching the Betty, a 2,000lb (907kg) bombload, and the capability to operate as a dive bomber as well as a torpedo bomber. This demanding specification led to a complex design resulting in difficult manufacture difficulties and consequent poor reliability and serviceability. These problems delayed entry into service until 1945, five years after work began on the aircraft. Eventually 1,098 P1Ys were built. During March–May 1945, the Gingas that were intended to be used to carry the new version of the MXY7, the Model 22, and the proposed Kawanishi Baika continued to be used as conventional bombers, and the two prototype carriers were destroyed during Allied bombing before they could be fitted with the Ohka.

Yokosuka P1Y Ginga. (*Author's Collection*)

Specifications (P1Y1a)

General Characteristics

Crew: 3
Length: 49ft 3in (15m)
Wingspan: 65ft 7in (20m)
Height: 14ft 1in (4.3m)
Wing area: 90 sq ft (55 sq m)
Wing loading: 39lb/sq ft (191kg/sq m)
Empty weight:16,017lb (7,265kg)
Gross weight: 23,149lb (10,500kg)
Maximum take-off weight: 29,762lb (13,500kg)
Powerplant: 2 × Nakajima NK9C Homare 12 18-cylinder air-cooled radial piston engines, 1,825hp each

Performance

Maximum speed: 340mph (547kmph) at 19,357ft (5,900m)
Cruise speed: 230mph (370kmph) at 4,000m (13,123ft)
Range: 3,340 miles (5,370km)
Service ceiling: 30,800ft (9,400m)

Armament

Guns:
1× flexible, nose-mounted 0.787in (20mm) Type 99 cannon
1× flexible rear-firing 0.512in (13mm) Type 2 machine gun
Bombs: Maximum 2,205lb (1,000kg) payload of bombs or 1× 1,764lb (800kg) torpedo

Ohka Attachment Mechanism to Betty

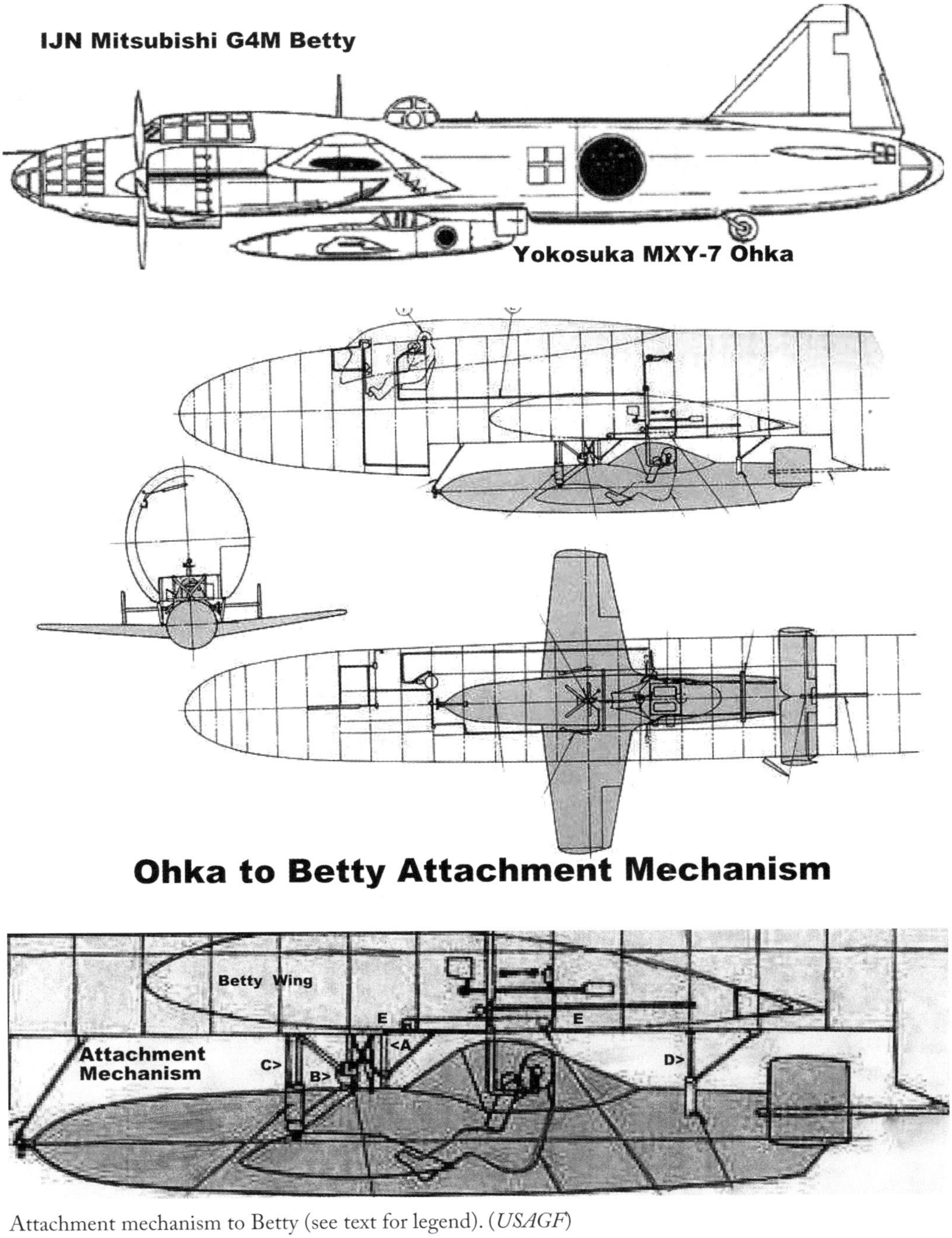

IJN Mitsubishi G4M Betty

Yokosuka MXY-7 Ohka

Ohka to Betty Attachment Mechanism

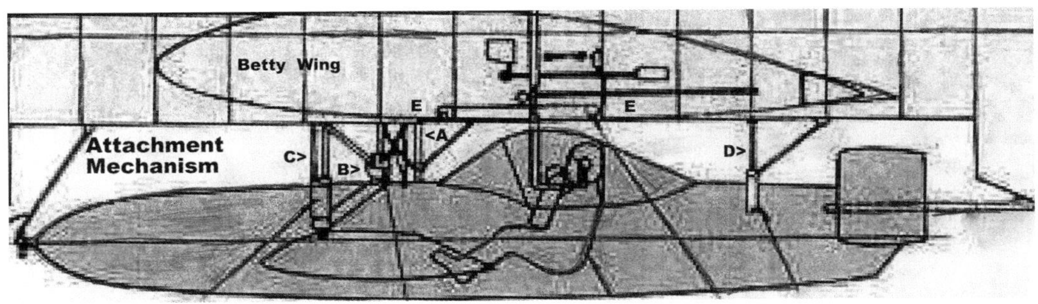

Attachment mechanism to Betty (see text for legend). (*USAGF*)

Retention lug eye. (*USAGF*)

(*Author/Lansdale*)

Loading the Ohka on to the Mothership

The Ohka was placed on its special three-wheel (one on the front and two in the rear) dolly that braced its wing supports and had a heavy canvas strap securing its fuselage. The dolly was a modified makeshift frame using Betty tail wheels for its two rear wheels and a Zero tail wheel as its front wheel. The dolly with its 4,718lb (2,140kg) Ohka was manhandled to its mothership, where the loading crew operated the pneumatic hand pumps on the dolly to slowly raise the Ohka until the lug retention rod hook extending from the Betty bomb bay (**E**, see photo) engaged the lug retention hook eye (**A**) located just forward the canopy. Two V-shaped hooks (**B**) dropped down from the bomb bay to attach to the Ohka's mid-wing just next to the fuselage. Two straight braces (**C**) dropped down to attach to the dorsal nose area just behind the warhead and the other brace (**D**) attached to the dorsal fuselage just behind the rear canopy. A cotter pin was inserted into the Ohka's bomb nose to prevent its fuse from spinning until the Ohka fell away. The next step was to plug the speaking communication tube into its port located just forward of the starboard side of the cockpit and insert the electric power cable into its plug located just forward of the portside of the cockpit. The speaking tube had a cone attached to its end for the pilot to speak into and was held in place by a neck strap. The large round earpiece fitted over the pilot's ear and was held in place by the flight helmet. The IJN helmet was a brown leather summer type with a chin strap, with the maker's and issue labels on the inside cotton lining. The IJA helmet had a five-pointed Japanese Army Star on the front. The goggles were the iconic, 'cat's eye' type as seen in Hollywood Second World War movies. They had yellow tinted lenses held in by place by aluminium frames cushioned by velvet linings.

The Ohka and Betty Composite

Testing

Although flight testing of the ten MXY7 prototypes was scheduled to begin during October 1944, the impatient IJN did not wait for the results of these to begin operations. During September, R Adm. Jiro Saba, Director Kugisho Naval Aeronautical Research laboratory, approached Lt Cdr Matsurra at the Munitions Ministry to organise Ohka production. To maintain secrecy, much of the work was directed to military contractors and not to the private aviation industry. The Ohka would be manufactured at Dai-Ichi Kai-gun Koku Gijutsu-sho (Yokosuka Aviation Technical Arsenal) as well as at Dai-Ichi Kaigun Kokusho (1st Naval Air Depot). Two private sub-contractors, Nippon Hikoki K.K. in Yokohama and Fuji Hikoki K.K. in Kanagawa, would provide wing and tail assemblies. Hikoki translates as aircraft and K.K. (Kabushiki Kaisha) translates as 'stock company', similar to Co. (Company) or Inc. (Incorporated). It had been projected that 100 Ohkas would be completed by November 1944, but it would not be until the first successful test of a rocket-powered Ohka Type 11 on 19 November 1944 that production would be authorised.

Unmanned, Unpowered Test Flights

Initially, unmanned, unpowered flights containing no explosives and employing a spring-loaded elevator control were conducted to assess the Ohka's flight characteristics and the first unpowered flight tests began at the Sagami Arsenal with an unmanned, unpowered Ohka dropped over Sagami Bay on 23 October 1944. All Ohka drops were made from G4M2e Betty bombers, with the Ohkas being directed out over Sagami Bay. Since the Ohka's weight far exceeded the bomber's standard bomb load, the G4M2e pilots experienced poor handling and performance.

During late October 1944, flight testing was transferred to Kashima, which was near the IJN base in Sasebo, Nagasaki. There the first manned flight of an Ohka took place in a K-1 trainer prototype on 31 October, piloted by Chief Petty Officer Kazutoshi Nagano. To simulate the combat weight of the Ohka, water tanks were used as ballast in place of the warhead. Because there was no room for a conventional landing gear, a special

Because there was no room on the Ohka K-1 trainer for a conventional landing gear, a central landing skid was installed to the fuselage underside and rounded skids were added under each wing tip to protect the wings from damage from striking the ground on landing. (*USAGF*)

central, under-fuselage, shock-absorbing landing skid was substituted and rounded skids were added under each wing tip to protect the wings from burrowing into the ground on landing. Before landing, the water in the nose was to be jettisoned, which slowed the landing speed to 138mph (223kmph). For Nagano's flight, a rocket booster was installed under each wing but no there were no fuselage rockets. At 11,500ft (3,505m) the G4M2e released Nagano and the Ohka dropped into a good, stable glide. A few minutes into the flight, Nagano activated the booster rockets but almost immediately the Ohka began to yaw. Nagano quickly jettisoned the rockets and further yaw was averted. The flight continued, with Nagano finally releasing the water ballast and landing perfectly on the skid. The reason for the yaw was subsequently found to be caused by the uneven thrust from the rockets. This flight was considered successful enough that series production of forty-five Ohka K-l trainers was authorised to immediately began.

Testing continued but on 13 November 1944, the Ohka claimed its first casualty. Lt Tsutomu Kariya in a K-1 made a flawless drop from 9,800ft (2,987m) and was descending for a landing when he inadvertently only released the water ballast from the nose tank, leaving the rear tank full. This action immediately caused the nose to pitch up, putting the Ohka into an unrecoverable stall. Kariya survived the crash but died from his injuries several hours later. On 29 November, FPO Kita Nubuo was killed during a similar K-1 test flight.

First Successful Test of a Rocket-Powered Ohka Type 11

The first successful test of a rocket-powered Ohka Type 11 occurred on 19 November 1944. As a result, production of the type was authorised to begin, with 155 to be assembled at Kugisho and 600 more Ohka Model 11s at the Yokosuka Naval Air Arsenal at Kasumigaura, although most of the main assemblies came from the Fuji Aircraft Company near Hiratsuka and Nippon Hikoki at Yokohama.

Flight testing of the powered Ohka continued throughout November. These tests revealed that when dropped from 19,500ft (5,944m) at a downward glide angle of 5.5 degrees the Ohka could attain a range of 37 miles (60km) at a speed of 230mph (317kmph), and in a nearly vertical dive it had a recorded (suicidal) speed of over 600mph (966kmph). However, under combat conditions the Ohka's range diminished to 15 to 18 miles (25 to 29km). From these tests and flight experience, a mission profile was developed for the Ohka's deployment. Flying at an altitude between 20,000ft and 27,000ft (6,096m and 8,230m), the G4M2e would release the Ohka when it was within 10 to 20 miles (17 to 33km) of the target. The pilot would then enter a shallow glide with an airspeed of between 230mph and 280mph (371kmph and 451kmph). At about 5 to 7 miles (8 to 12km) from the target, and from an altitude of approximately 11,500ft (3,505m), the pilot would activate the rocket boosters, increasing the speed to 403mph (649kmph). Prior to crashing into the target, he would put the Ohka into a 50-degree dive, which increased the speed up to nearly 580mph (934kmph). At the last instant, the pilot would pull up the nose to strike the targeted vessel at the waterline.

Yokosuka Naval Air Arsenal Ohka Assembly Plant

Yokosuka Naval Air Arsenal at Kasumigaura as seen in late 1945, as indicated by the two large US Navy LSTs docked outside the two hangars. (*USN*)

Ohkas awaiting final main assembly from fabrications provided by Fuji Aircraft Company Nippon Hikoki. (*USN*)

Two US technical personnel examine a completed Ohka. Note the Hinomaru rising suns painted on the fuselages, which were not present on the captured Okinawa Ohkas. (*USN*)

Kugisho MXY7 K-1 Ohka Glider Trainer

The development of the Ohka trainer MXY7 K-1 commenced almost at the same time as the Model 11 during August 1944 and had the same basic aerodynamic design. The K-1's differences included installation of the landing skid and protective wing tip outriggers; including wing flaps to slow the landing speed to an allowable but still high 138mph (222kmph); replacing the bomb load and the booster rockets with two water ballast tanks, simulating the design take-off weight and centre of gravity position; the outlet of the future rocket engines was faired over by a metal panel; and painting it in trainer aircraft orange.

The Ohka K-l training gliders were manufactured at the Kugisho plant at Yokosuka. The K-l landed safely on a special under-fuselage, shock-absorbing skid. Production of the gliders began in October 1944, after a month a subcontractor had constructed eighteen pairs of wings and tail sets, and by March 1945 forty-five K-ls had been assembled. These gliders were used for training future suicide pilots who had little experience in flying and navigation. After release from the carrier aircraft, the pilot performed a pre-set flying training agenda, following which he jettisoned its water ballast. However, it was found that the water was difficult to release, and some K-1 versions had these tanks removed. The K-1's landing speed on its skid was a rather fast 92mph (152kmph), which could be somewhat unnerving when skidding over a grassy field waiting to come to a stop.

(*Author's collection*)

The Kamikaze 'Recruit'

Once the Japanese officially authorised kamikaze operations, the next step was to organise the recruitment of pilots and crews. Generally, there were three types of kamikaze recruits mostly chronologically categorised as 'fully aware' volunteers, 'uninformed' volunteers, and later, as a result of heavy losses, conscripts. The initial small number of special attack recruits were fully informed volunteers who understood exactly that they were volunteering for a suicide mission. These volunteers were gleaned from 'eager' and patriotic flight instructors, both officers and non-commissioned officers (NCOs), and mainly navy petty officers.

In the main there were three types of kamikaze recruits: 'fully aware' volunteers, 'uninformed' volunteers, and later, as a result of heavy losses, conscripts. (*Author/Lansdale*)

As the losses of irreplaceable flight instructors within the Special Attack Force mounted during the Philippines campaign, enthusiastic experienced pilots, and then newly trained pilots were asked to volunteer. These also were idealistic men, devoted to the Emperor, the nation, and wanting to bringing honour to their family. But as their ranks also thinned, more new volunteers and an increasing number of conscripts joined the ranks, often under coercion and peer pressure, and often they were not informed of their future suicide mission. They were trained, like the 9-11 New York World Trade Center bombers, in one-way rudimentary flying, being able to take off, follow a navigation aircraft, and then dive and crash their aircraft. The conscripted pilots were known as 'boy pilots', teenagers who left school as an alternative to their conscription or enlistment, often unknowingly into a suicide unit. Like other regular Japanese military personnel, the kamikaze pilots were also programmed with the following oath: 'Loyalty is your obligation. Propriety is your way of life. You must esteem military valour highly. You must have the highest regard for righteousness. You must live a simple life.'

Ohka Unit Creation and Training

The Ohka unit, known as the Thunder Gods Special Attack Corps and designated as the 721st Kokutai, was officially formed in October 1944 along with the initial organisation of Adm. Ōnishi's conventional kamikaze Special Attack Corps for defence of the Philippines. However, it did not see action as the Ohkas were lost on their to the Philippines aboard the *Unryū*, *Ryūhō*, and *Shinano*, which were sunk. The Thunder Gods were a mixed unit of 1,000 volunteers and 3,000 conscripted pilots. Since there was such a large number of pilots available to fly the limited number of Ohkas, many were trained to fly conventional kamikaze fighters and bombers in a unit known as the Kemmu Squadron, which remained closely associated with the Ohka operations.

721st Kokutai

As flight testing and production of the Ohka got under way, the 721st Kokutai was formed at Konoike Airbase near the Yokosuka Arsenal on 1 October 1944 as the first Ohka-flying Shimpu Tokko Tai unit (Kamikaze Corps) to train the pilots for the Tokko mission. The 721st was allocated the specific unit identification of Jinrai Butai ('Divine-Thunder' Wing), as it had become traditional to honour all Tokko-designated units by individual salutary names. This unit, under the command of Cdr Motoharu Okamura (former CO of the 341st NAG), did not report to any of the naval air fleets, but rather to Imperial General Headquarters, from whom R Adm. Ōnishi apparently managed to keep the project secret. The 721st Air Group was issued twin-engine Mitsubishi G4M bombers with bomb bays modified to suspend the manned bomb under the fuselage. The unit was also issued its own protective fighters, mostly Zeros. By the end of October 1944, the upper echelons of Japanese military and political hierarchy had accepted the concept of aerial suicide attack, and the air group came out of its cover. The 721st Kikotai (Naval Squadron) consisted of the 708th Hikotai (Attack Squadron) under Lt Cdr Adachi Jiro and the 711th Hikotai under Lt Cdr Goro Nonaka (former squadron leader of the 752nd NAG), each with eighteen G4M2e bombers flying in four units: Shinken, Shichisei, Tsukuba, and Shōwa. As the commander of the Betty bomber units that would carry the Ohkas, Nonaka was originally openly critical of the project as he felt that his crews were as condemned as the Ohka pilots. However, when leading the first Ohka mission he vowed to, and succeeded, in not returning with his kamikaze Betty bomber. The 721st was nicknamed the Jinrai Butai, translating as 'Thunder God Corps' but better known today in popular literature as 'Divine Thunder'.

Cdr Goro Nonaka, K711 Betty squadron commander. (*Author/Lansdale*)

The 306th Hikotai and the 308th Hikotai fighter units were assigned to escort the Ohka-carrying Bettys, with each squadron providing thirty-six Mitsubishi A6M Zero (Reisen) fighters. The 721st Kokutai's initial ten Ohka aircraft were supplemented by forty Mitsubishi A6M5s equipped with two 551lb (250kg) bombs.

With Japan's declining resources and its inability to train replacement pilots quickly and efficiently due to fuel and instructor shortages, inexperienced pilots ultimately became the kamikaze vanguard. Throughout October the 721st Kokutai received many hundreds of volunteers from the ranks of IJN pilots but being a suicide squadron those who were married, were only sons, were oldest sons, sons with one surviving parent, those with weighing family responsibilities, or already combat pilots, were rejected, and finally the unit was able to select 600 pilots. Capt. Okamura remarked that there were so many volunteers for suicide missions that he referred to them as a swarm of bees, adding that bees died after they had stung.

Training began with the arrival of K-l trainers. At this point in the war basic training aircraft, fuel, and instructors were at a premium and used to train combat pilots. So the prospective Ohka pilot would become familiar with the aircraft while on the ground. Afterward, they were given an initial test flight in the K-1 from an altitude of 9,000ft (2,743m) and two more from 16,000ft (4,877m), at which time they were considered combat qualified.

The MXY7 K-1 training flight check-outs were not without difficulties. The relative attitudes and aerodynamic forces between the Ohka and the mothership were critical, particularly at separation. To balance the forces at separation, the water ballast tanks fore and aft of the K-1 cockpit had to be emptied before landing, in a correct sequence. A pilot was killed when he mistakenly emptied the front tank first, causing his K-1 to pitch upwards into a spin and crash. As training continued, mothership airspeeds were modified until a safe launch could be made without water in the ballast tanks.

Kamikaze Tactics

By 1944, the US Navy's air defence system had evolved to counter conventional attacks by large formations of enemy aircraft. During 1942, the greatest challenge had been effective fighter direction, intercepting an incoming attack with the CAP in time to break it up and reduce its strength. Despite the navy's best defensive efforts, in each of the four carrier battles that year, enough attacking aircraft got through to sink at least one then very valuable carrier (Java Sea/*Langley*, Coral Sea/*Lexington*, Midway/*Yorktown*, and Santa Cruz/*Hornet*). Increasingly sophisticated radars and refined Combat Information Center (CIC) techniques allowed the navy's fighter direction procedures to improve so that, by June 1944, the relationship between offence and defence had reversed. At the Battle of the Philippine Sea, Adm. Raymond Spruance waited close to the Saipan invasion fleet, confident that Task Force 58's CAP would intercept the attacks of V Adm. Jisaburō Ozawa's Mobile Fleet. In the resulting 'Marianas Turkey Shoot' the Japanese lost 243 planes out of 373 sent against TF 58; a high price to pay when none of Spruance's carriers were hit.

Throughout the war IJN commanders constantly sought out weaknesses in the US Navy's air defence system to be exploited by their torpedo bombers. They found that if the bomber formation orbited outside the range of USN radar-directed gunfire and then broke off one at a time to attack the ships of the fleet independently, it made them more difficult to detect and shoot down as CIC teams often failed to notice the lone attacker in time to alert and bring the guns on the quickly closing target.

Kamikaze commanders also integrated this lone attacker tactic but also integrated several other innovative techniques also designed to exploit weaknesses in the navy's air defence system. Kamikazes approached as a group, but once within range of the task force's fighter/radar direction system, they dispersed and made their way toward a specific target area individually or in small groups. The many approaching aircraft would overwhelm CIC teams because there were too many targets to track. By closely following USN strike aircraft that were returning to their carriers, kamikazes could blend into their radar return and approach undetected. Low-altitude approaches reduced the distance at which search radars could detect kamikazes; often, defending fighters could make just one pass on these low flyers before they dived at their targets. Other kamikazes loitered in the radar 'blind spot' directly overhead until they suddenly attacked. The use of 'window' (chaff) allowed kamikazes to inhibit radar tracking just long enough to close. Finally, because navy search radars had difficulty detecting targets over land, kamikazes learned to fly over it before attacking. Clever use of altitude, terrain, and radar countermeasures all minimised the effectiveness of the navy's air defence system.

V Adm. Lloyd Mustin's investigation described the problem:

> The confusion factor is as intense as he (the enemy) can make it, and the business of picking out which target you want … picking out which (radar) pip is a target, and then which of many targets is the proper one … is a bit complicated. It's an identification process that taxes a well-trained group of people typically found in a ship's CIC … Along their way to the target, kamikazes made radical changes in course and altitude, complicating the process of interception. To further reduce the chances of shooting them down, kamikaze pilots creatively used cloud cover to hide from CAP fighters.

These tactics meant kamikaze raids were an estimated seven to ten times more successful than conventional ones. During the first four months of kamikaze attacks, from October 1944 to January 1945, the Navy's Operations Research Group (ORG) estimated that 1,444 Japanese aircraft had attacked, of which 352 were kamikazes that recorded 121 hits, a more than 34 per cent success rate. Conventional attacks recorded only twenty-three hits for only a 2 per cent success rate.

During the Okinawa campaign the ORG estimated 793 kamikazes attacked, of which 181 (23 per cent) hit their targets and another 95 (12 per cent) crashed near enough to cause damage. Meanwhile, conventional attacks were much less effective as, of 1,119 attacks, only 16 (1.4 per cent) damaged Allied shipping. During the Okinawa kamikaze campaign, due to the widespread use of radar pickets, a higher percentage of kamikazes attacked smaller vessels, with 86 per cent targeting nothing larger than a destroyer, compared to just 61 per cent in the Philippines.

Ohka Operational Procedure and Tactics

The Imperial Japanese Navy's attack protocol for Ohka combat sorties originally intended to send at least four fighter escorts for every Betty/Ohka combination taking part to within 20–25 miles (32–40km) of the Allied fleet. Because of their heavy Ohka load, the mother G4M2e were restricted to flying at 16,400 to 18,000ft (5,000 to 5,500m). The Ohka's estimated maximum practical horizontal range after release from the Betty at about

17,000ft (5,182m) was from 20 to 25 miles (32 to 40km), based upon a minimum glide angle of 5 to 6 degrees. At lower launching altitudes, maximum range was slightly decreased.

On the approach to the target area, the Ohka pilot was a passenger in the Betty mothership seated on the dorsal gunner's bench that was the Betty's landing gear gearing box. The top of the bench opened above the Ohka cockpit canopy, which slid aft so the pilot could drop down into a roaring slipstream and on to its metal seat. This access area was known as the 'Devil's Gate'. Once seated in the cockpit, before launch the pilot buckled his seat and shoulder belts and removed the bungees that secured the rudder foot bars at the eight and four o'clock positions to the floor to prevent rudder activation while the

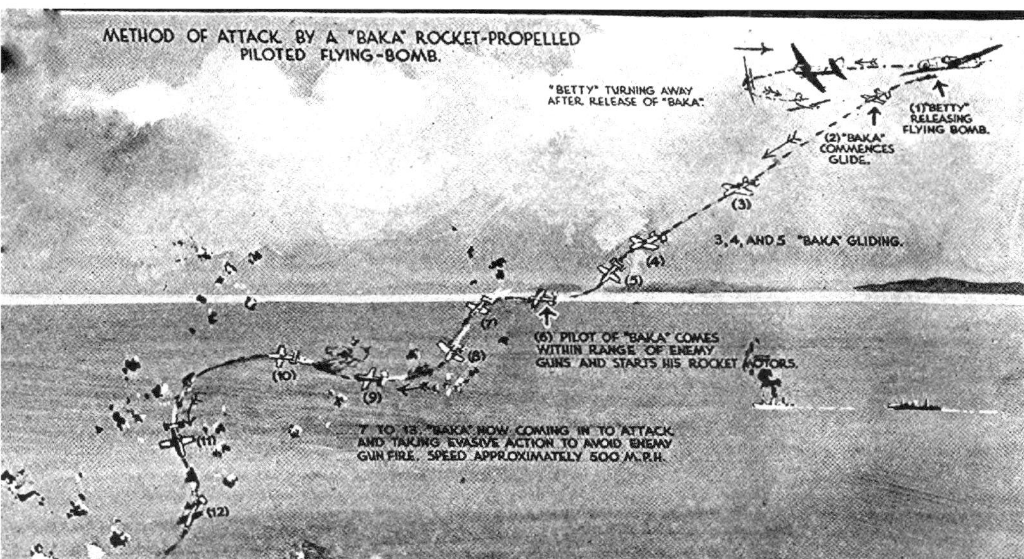

A US Navy wartime drawing depicting a 'method of attack by a Baka rocket-propelled flying bomb'. At this time the Ohka was dubbed the 'Baka Bomb' by the Allies, as Baka's Japanese translation is 'foolish' or 'idiotic', and the Japanese strategy of using them was, in the view of the Allies, foolhardy. Another Baka naming version was that fifteen Ohkas were captured by the US Marines on the first day of the invasion, 1 April 1945, April Fool's Day, and as a result were dubbed 'Baka'. (*USN*)

Ohka was being carried. He then disconnected the metal rods that held the joystick in neutral at the ten and two o'clock positions. The pilot handed the bungees and rods up to an assistant in the bomb bay as a safety measure to not have them jam the controls in flight. The pilot pulled the canopy forward with a small wooden block handle to snap it shut. While waiting to be released, the pilot switched the rocket motors to standby and activated the fuse handle to arm the warhead. When he was ready to be launched, the Ohka pilot informed the Betty via a microphone attached to the mothership by wire. He also tapped out a Morse code message to confirm his voice message, which was verified visually by the Betty pilot by a flashing light on the instrument panel. Once the target's location had been determined and before launch, the Betty initiated a shallow dive until reaching the Ohka's release speed of between 175 to 200mph (280 to 325kmph). The Ohka pilot would then signal that he was ready and pull the release handle. The Ohka was held under the Betty bomb bay by the pivoting lug retention hook that was held in place by an internal spring and explosive disintegrating bolt. The explosive bolt was ignited by the Betty co-pilot to cause the spring to retract, pivoting the hook upward and away from the suspension lug. Gravity then caused the Ohka to drop away and severed the communication and electrical cables. An I-hook was attached to a spring on the joystick to prevent the pilot from pulling it back on release to stop the Ohka lurching up into the Betty. After launching, this was removed by the pilot and he would then take control of his aircraft. The Ohka initially descended in a shallow glide, first to clear the Betty mothership and then to gain speed. After launching their drag-inducing Ohka parasites, the Betty pilots would head back to base ASAP, relieved at not having been intercepted by US Navy CAPs Corsairs and Hellcats.

A Betty of the 721st Kokutai Naval Squadron loaded with an Ohka at Kanoya Airbase on Kyushu, at the south end of Japan's southern-most island. (*Author/Lansdale*)

Ohka launch sequence. (*USN*)

The Ohka flight started as a shallow, unpowered dive, on a 5–6 degree gliding angle, reaching a cruise speed of between 230–280mph (370–450kmph). While in the glide towards the target area, the pilot used the little manoeuvrability and course deviation afforded by the Ohka's small wings to attempt to select a choice target among the numerous warships off Okinawa. At anywhere between 9,850–26,250ft (3,000–8,000m) from the target, the pilot pressed the button on the top of the control stick to start the electric ignition of the Toku-Ro.1 Type 4 Mark 1 Model 20 solid-propellant rocket motors at the rear of the fuselage. He could then ignite all three rockets simultaneously or, to extend the Ohka's range, they were selected #1-#2-#3 with the last rocket saved to increase speed as it neared the target. Rockets could not be shut off. After the ignition, the pilot initiated the final 50-degree dive on the target, reaching a terminal speed of 575mph (930kmph). The pilot could not alter course as the pressure on the tail surfaces at near transonic flight was more than any pilot application to the flight controls. The speeding Ohka could not be intercepted by enemy fighters at this point and due to the inertial momentum of the heavy warhead, its course could only be altered by a direct hit from the heavy AA.

Chapter Two

USN Kamikaze Detection and Defences: Picket Ships, CAP, and AA Defences

Operation Iceberg: Invasion of Okinawa

On 1 April 1945, the American invasion of Okinawa, Operation Iceberg, began with the Japanese facing the most powerful armada ever assembled: the US Fast Carrier Task Force 58 with its 11 fleet carriers, 6 light carriers, and 22 escort carriers, as well as 8 fast battleships, 10 old battleships, 2 large cruisers, 12 heavy cruisers, 13 light cruisers, 4 anti-aircraft light cruisers, 132 destroyers, and 45 destroyer escorts. The British Task Force 57 included 5 fleet carriers, 4 light carriers, and 9 escort carriers, 2 battleships, 7 light cruisers, and 14 destroyers. Total US Navy, Marines and Army Air

On 1 April 1945, the American invasion of Okinawa, Operation Iceberg, began with the Japanese facing the most powerful armada ever assembled. (*USN*)

Force fighters, attack aircraft, scout planes, bombers and dive bombers would exceed 3,000 during the 82-day battle.

On day 1 some 50,000 Allied troops landed on Okinawa expecting strong opposition from Japan's 32nd Army of 130,000 men commanded by Lt Gen. Mitsuru Ushijima. However, there was virtually no Japanese land or air opposition to the landing, mainly because of effective carrier air attacks on southern Kyushu airfields and their aircraft. Since the Japanese Combined Fleet had been virtually decimated in the large sea battles off the Marianas and Philippines, the kamikazes were Japan's last hope of inflicting severe losses on the Allied fleet.

Allied Tactical Response to Kamikazes

Directing a kamikaze aircraft to crash into a manoeuvring warship was easier than hitting one with a bomb or torpedo. However, crashing into a target was not easy as suicide pilots were primarily novice pilots and accurate manoeuvring in their final high-speed dives on their targets was difficult to achieve, with many missing their target or being shot down. Nonetheless, during the Okinawa campaign besides 7 carriers, the kamikazes struck 40 other ships (5 sunk, 23 heavily damaged, and 12 moderately damaged) and inflicted 3,389 US fatalities along with 26 British losses. These losses inflicted by these unanticipated new suicide tactics were so serious and concerning that it led the American high command to modify its conduct of the Pacific War, changing its battle tactics and task force organisation.

During December 1944, Adm. William Halsey, Commander of the Third Fleet, wrote:

> The Japanese air command ... has ... evolved a sound defensive plan against carrier attacks. He has coordinated and centralized his command responsibilities, but decentralized and dispersed his air forces. Kamikaze attacks, because they could be made by lone attackers and small groups, allowed more dispersion of planes and pilots.

Halsey and other senior officers rapidly introduced tactical adaptations designed to minimise the effectiveness of kamikazes. It was found that the most important kamikaze defence was to detect and destroy the attackers as far from the important carriers and battleships of the main fleet as possible. Two broad paths were pursued. In the combat theatre, task forces introduced new, adaptive tactics based on first-hand combat experience. At the same time, a new experimental unit was formed in the United States to investigate more fundamental challenges and improve the navy's underlying capabilities. The combination of these two allowed the navy to overcome the determined efforts of Japanese pilots.

By 1945, the US Navy had developed a multilayered fleet air defence system that integrated radar picket ships and fleet radar, CAPs, and anti-aircraft guns.

Radar Picket Destroyers

Until late 1944 the standard US Navy carrier task force air defence formation had been a circle of carriers with a 2,000-yard (2,030m) radius centred around a single fleet carrier, usually the flagship. Another ring around the carrier circle would be at 4,000 yards

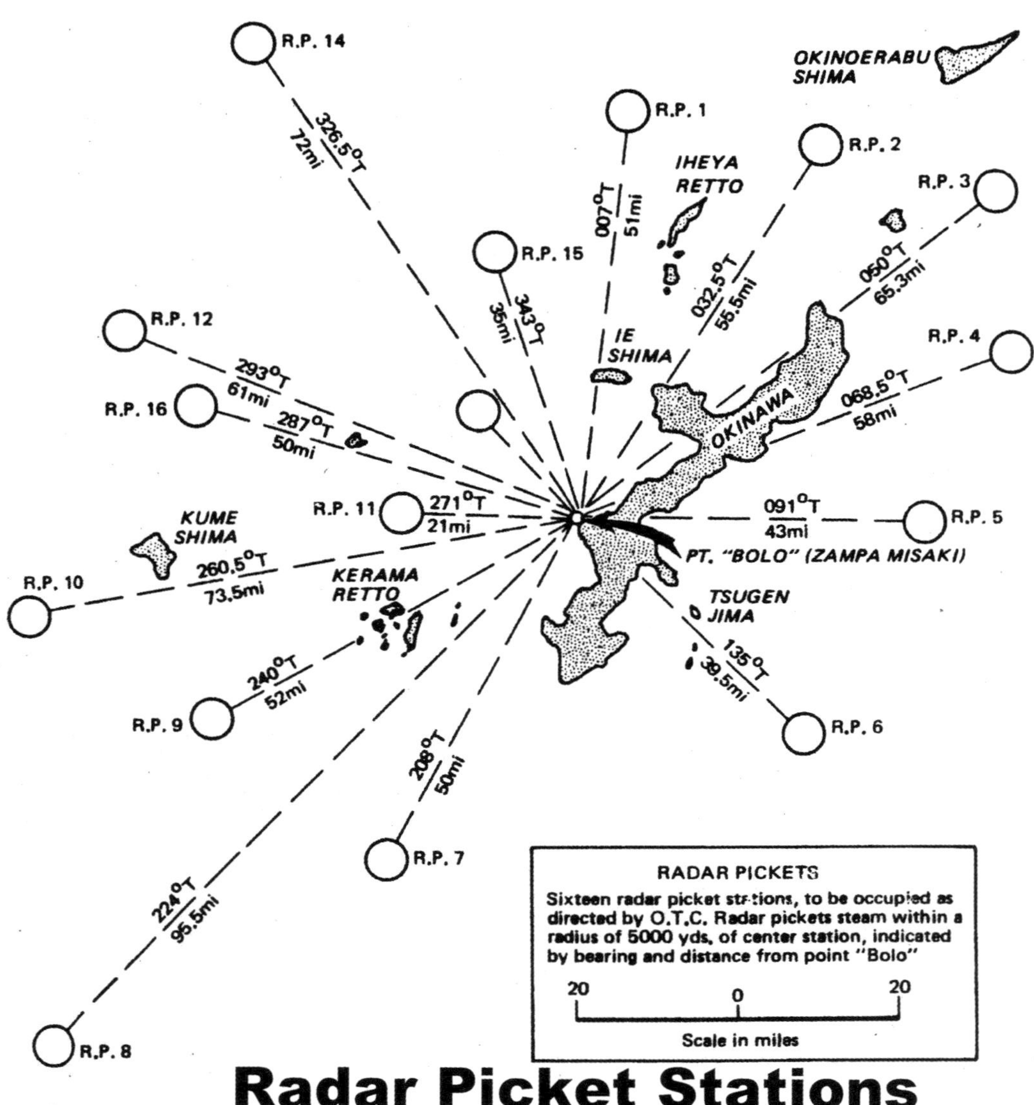

(4,060m) consisting of battleships, cruisers, and destroyers, all equipped with various-calibre defensive AA gunnery. The kamikaze attacks during the battle for the Philippines alerted Allied strategists that this defensive disposition would not sufficiently defend against the expected even more ferocious suicide attacks off Okinawa as ships on the outer circle's periphery were too close to give timely warning and defence.

The solution to the kamikaze saturation attacks was the use of destroyers, called pickets, which over the previous years had been included in the navy's tactical doctrine to track and intercept incoming attackers long before they threatened the main fleet. However, they were to be used much more often and in greater numbers once kamikaze attacks began. The navy did equip several submarines for use in the radar picket role, though those equipped with advanced radars never performed the picket function.

Radar picket destroyer USS *Aaron Ward* (DD-773). (*USN*)

During the Okinawa campaign, to cover all possible approaches to the island and the Allied fleet and to provide early warning, fighter direction, and direct AA engagement, fifteen radar picket stations were established around the island arranged at distances from 20 to 90 miles (32 to 145km) from the main body of the fleet surrounding the island

Landing Craft Support (Large) LCS(L). (*USN*)

Landing Ship Medium (Rocket) LSM(R). (*USN*)

and the invasion fleet. Picket stations were identified by their numbers, 1–15, with No. 1 directly to the north and successive stations located at various distances counterclockwise around the perimeter of the island, with No. 15 north-west of Station No. 1 (see map). Originally, a typical picket station had one destroyer, supported by two landing ships, usually Landing Craft Support (Large) LCS(L) or Landing Ship Medium (Rocket) LSM(R), providing additional AA firepower.

By mid-April 1945, vulnerable picket stations were reinforced to include a destroyer or destroyer-minesweeper with a fighter director team on board, a second destroyer to 'ride shotgun', one or more landing craft, and a two-plane CAP.

Eventually, the number of destroyers and supporting vessels were doubled at the most vulnerable stations. The pickets normally patrolled within a 5,000-yard (4,572m) radius in their assigned circular station at 15 knots (17mph/27kmph) but the picket CO was guided by prevailing conditions regarding fuel conservation and had discretion to change speed, especially to increase speed if attack appeared imminent.

Destroyer pickets were modified for their new role by removing torpedo tubes and installing radars, along with additional anti-aircraft guns. The pickets were painted in dazzle camouflage, which was introduced and extensively used during the First World War and reintroduced during the Second to a lesser extent. Dazzle measures 31, 32 and 33 referred to dark, medium, and light colour combinations on USN destroyers and destroyer escorts. Dazzle consisted of painting a mixture of obtrusive polygon patterns on vertical hull surfaces in combinations of Ocean, Haze, and Pale Greys, Deck and Navy Blues, and Dull Black. Different from other types of camouflage, the very visible dazzle

Dazzle Measure 33 depicted on Sumner-class destroyer Picket *John W. Weeks* (DD-701). (*USN*)

was not to conceal but to make it difficult to estimate a target's range, speed, and heading by enemy aircraft and submarines. Each ship's dazzle pattern was distinctive, making it more difficult for the enemy to identify different classes of vessels, and this resulted in a plethora of dazzle schemes. As directed in the *World War II US Navy Dazzle Camouflage Measures 31, 32 and 33: Destroyers*: Dazzle painting was not required to be 'exact or carried into corners. Small gear, wires, rigging, and areas permanently in shadow, as under boats, etc., need not be painted with camouflage colours. There is no objection to exact or careful painting which may be desired for the sake of good appearance at close range. All bright or shiny objects, no matter how insignificant, shall be painted, covered, or removed. Glass windows shall be covered or removed, especially during the day in sunny weather, and at night when anticipating searchlight discovery.' The effectiveness of dazzle was deemed by the navy as 'mixed at best'.

Inexperienced and barely trained kamikaze pilots approaching the invasion fleet from Kyushu or Formosa tended to attack picket ships that presented the first and most accessible targets and a single hit usually put one out of action, at a minimum. Nonetheless, destroying a picket was of some importance as it eliminated the early warning supplied by the picket and also the picket's AA interference encountered by other kamikazes on their way to attack the fleet. Nervous Betty mothership pilots, not on a personal suicide mission, approaching the invasion fleet from Kyushu often sighted the pickets first and immediately launched their hapless Ohkas, then quickly retreated back to base before meeting swarming navy and Marine CAP.

Battle Experience: Radar Pickets and Methods of Combating Suicide Attacks Off Okinawa (20 July 1945) listed directions for pickets while waiting on station or under attack:

1) To be constantly occupied by destroyers, controlled by the Officer in Tactical Command (OTC), to cover the most likely direction of enemy aircraft approach.

2) Maintain constant visual searches using all available bridge and control personnel as lookouts on meticulous sector watch.
3) Maintain constant radar search. SG Microwave Search Radar was considered invaluable for early warning on low-flying bogies.
4) If possible, every Picket was to have an assigned fighter direction team, and the Stations were to be spaced so that the CAP be controlled on an individual raid could easily be passed from picket-to-picket.
5) The Pickets were to report all contacts in terms of range and bearing from Point Bolo on Okinawa to the OTC's fighter director and were to insure they got an acknowledgment for every transmission.
6) Generally, all aircraft, on radar or observed, were to be considered suicide and were to be kept on beam.
7) When under observation by aircraft, the Picket was to change course frequently 10, 20, or 30 degrees. Then, while under attack change direction of turn at the last moment, when possible.
8) When an attack began, or before, the Picket was to go to maximum speed and stay there.
9) The Picket Captain was to hold steady if oncoming aircraft were in low approach and manoeuvre if oncoming aircraft were in high approach (above 30 degrees).
10) Manoeuvre to bring maximum number of guns to bear on each attack.
11) AA weapons were to be always manned and ready and were to open fire on any unidentified airplane that came within 12,000 yards (7 miles/11km) whether they had a good fire control solution or not. Rapid continuous fire was to be used, with an ammunition ratio of four VT to one AA Common. 100 per cent VT fused projectiles were recommended to be employed.

CAPs and Pickets

Early in the Okinawa kamikaze campaign, after a radar picket reported enemy contact, control of all or part of a CAP orbiting at a point nearest that contact was often moved by the Force Fighter Director (FFD) to defend that picket. Later specific protective CAPs were assigned to directly cover pickets in especially vulnerable stations. However, good communications were essential between the pickets and CAP since the pickets were directed to open fire on all unidentified aircraft approaching within 12,000 yards (7 miles/11km) range.

CAPs were maintained day and night over the picket stations, which could also call for aid from the routine combat air patrol of from 48 to 120 aircraft airborne during the daytime, orbiting in depth around Okinawa. This cordon of fighter protection intercepted the incoming kamikaze formations as far from the US fleet as possible by direction from a series of concentric picket lines formed by radar-equipped destroyers.

Because destroyer Combat Information Centers (CICs) could track and intercept only two incoming kamikazes at a time, only a few more could overwhelm a radar picket. In response, these pickets could vector their CAP fighters to intercept incoming Japanese further out, beyond the 50 to 60 miles where kamikaze formations tended to separate for their attacks. This ensured that Japanese formations were attacked before they dispersed and overwhelmed CIC capacity. To prevent kamikazes from following returning USN missions, the destroyers of the picket line used their CAP fighters to 'filter' incoming formations, visually investigating them and shooting down any Japanese shadowers. During the Okinawa campaign, the picket line CAPs used these techniques to destroy an estimated eighty-six enemy planes; the destroyers shot down twenty-seven more with their guns.

In 1945 the Commander Cruiser Division Six commented the following about the picket destroyer operations:

> In this operation it was necessary to station pickets at considerable distances (75 miles) from the centre of the area in order to cover the most probable directions of approach of aircraft from enemy bases and at the same time to prevent approaching enemy planes from taking advantage of adjacent land masses. While the picket stations were close enough to each other to permit passing control of friendly fighters from one ship to another without losing contact, the stations were not close enough to permit mutual support against either air attack or surface raiders. Steps were taken to alleviate the condition by the assignment of an additional destroyer to each of the pickets in the 'more vulnerable' stations and by stationing various small craft such as LCSs and LCMs in position to support the Pickets. Nevertheless, the attacks continued, and severe damage and painful losses were incurred.

As soon as possible, radar stations were established on the islands surrounding Okinawa, which allowed some of the picket radar ships to be cancelled or moved elsewhere to augment more vulnerable stations. However, the pickets at longer ranges from Okinawa remained in operation through the end of the campaign.

TF 58 Fast Carrier Task Force Radar Pickets

During this time, TF 58 Fast Carrier Task Force commanders decided that rather than dispersing their own pickets alone or in pairs, they would also organise them in a radar picket line, consisting of two or three destroyer divisions. The line had at least four pickets, but generally six or eight, ensuring that the picket line had the firepower to fight off kamikaze attacks. TF 58 was able to concentrate its destroyers and position them along the 'most probable line' of Japanese approach. This was due to its mobility in contrast to the static invasion shipping forces off Okinawa; TF 58 did not stay in a fixed location. Because of this picket procedure, only two picket destroyers were damaged, and none were sunk during TF 58's support at Okinawa.

Summary and Conclusions

The radar picket operations were crucial but were also costly as of the 101 destroyers assigned to radar picket stations, 10 were sunk and 32 were damaged by kamikaze attacks while on Okinawa picket line duty. Of the 88 Landing Craft, Support (Large)/LCS(L) assigned to picket stations, 2 were sunk and 11 damaged by kamikazes, while the 11 Landing Ship, Medium (Rocket)/LSM(R)s had 3 sunk and 2 damaged.

Though picket losses were high, the strategy was effective, as the radar screen enlarged US defences and greatly decreased surprise attacks. Using reports supplied by the picket, CAP fighters could be vectored to intercept incoming attacks. Pickets were so effective that the increased use of them was planned for the anticipated invasion of Japan.

Despite the alarming kamikaze numbers and USN ship losses, *Battle Experience: Radar Pickets and Methods of Combating Suicide Attacks Off Okinawa (20 July 1945)* reported that radar pickets had been an 'unqualified success' in:

> Early radar reporting
> Fighter direction at extended distance from objective
> Shooting down enemy planes
> Breaking up enemy raids with gunfire
> Rescuing personnel from crashed CAP aircraft

Combat Air Patrol

The Navy, Marines, and Army CAP Air Units

After the Philippine kamikaze attacks, the American command was aware of the likelihood of formidable attacks by both air and sea on Okinawa assault forces as it was near the Japanese homeland, where the remaining strength of the enemy's naval and air forces was concentrated.

In early 1945, famed USN aviator and tactician Cdr John Thach, already recognised for developing the 'Thach Weave' as an effective aerial combat tactic, developed a defensive strategy against kamikazes dubbed the 'Big Blue Blanket' (named for the blue paint schemes of navy and Marines aircraft), which would establish USN and USMC air supremacy distant from the main Allied carrier and capital ship force. Sizeable CAPs would operate further from their carriers than ever before, while picket destroyers and AA armed landing ships at stations circling Okinawa, distant from the main fleet, provided improved coordination between carrier fighter directors and earlier radar interception for the CAP. Thach's strategy necessitated 24/7 fighter patrols over the Allied fleets, but this was difficult even though the US Fast Carrier Task Force itself had more than 1,000 fighter aircraft available as more were necessary for this extent of CAP cover. Also, at this point in the war, the navy had reduced fighter pilot training, consequently there were not enough navy pilots available. The final component in Thach's anti-kamikaze scheme were intensive fighter sweeps to be deployed on Japanese kamikaze airfields on Kyushu, bombing runways, using delayed-action bombs to make repairs more difficult and dangerous.

To meet the expected air offensive over Okinawa from the nearby fields of Kyushu. Shanghai, and Formosa, the Americans relied upon the Fifth Fleet, the Tenth Army's Tactical Air Force (TAF), the guns of the fleet and supply ships, the British task force, and land-based anti-aircraft artillery. Adm. Raymond Spruance's Fifth Fleet was readied for what was to be the last major naval action of the Pacific War. It was comprised of

Cdr John Thach, earlier recognised for developing the 'Thach Weave', developed a defensive strategy against kamikazes dubbed the 'Big Blue Blanket'. (*USN*)

Adm. Marc Mitscher's Task Force 58 and V Adm. Richmond Kelly Turner's Task Force 51, with V Adm. Sir H. Bernard Rawlings's Task Force 57 of the newly formed British Pacific Fleet providing air cover support between Okinawa and Formosa.

A major countermeasure used to combat the kamikaze threat was to increase the number of combat air patrol aircraft and increase their patrol range out beyond the massed fleet. These CAPs comprised Navy and Marines fighter-interceptors and later Air Force aircraft after the capture of Japanese airfields on Okinawa that placed AAF aircraft within range to furnish air and ground support. However, adding more CAP interceptor aircraft to carrier complements, would be at the expense of Navy and Marines attack aircraft, such as fighter-bombers that would be used to attack Japanese stubborn ground-based positions on Okinawa. This necessity for increased CAP to protect the fleet caused some ground commanders concern that their own close air support would be reduced but Navy (and some Marines) squadrons from the escort carriers filled that need, flying more than 60 per cent of the close air missions. During the Okinawa campaign, between 1 April and 21 June, the combination of TAF and V Adm. Calvin Durgin's Escort Carrier Force would mainly fly ground-support missions, conducting 18,133 sorties on Okinawa and expending

2,000 tons of bombs and 30,000 rockets that destroyed numerous ground targets and also claimed 280 enemy aircraft in the air.

Task Force 58, deployed just to the east of Okinawa, with its own picket group of from six to eight destroyers, maintained thirteen carriers (seven CV and six CVL) on duty from 23 March to 27 April and a lesser number subsequently. Until 27 April, from fourteen to eighteen converted carriers (CVEs) were in the area at all times, and until 20 April, British Task Force 57, with four large and six CVEs, remained off the Sakishima Islands to protect the southern Okinawa flank.

The Tenth TAF, commanded by USMC Maj. Gen. Francis Mulcahy, was a joint aviation command of the Tenth US Army that was comprised of both USMC and AAF aviation units. It was assigned to direct all land-based aviation, aviation command, and control units during the Battle of Okinawa. The force would grow to include a total of fifteen Marine fighter squadrons, ten Army fighter squadrons, two Marine torpedo bomber squadrons, and sixteen Army Air Force bomber squadrons. Other Marines and Army Air Groups were added later. In the execution of the air superiority missions, the Marines fighter squadrons flew Chance Vought F4U Corsairs, and the Marine night fighter squadrons flew radar-equipped Grumman F6F Hellcats. Army Air Force fighter pilots flew Republic P-47 Thunderbolts, while their night fighter squadron was equipped with the Northrop P-61 Black Widow.

The most effective fighters against kamikazes over Okinawa were F4U-1D Corsairs of VMF-323. (*Author collection*)

Two Marine fighter groups, MAG-31 and -33, flying from Yontan under the Tenth TAF, provided most of the CAP missions over the fleet during the first several weeks of the battle. Marines CAP requirements escalated from twelve aircraft on patrol initially to as many as thirty-two on station, with an additional dozen on ground alert. By the end of April the TAF aircraft had flown 3,521 combat air patrol sorties and were responsible for assisting in the shooting down of 143 enemy aircraft. There were two Marine aircraft groups ashore giving them six Corsair squadrons and two Hellcat -3N and -5N-equipped night fighter squadrons.

May 1945 saw TAF strength increased with the addition of Marine Aircraft Group 22 and the 318th Fighter Group. With the additional aircraft assigned, combat air patrols were pushed further north of Okinawa. During May, TAF aircraft flew more than 6,700 sorties in defence of the island and with naval shipping claiming 369 enemy aircraft shot down. During the same period TAF lost 109 aircraft, with only 3 lost to direct enemy action. At the end of May and into June, the remainder of the fighter squadrons from the AAF's 301st Fighter Wing and Marine Aircraft Group 14 arrived. Eventually, ADC commanded a total of twenty-five fighter squadrons.

Between the beginning of the Okinawa campaign on 1 April and its end on 21 June, the combination of TAF and USN carrier pilots flew 14,244 air support sorties. Overall, TAF pilots shot down 625 Japanese aircraft of all types. Col Ward Dickey's Marine Aircraft Group 33 set a record with 214 kills; more than half claimed by Maj. George Axtell's Marine Fighter Attack Squadron (VMF) 323, the 'Death Rattlers'. At 22, Axtell was the youngest squadron commander in the Marine Corps. On 9 April 1945, twenty-four Death Rattler F4U Corsairs flew into recently captured Kadena Airfield to begin CAP and ground-support missions for Operation Iceberg. Between then and the Japanese surrender

Ten of twelve VMF-323 aces (left to right): Maj. George Axtell, CO, 6 kills; Maj. Jeff Dorroh, XO, 6 kills; 2nd Lt Stuart Alley, 5 kills; 2nd Lt Al Wells, 5 kills; 2nd Lt Francis Terrell, 6 kills; 2nd Lt Bill Drake, 5 kills; 2nd Lt Joe Dillard, 6.33 kills; 2nd Lt Jerry O'Keefe, 7 kills; 2nd Lt Dewey Durnford, 6.33 kills; and 1st Lt Bill Hood, 5.5 kills. Missing are 1Lt John Ruhsam, 7 kills and 1Lt Bob Wade, 7 kills. (*Author's collection*)

in August, VMF-323 shot down 124 Japanese aircraft, mostly kamikazes, without loss, the highest total of any squadron during the battle and with 12 Death Rattlers becoming aces.

Cdr Albert Momm, commander of the destroyer *Mullany* (DD-528), evaluated the CAP and CAP night fighter capabilities after his ship was hit and put out of action by a kamikaze on 6 April:

> The CAP has done an excellent job in keeping the figures high in the 'splash' column, flying in difficult weather and until dark in several instances. The night CAP has proven valuable in many interceptions, but there is still much to be desired if control of the air at night is to be obtained. Night fighters were airborne occasionally with no attempt made at intercepting the night 'hecklers'. This shows a need for more specially trained intercept officers in the forward areas. With two operational airfields and qualified intercept officers present, there should be no excuse for not utilizing the night fighter to the utmost. Fortunately, the Japs did not see the capabilities of a full-scale night bombing attack on Kerama Retto, where the anchorage was filled with damaged ships and other high-priority targets.

CAP Tactics V. the Ohka

For the Betty/Ohka composite to be most effective, its approach needed to be at higher altitudes and longer ranges but this made it easier for the navy radar-equipped picket ships to detect the enemy composite, which then allowed more CAP alert and intercept time. However, once launched, the Ohka's short 20ft length, 16ft wingspan, and partial stealth wooden construction reflected only a small, fast-moving pip on navy radar screens, making it difficult to detect. The Betty turned back to Japan immediately upon releasing its Ohka, causing the picket radar operators to tend to follow the mothership's larger radar track, while overlooking the smaller Ohka's echo on the first radar sweep and then, perhaps, losing it altogether on succeeding sweeps as the attacker sped in. The Betty's speed, altitude, and manoeuvrability was reduced when carrying the Ohka, making CAP interception prior to release point imperative. Once the Ohka was released, the chances of both interception by the CAP and shipboard AA firepower were limited by the 500mph+ speed of a diving Ohka. Therefore, the USN's priority was the early detection, interception, and destruction of the Betty/Ohka coordinated by the USN's radar and CAP team before the Ohka was near enough to the fleet to be released. If the CAP interceptors could engage an Ohka kamikaze raid more than 50 miles from the fleet, the attack would often be disrupted and scattered. The Bettys, still carrying their Ohkas, being easy targets, would often drop their load (the Ohka pilots had not entered their aircraft at this point) and try to head back to Kyushu as quickly as possible. If the CAP interception occurred closer than 25 miles out, most of the Bettys would be in position to release their Ohka, which could then reach Allied ships. Therefore, long-range interception was so decisive that USN commanders continually changed the composition of carrier air groups to include more fighters and fewer carrier bombers, even knowing that it reduced the tactical and ground-support capacity of the fleet.

F4U gun camera footage of the pursuit and destruction of a Betty-carrying Ohka. (*Author's collection*)

The picket *Mannert L. Abele*'s captain, Lt Cdr Alton Parker, stated:

> In this officer's opinion there can only be one certain defense against the suicide attack and that is in maintaining a large CAP in the air at all times with each picket having control of at least eight planes, four of which could be directed visually.

Cdr Leonard Chamberlain, the captain of the picket USS *Hugh V. Hadley*, recorded:

> The aviators who comprised the Combat Air Patrol assigned to the *Hadley* gave battle to the enemy that ranks with the highest traditions of our Navy's history. When the leader was asked to close and assist us, he replied, 'I am out of ammunition, but I am

> sticking with you.' He then proceeded to fly his plane at enemy planes attacking in attempting to head them off.

Cdr William Sanders, CO USS *Aaron Ward*:

> The CAP has done a magnificent job in these operations but often too few have been available. The CAP must be large enough and carefully stacked (to meet massed attacks).

Anti-Aircraft Defences

Anti-Aircraft Guns and Gunnery

Because US Navy anti-aircraft defences were designed to resist conventional air attacks, kamikazes exploited the limitations of such guns. Conventional attacks could be deterred by the mass of automatic anti-aircraft weapons mounted on-board USN ships late in the war, but kamikazes had more resolve, often crashing into their targets after extensive damage. To reliably defeat a kamikaze, it had to be completely destroyed before closing on its target.

Pre-War US Navy Anti-Aircraft Guns

During the late 1930s, the 1.1in gun was intended to replace the too light Browning .50 calibre machine gun, which lacked range and firepower as an anti-aircraft gun. The first 1.1in guns were mounted in 1939 and were widely used before and during the first years of the Second World War. Unfortunately, during their early combat use these heavy guns were found to be unreliable, four barrels were required to duplicate the .50 calibre's rate of fire, they were likely to jam and were generally ineffective as an AA weapon. They were replaced by the superior 20mm Oerlikon and 40mm Bofors AA guns as soon as their production accelerated.

20mm Oerlikon AA Gun

The Swiss-developed 20mm Oerlikon was initially developed as an aircraft gun but became best known in its naval applications. The Royal Navy manufactured and mounted large numbers under licence. From 1942, the USN replaced the 1.1in-calibre gun with the Oerlikon, where it succeeded in the naval anti-aircraft role. It provided an effective defence at short ranges, up to almost a mile (1.5km), a range at which heavier guns had difficulty tracking a target. Between December 1941 and September 1944, 32 per cent of all Japanese aircraft downed by the USN were credited to this weapon, with the high point being 48.3 per cent for the second half of 1942. In 1943 the innovative Mark 14 Gunsight was introduced, which made these guns even more effective. By late 1944, the USN had found that the Oerlikon's 20mm shells were too light to destroy kamikazes and their higher approach speeds made manually controlled guns obsolete. As a result, Oerlikons were replaced by 40mm Bofors wherever possible during 1944–1945.

20mm Oerlikon AA guns. (*USN*)

40mm Bofors AA Gun

The Swedish-developed water-cooled 40mm Bofors gun was employed on almost every major US and Royal Navy warship of the Second World War. It was licensed to the BuOrd during mid-1941 and this made major improvements with the addition of power operation to both twin and quadruple mounts (essentially mounting two twin mounts side by side). Many considered that these improvements made it the best automatic cannon anti-aircraft weapon of the Second World War and it remained in service long after the conflict ended. The Mark 14 gunsight used with the Oerlikon was later adopted as part of the Mark 51 director that was used to control the 40mm Bofors, significantly increasing its effectiveness.

40mm Bofors AA guns. (*USN*)

A barrage of 20 and 40mm shells splash into the sea behind a Kate torpedo plane bearing down on the battleship USS *Texas*. The kamikaze missed its target and crashed into the Pacific. (*USN*)

Comments on the Effectiveness of Picket Ship Guns and Gunnery

Cdr Baron Mullaney, CO *USS Hugh V. Hadley:*

> I was amazed at the performance of the 20mm and 40mm guns. Contrary to my expectation, these smaller guns shot down the bulk of the enemy planes. Daily the crews had dinned into their minds the following order: 'LEAD THAT PLANE.' Signs were painted at the gun stations as follows: 'LEAD THAT PLANE.' It worked; they led and the planes flew right through our projectiles.

Cdr David Martineau, CO *USS Metcalf*:

> The ability to hit fast-moving planes with machine guns and automatic weapon is acquired only through constant practice and is an art which must be either continually practiced or rapidly lost.

5in/38-calibre Dual-Purpose AA Gun

The navy's 20mm and 40mm guns lacked the destructive power to bring down a determined kamikaze. The only calibre of anti-aircraft weapon large enough to completely destroy a kamikaze before it crashed into its target was the 5in gun, which quickly became the preferred weapon for fighting off suicide attacks, especially when coupled with the VT or proximity fuse. (VT, or variable time, was the navy's verbiage to obscure the substance of the new proximity fuse, which used a small radar to ensure detonation when an enemy aircraft was nearby.)

The 5in/38-calibre (12.7cm) was considered the superlative dual-purpose naval gun of the Second World War. It was initially designed to arm new 1930s destroyers, but ultimately was used on virtually every major US warship built between 1934 and 1948 and continued to arm new warships as late as the 1960s. The guns were commonly controlled by the advanced Mark 37 Gun Fire Control System, which provided accurate and timely firing against surface and air targets. To engage enemy aircraft using surprise attacks, 5in batteries were placed under the control of manually operated auxiliary gun directors. If targets were identified at long range, 5in gun control was to be controlled by the main Mark 37 gun director. For a gun of its calibre, it had a relatively high rate of fire, which gave it its prominence as an anti-aircraft weapon, a role in which it was utilised regularly by the navy. However, even using this advanced fire control system, approximately 1,000 rounds of ammunition needed to be fired per aircraft kill. These kills were generally achieved by shell fragments from barrage fire rather than direct hits. Attacking enemy aircraft met large walls of shell fragments from many guns firing in the air at once. However, this standard procedure of massing multiple ships together to form the tightest collection of gun coverage led to a marked increase in 'friendly fire' incidents as shrapnel and shells from neighbouring ships' anti-aircraft guns rained down on other ships, killing 65 and wounding 368. As good as the 5/38 was, it was the introduction VT (proximity-fused) AA ammunition that made it outstanding.

A dramatic photo, on 11 April 1945, of a Zero kamikaze crashing into the USS *Missouri*'s (BB-63) ship's 5in gun defences (the Mk 37 gun director is in the right foreground). (*USN*)

3in/50 AA Gun

A promising new semi-automatic 3in gun mount was scheduled to replace the existing pair of 40mm mounts, with one 3in for each pair. This gun was the smallest that could fire proximity-fuse projectiles that could destroy a kamikaze. Preliminary analyses indicated that this new 3in would be nearly equal to the 5in in effectiveness and replacing 40mm guns with 3in ones would increase anti-kamikaze firepower by two to five times, even with the reduced number of barrels. In late June 1945, the BuOrd assigned priority for the 3in project, but the end of the war slowed development and funds were redirected to the 3in/70 (7.62cm) AA gun project, delaying the delivery of this gun to the fleet until 1948.

Proximity (VT) Rounds

The small, fast-moving Ohkas made AA fire control especially challenging but by 1945 large quantities of newly developed anti-aircraft variable time (VT) proximity fused AA shells became available. A conventional AA shell that just misses the target will not explode. A time- or altitude-triggered AA fuse required expert prediction by the gunner and accurate timing by the fuse. If either was wrong, then even accurately aimed rounds would explode without effect before or after reaching the target. Armed with a proximity fuse, the AA shell only needed to pass near the target at some time during its flight to explode. However, to function in shells, the fuse needed to be miniaturised, survive the high acceleration of firing, and be dependable. In 1942, the National Defense Research Committee (NDRC) delegated physicist Merle Tuve at the Department of Terrestrial Magnetism at the Johns Hopkins University Applied Physics Lab (APL) to develop proximity fuses for shells. After Tuve's group succeeded, over 100 American companies were mobilised to build some 20 million shell fuses during the war. The proximity fuse was one of the most important technological innovations of the Second World War and was considered so significant that it was regarded as secret as the atom bomb project or the D-Day invasion. The VT sensor was a small radar set that transmitted signals and listened for their reflections from nearby objects and when a target closed enough to be damaged or destroyed, the fuse would explode the shell. VT shells were seven times more successful on average than conventional shells and were highly effective in their use against conventional prop-driven kamikaze attacks.

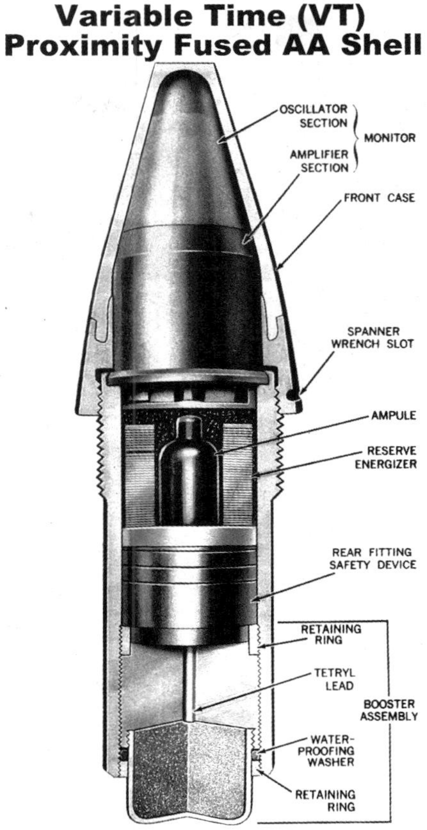

Variable Time (VT) Proximity Fused AA Shell

(*USN*)

However, the ORG also showed that it required about 500 VT rounds to destroy an enemy aircraft during conventional attacks, fewer for prop-driven kamikazes, the reason being their simpler unswerving trajectory. By contrast, the non-VT-fused 5in results showed an expenditure of 2,000 rounds per destroyed enemy aircraft, slightly less for kamikaze attacks, again related to the kamikaze's constant trajectory. However, because of their high speed and small size, proximity fuses would be triggered by an Ohka at a more distant 30 to 45ft proximity and it was estimated that approximately four times as many of the proximity shells would have to be fired by anti-aircraft gunners to destroy an Ohka.

Fleet Anti-Aircraft Tactics

Throughout the Pacific War, the USN had continually improved its anti-aircraft doctrine, guns, rounds, and accuracy. By 1945, fleet carriers averaged 136 separate guns of various calibres, battleships 149 guns, while heavy cruisers averaged 83 guns and destroyers 42. AA defences had to be effective at long range to engage early-detected Japanese aircraft, and also at very short ranges, during the decisive split second of the kamikaze attack. The fleet's anti-aircraft tactics depended on the types of ships involved, the Fast Carrier Task Force or the supporting naval units, and the situation for either at the time.

Fast Carrier Force

The Fast Carrier Task Force, the main target of enemy air attacks, was to put up an aggressive defence utilising heavy AA firepower, high speed, manoeuvrability, and the newest radar equipment and AA directors available.

Normally operating 60 miles or more from land, the task force's anti-aircraft dispositions sited battleships, cruisers, and destroyers in the same circular screen, with aircraft carriers at the centre. AA policy mandated opening fire at 12,000 yards or more, using a high proportion of VT shells.

During early 1945 fast carrier task groups developed AA coordination plans, devised to provide concentrated 5in gunfire against targets at long range, while protecting against further undetected attacks. Under this plan, a task group AA coordinator was assigned to filter all target information to and from ships over a special VHF circuit. The task group was divided into four sectors, and ships in each sector, when alerted, would supplement search radars with fire control radars. The plan imposed no restrictions of freedom of action by individual ships in repelling air attacks.

The US Pacific Fleet prepares for Okinawa: USS *Wasp*, USS *Yorktown*, USS *Hornet*, USS *Hancock*, USS *Ticonderoga*, and other warships at Ulithi Atoll, Caroline Islands, 8 December 1944. (*USN*)

Supporting Naval Forces

Supporting forces consisted of screening and picket destroyers, convoy transports and tankers, and bombardment, amphibious, auxiliary, and landing craft. Unlike the fast carrier force, these supporting naval units, except for destroyers, mostly opposed enemy aircraft less forcefully as they were generally less well equipped with AA armament, radar, and fire control equipment. Their comparative lack of speed and manoeuvrability, and the necessity for them to operate close to land, also limited their defences against enemy air attacks. Most of these supporting ships were anchored or were limited by their assigned duties and depended for protection against attack upon smokescreens, camouflage, or concealment in cloud shadows, rain squalls, and against the dark side of nearby land masses.

Radar picket destroyers were to fire upon enemy aircraft well before they approached the main fleet body. (*USN*)

The comparatively well-armed and radar-equipped screening destroyers were to connect task groups and fire upon enemy aircraft attempting to pass between them. Picket destroyers, supplemented by armed landing craft, were stationed in the direction of an expected attack, widening the task force's radar range. Picket stations, usually consisting of a division and sometimes a squadron of destroyers under its division or squadron commander, were to engage and fire upon enemy aircraft, direct CAP fighters assigned to it, and direct returning aircraft.

US Navy Task Force Operational Response to Kamikaze Attacks

Protective AA Screening

After the early carrier v. carrier battles of 1942, the USN discarded their single-carrier formations and alternatively adapted their task forces around multiple carriers. The momentous 1944 sea battles of the Philippine Sea in June and the Leyte Gulf in October established the value of two or more carriers operating mutually and protected by one or more escorting ship AA screens.

By late 1944, USN anti-aircraft doctrine specified that screening ships were to be stationed between 1,500 and 2,000 yards from ships they were to shield and from other escorting ships. This distance provided massed AA fire while furnishing individual vessels areas to manoeuvre if attacked. But as Japanese massed kamikaze attacks progressively threatened task force shipping, USN commanders constricted their formations and sought other approaches to strengthen defences.

In protecting Okinawa shipping from enemy air attack, USN planners recognised that the most effective defence against kamikazes was the closest possible formation with a single circle of escorting vessels spread 1,000 yards apart around the screened warships. There were recommendations for even tighter screens, with escorting shipping to close to within 200 yards of screened ships when attacks were impending. However, tighter screens increased the probability of hitting nearby ships when firing at low-level attackers, so the necessity for anti-aircraft fire coordination, fire discipline, and thorough training for gun crews was emphasized.

As soon as approaching kamikazes were detected, navy ships were instructed to collectively initiate high-speed repeated evasive tight turns, placing the target on the beam for maximum firepower, and open anti-aircraft fire at maximum range, using a high percentage of VT fuses, and maintaining heavy gunfire until the target was destroyed. When the kamikazes initiated their final attack runs, these ships were directed to as quickly as possible manoeuvre to bring their gunnery directors and the maximum number of AA guns to bear. This generally meant that ships would turn to present their beam to high-diving attackers, which had the further advantage of increasing the probability that a diving kamikaze would miss its target. Targets facing low-level attacks were instructed to turn away from threats, presenting as narrow a target as possible and protecting its control station on the bridge. However, there were problems regarding high-speed, zigzagging, evasive manoeuvring, particularly concerning destroyers and smaller escorting AA ships. This 'jinking' could cause aiming to be disrupted for ship's AA gunners and all but the most advanced radar-equipped, gun-direction systems. Nonetheless, while under a harrowing kamikaze attack, few ships' captains could not resist exploiting the most extreme evasive manoeuvres possible.

A fleet gunnery directive posted to picket ships recommended the following:

In General, Consider All Planes Suicide
Go to Maximum Speed and Stay There
Manoeuvre
Keep Good Relative Wind
Get Planes on Beam
Hold steady if in Low Approach
Manoeuvre on a High Approach (Above 30 degrees)

Anti-Kamikaze Gunnery Tactics

US Navy shipboard gunners had to develop new methods to counter kamikaze attacks as once within firing range, these attacks developed very quickly, especially the rocket-propelled Ohka attacks. The kamikaze's vulnerability was its requirement to maintain a collision course, which meant that their relative bearing had to remain constant. Given sufficient time to manoeuvre, the targeted ship, not the kamikaze, could dictate that bearing; one that would permit the ship to concentrate its firepower. To do so, general quarters were to be called only if a bogey (an unidentified aircraft) closed to 20 miles (32km). When a target closed to 16,000 yards (9 miles/14,630m), the targeted ship was to manoeuvre to position it on a 110-degree relative bearing and remain there, and never allow a bogey to approach from astern where minimal firepower could be directed. The target was to maintain a patrol speed 10 to 15 knots until the kamikaze closed to

10,000 yards (9,144m) and then accelerate to full speed. At this range the 5in/38-calibre (127mm) guns were to commence firing initially using salvo fire. Once the attacker was at 5,000 yards (4,572m) and plainly visible, the 40mm Bofors and then the gyroscopically stabilised 20mm Oerlikon autocannons were to commence their continuous, rapid fire, followed by machine gun fire. The 5in main battery would change to rapid continuous fire at 3,500 yards (3,200m) to give relief to the fatigued gun loaders loading the 54lb (24.5kg) projectiles. Although 40mm and 20mm guns destroyed more attacking planes, it was desirable that the 5in guns destroy the kamikaze at a safe distance from the attacked ship, as once the kamikaze, even when heavily damaged, closed to within range of the lighter 20 and 40mm AA guns, its momentum could continue it to crash into its target.

A fleet gunnery directive posted to picket ships instructed:

> Commence firing main battery at maximum range possible and keep firing. Even if no hits are made, it will frequently drive them off. At the same time, however, it may cause them to turn on weaker ships in the vicinity ... Use all available guns that can bear and range ... Rates of fire vary widely between ships. Make sure that you are obtaining the maximum efficiency that your guns are capable of performing. Watch the condition of your ready ammunition supply.

Combat Information Center (CIC)

The Combat Information Center (CIC), the nerve centre of a warship, was developed in 1942, and was continually improved. It was critical in providing a comprehensive tactical analysis during confused and quickly changing air and sea battles. The CIC acted as a tactical centre to coordinate, analyse, and communicate enemy threat information received from the ship's radars, radios, electronic countermeasures (ECM), lookouts, the bridge, and naval gunfire spotters to determine real-time tactical action to relay to their bridge and gunnery crews, along with other ships and aircraft of the task force. To maximise the effectiveness of task force anti-aircraft defence, the task force command assigned explicit defensive duties, such as fighter direction or air search, to individual ships or groups of ships while acting as the principal information and direction centre for the entire task force.

During the war, the CIC's most important and unsolvable limiting factor involved the Fighter Direction Officers (FDOs), who were central to the CIC process. They wanted quicker updates and more accurate information on the developing combat situation to make more informed decisions. The CIC operators complained that the display of information was slow, complicated, and incomplete, making it difficult to comprehend the entire situation rapidly or correctly. Consequently, only a few enemy attacks could be managed simultaneously by a single CIC. The solo, dispersed character of kamikaze attacks tested the effective bounds of the CIC system and its operators. During the war the navy attempted to network task force CICs, but the ultimate solution was to automate (computerise) much of the necessary information processing, which was ultimately systematised as the Naval Tactical Data System in the 1960s.

The Combat Information Center (CIC) was maintained as a source of accurate up-to-the-minute information on own and enemy surface and air units and on navigational objects. Its primary purpose was to supply this information to flagship and gunnery control stations to further the fighting efficiency and safety of the ship. (*USN*)

Fighter Direction, Radar, and the Fighter Direction Officer (FDO)

Naval radar played a decisive role in ending the Pacific War as not only was it used to detect and track air and surface targets, but also became a primary method of directing shipboard gun fire, especially as it was also very effectively employed in the new VT fuses. Search and height-finding radars provided huge amounts of data that required skilled operators, plotting teams, and fighter directors for their effective use by the fighter pilots, who were the spearhead of the air defence team.

Naval fighter direction progressed constantly during the war's final year due to wartime experience, by extending and improving FDO training and curricula, and by the continually improved equipment and facilities. The FDO's primary frustration was with his facilities and equipment as there were times during the air campaign when massed Japanese air attacks forced fighter direction teams to the limits of their abilities and capacities and that of their equipment. They continually found their greatest difficulty to be their inability to effectively employ all the data that their radars could potentially provide. Generally, the FDO's equipment served them adequately during small-scale attacks; but problems occurred in saturation raids while trying to keep up with and maintain the total tactical picture. The solution was to be 'some sort of automated aid to the plotting teams and fighter directors'. Also, unlike the FDOs on carriers, those on destroyers had the problem of not having previous regular personal contact with the pilots they were directing. Carrier FDOs knew their pilots from their ship, which helped them to understand each other and help pilots successfully carry out directions. Also, pilots sometimes did not keep destroyer FDOs informed and sometimes did not turn on their IFF equipment.

While the radar pickets were generally outstanding in providing early warning of incoming strikes and vectoring CAP to interceptions (about 60 per cent of the time), many enemy aircraft succeeded in reaching their targets. Radar provided the Navy with a valuable anti-aircraft apparatus, but one that required continual complicated maintenance and its effective use was problematic. Inspections revealed that many radars gave inaccurate readings due to maladjusted antennae and inadequately trained operators. The slow, wood and fabric biplane trainers the IJN used as kamikazes were difficult to detect on radar until they were close to their targets and then, unexpectedly manoeuvrable, became difficult targets for anti-aircraft fire. The Ohkas would also become difficult AA targets but because of their carrying Bettys and their high speed.

Ohka Radar Interception

Because the Betty parent aircraft usually reversed course to head home immediately upon releasing its Ohka, there was an inclination for radar operators to follow this initial larger track of the Betty while not noticing the smaller echo of the Ohka that was then closing rapidly on its target. Radar operators would also assess the released Ohka's echo as anti-radar detection window on the first sweep, then lose it entirely on succeeding sweeps.

An action report by commander Task Force 58, R Adm. Marc Mitscher, telling of kamikaze tactics during the Okinawa operation, stated:

> Fighter direction met its most strenuous test in the present Kyushu-Okinawa operations. Rarely have the enemy attacks been so cleverly executed and made with such reckless determination. These attacks were generally by single or few aircraft making their approach with radical changes in course and altitude, dispersing when intercepted and using cloud cover to every advantage. They tailed our friendlies home, used decoy planes, and in at any altitude or on the water. Only once during the entire present operation did the enemy attack in the old orthodox fashion. Here a raid of 32 Bettys with 16 fighters as cover stacked 14–18,000ft was annihilated 60 miles from this force. Fighter Director teams and radar personnel operating in this task force were well trained and experienced and every effort was made to increase efficiency by practice and experience. Never before, however, have the limitations of our present equipment become so pronounced, and the enemy, fully aware of these limitations gained by experience and other means, made every effort to attack this force under the cloak of these limitations and with quite effective results.

Mitscher's report then summarised the limitations of our air defence against the kamikaze attack:

> Even the new SM and SP height-finding radars [Author: only used on carriers and battleships] could not consistently detect low fliers in time to deploy fighters, especially of singles or small groups. When fighters were deployed, the attackers were usually so close that the CAP could get in only one pass.
>
> There was an unusually high percentage of uncompleted interceptions against small formation kamikazes at ranges beyond 50 miles because the CAP never sighted them. This was due to inability of height-finding radars to reach beyond this range, and due to the two-degree bearing accuracy of SC-2 and SK search radars that resulted in seven-mile distance errors at a range of 100 miles. [Author: However, SC-2 radar was the only one with directional IFF, which allowed quicker differentiation between friendly and enemy units.]
>
> Present radars had difficulty in maintaining tracks on small groups or single attackers that made sudden changes in course, altitude, and speed. Tracking was even more difficult when friendly aircraft were also in the picture. The Japanese use of window could be very effective.

Height-Finder Radars

There were mainly three types of height-finder radars: the newer SM and SP units and the older SG units. The SM radars were used on fleet carriers and battleships because of the unit's weight (18,000lb/4,283kg) and the antenna's size (6ft/1.8m in diameter) while the smaller, but still bulky, SP radar was installed on smaller carriers. The older smaller SG units were used by cruisers and destroyers. To overcome a failing in previous air search radars, these radars were developed to gather more precise information about the height of enemy planes.

The first operational Raytheon SG set was installed on the cruiser USS *Augusta* in April 1942, they were generally operational by fall of 1942, and were installed on all cruisers and destroyers by early 1943. The SG unit weighed 3,000lb (1,350kg) and was equipped with a 48 × 15in (122 × 38cm) rotating elliptical parabolic antenna that scanned at 4, 8, or 12 rotations per minute, producing a beam 5 degrees wide and 15 degrees high to a range of 17 miles (28km) tracking a low-altitude bomber with an accuracy of 200 yards (183m). SG radar was a vast improvement over the previous SC radar, providing naval radar operators a more precise electronic map of their surroundings on their PPI scope. The picket destroyer captain was able to see incoming low-level enemy aircraft 360 degrees around his ship in daylight, night, and fog.

R Adm. C.T. Joy, Commander Cruiser Division Six, wrote this in his action report of the role of fighter direction in the Okinawa campaign:

> Fighter direction during this operation was well handled, particularly in view of the many new problems imposed on account of the large size and geographical location

US Navy SG search radar's microwave frequencies provided good performance and smaller units and antennas, making it possible for them to become standard on cruisers and destroyers by early 1943. (*USN*)

of the area in which our forces were operating. There were no surprise raids and the great majority of enemy planes which approached during daylight failed to reach the most vital targets in the transport area at the objective. The many successful interceptions resulted from splendid coordination of fighter direction by the Force Flagship and efficient work of numerous other vessels – especially the destroyer types which acted as radar pickets.

In a secret letter on 8 October 1944 to the Chiefs of the Bureaus of Ordnance, Aeronautics and Ships the CNO, Admiral Ernest King, summarised the fleet's needs for improved radar facilities and equipment. He called for:

1) Height-finding radars that could measure altitudes at up to 150 miles range, without the need to stop the antenna, and with elevation accuracy on the order of forty to sixty minutes of arc.
2) Radars with consistent detection ranges beyond 300 miles on aircraft up to altitudes of fifty thousand feet.
3) Airborne radars with detection ranges of 100 miles on aircraft and missiles.
4) Airborne radars with sufficient accuracy to direct fighters to interceptions at ranges up to twenty miles.
5) Search radars that could discriminate and detect air targets over land masses, and regardless of atmospheric problems or 'window' countermeasures.
6) Positive identification between friend and foe, and determination of individual unit or aircraft identity.

Project Cadillac: Improved Shipboard Radar

The navy urgently needed improved radar coverage to augment shipboard radars with airborne ones as Adm. King had suggested. Project Cadillac, code-named after the tallest mountain on the US Eastern Seaboard (in Maine), had been conceived in 1942; its original objective was to allow surface search beyond the horizon. In early 1944, Cadillac's requirement was changed to detect low-flying aircraft approaching below the beams of shipboard radars. Cadillac mounted the APS-20 aerial radar in a converted Grumman TBF and connected this radar's display to the host ship's CIC via radio link. The airborne APS-20 successfully operated as one of the ship's own radars. Beginning in February 1945, tests were conducted in response to the kamikaze threat. Although they revealed problems with the radio link, the tests were considered promising. Shipboard trials began in May and proved that Cadillac would increase the fleet's ability to detect and intercept low-flying kamikazes. When the war ended, plans were under way to equip four fleet carriers with the necessary planes and equipment. The Cadillac concept merged with the success of the destroyer pickets to prompt plans for an airborne CIC that could direct fighters, designated as Cadillac II. Although it also used the APS-20, this new concept was fundamentally different. Instead of augmenting shipboard capabilities, the radar was used by CIC operators within the host aircraft, a converted Boeing B-17. The goal was to augment fighter-direction capabilities and provide a new mechanism for vectoring CAP fighters to intercepts. Patrol Bombing Squadron 101 was formed on 2 July 1945 and, had the war continued, Cadillac II would likely have provided fighter direction for navy TFs during the assault on Kyushu.

Project Cadillac mounted the APS-20 aerial radar in a converted Grumman TBF and connected this radar's display to the host ship's CIC via radio link. (*USN*)

Pre-Emptive Raids on Kyushu Kamikaze Airfields

After the initial limited but successful kamikaze attacks in the Philippines, the American High Command realised that no matter how responsive the air and surface defences surrounding Okinawa were, a number of suicide aircraft were going to strike their targets. They anticipated that by repeated air strikes against the kamikaze airbases on the southern

TF 58 Grumman F6F Hellcats of VF-17 and VBF-17 on the flight deck of the Essex-class fleet aircraft carrier USS *Hornet* (CV-12) carried out fighter-bomber attacks against Kyushu kamikaze bases (below) on 18–19 March 1945 in preparation for Operation Iceberg that destroyed an estimated 528 enemy aircraft in the air and on the ground. (*USN*)

Japanese home island of Kyushu, kamikaze raids could be limited in size and frequency. Navy commanders ordered TF 58 carrier-borne fighter-bomber attacks against southern Kyushu kamikaze bases on 18–19 March 1945, in preparation for Operation Iceberg. The British Pacific Fleet (BPF; known as Task Force 57) was comprised of 50 warships, of which 17 were aircraft carriers that provided about a quarter of Allied naval air power (450 aircraft). TF 57 attacked and neutralised Japanese airfields on Formosa and the Sakishima Islands in late March and early April. Meanwhile, the Twentieth Air Force diverted 2,000 B-29 sorties from their strategic priority of bombing of Japanese cities to the tactical bombing of identified kamikaze airbases and aircraft manufacturing targets. Fifth Air Force bombers flew 138 sorties against airfields on Kyushu and the Seventh Air Force conducted a further 784. While these air force and navy air raids destroyed more than 1,000 Japanese aircraft on the ground, they did not appreciably reduce Japan's ability to mount kamikaze attacks during the Okinawa campaign. Although these raids successfully delayed some kamikaze sorties taking off from damaged airfields, the Japanese were successful in quickly repairing the damaged runways adequately for the kamikazes to take off and continue to form to be led to their targets.

Kamikaze attacks tapered off near the end of the campaign only because Tokyo wanted to conserve kamikaze aircraft and pilots for the defence of the Home Islands. By August 1945, Japan had amassed more than 6,000 aircraft of virtually every type to engage as kamikazes against the anticipated US invasion armada. During the month the XXI Bomber Command assaulted the Japanese with 15,712 tons of bombs. Some 36 per cent of the tonnage had been dropped on Kyushu airfields in support of the Okinawa operation, 29 per cent on the Japanese aircraft industry, and 34 per cent on other Japanese urban industrial areas. Formosa was being struck from the Philippines.

Chapter Three

Conventional Kamikaze Attacks: A Synopsis

The First Kamikaze Attacks Endorsed for Defence of the Philippines

After Adm. Takijirō Ōnishi and Cdr Motoharu Okamura established the basis for the kamikaze, the precept was met with fits and starts until 17 October 1944, when Allied forces began operations around Leyte Gulf, where the Japanese defenders found themselves severely outnumbered in men and aircraft. As commander of the Philippines' aerial defence (*tokkotai*) and First Air Fleet Commander, Ōnishi then coordinated the planned employment of a suicide offensive force, the Special Attack Unit. In a meeting at Mabalacat Airfield (former Clark Airbase), on 19 October 1944, Ōnishi, who was visiting the 201st Navy Flying Corps headquarters, stated that considering the navy's diminished strength, only suicide attack units would be effective in countering the US carrier fleet and ordered them to proceed.

During the Philippines campaign, R Adm. Masafumi Arima, the commander of the 26th Air Flotilla (part of the Eleventh Air Fleet), is sometimes recognised with originating the kamikaze scheme. On 15 October 1944, Arima flew a Betty to attack the large Essex-class carrier USS *Franklin* (CV-13) near Leyte Gulf. He was killed and 'part of an aircraft' hit the *Franklin*. The Japanese High Command and propagandists gave Arima official credit for making the first kamikaze attack, promoting him posthumously to vice admiral, even though official Japanese accounts of Arima's attack bore slight resemblance to the actual circumstances. The *Franklin*'s combat report stated that a 'wounded Japanese Betty Mitsubishi G4M bomber went down fighting when it turned toward *Franklin* in a kamikaze attempt. Thankfully, it skimmed her flight deck and caused only minimal damage.'

R Adm. Masafumi Arima, the first kamikaze attacker. (*Author/Lansdale*)

The first Philippines kamikaze corps, under the command of Capt. Yukio Seki, consisted of four squadrons: 'Shikishima' (the poetic name of Japan), 'Asahi' (Rising Sun), 'Yamazakura' (Wild Cherry Tree) based in Mabalacat, and 'Yamato' (the name of the region of Kyoto), based in Cebu. Concerted Japanese suicide attacks in the Philippines began on 25 October 1944 during the US invasion of the Philippines, when kamikazes sank the escort carrier *St. Lo* (CVE–63), killing 113 crewmen, and damaged 3 large escort carriers: USS *Sangamon*

(CVE-26), *Santee* (CVE-29), and *Suwannee* (CVE-27), and three smaller escort carriers: USS *White Plains* (CVE-66), *Kalinin Bay* (CVE-68), and the *Kitkun Bay* (CVE-71).

Seki led the first kamikaze mission on 25 October 1944 and was credited with damaging the USS *Santee.* Five days later, kamikazes crashed into and badly damaged the carriers *Franklin* (CVE-13) and *Belleau Wood* (CVL-24). A kamikaze crashed through *Franklin*'s flight deck, killing fifty-six, and immediately afterwards another kamikaze bomb just missed the *Franklin* before crashing into the *Belleau Wood*, causing heavy damage and leaving ninety-two dead or missing. Between October 1944 and March 1945, kamikazes struck or damaged 130 USN and Allied combat vessels during the Philippine campaign, sinking 20. The largest ship to sink was the escort carrier *St. Lo* (CVE-63), and three destroyers were also lost. The *Franklin* had to return to the US for repairs and did not rejoin the fleet until 15 March 1945. In total 6 fleet, 2 light, and 10 escort carriers; 5 battleships; 1 USN and 2 Australian heavy cruisers, 6 light cruisers; and 25 US and 1 Australian destroyer were damaged. At least 1,400 sailors were killed.

An estimated 650 IJNAF and IJAAF aircraft were expended in sorties between 25 October 1944 and late January 1945, when the remaining Japanese air units were evacuated from the Philippines. Of 364 kamikazes that appeared over USN and Allied ships, anti-aircraft guns claimed 231 kills and deflections (including near misses), a success rate of 64 per cent. However, 115 kamikazes hit ships (32 per cent) and another 56 crashed close enough to cause damage (hits + near misses were 47 per cent). In comparison, 1,092

USS *Franklin* (CV-13) on right and USS *Belleau Wood* (CVL-24) afire after being struck by kamikazes on 25 October 1944. (*USN*)

conventional Japanese attackers were also fired upon, of which 156 (14 per cent) were shot down and only 23 scored hits on ships (1.3 per cent). While these suicide attacks did not prevent Japan's defeat in the Philippines, they considerably surpassed the results achieved with conventional air tactics alone and ensured the increased use of kamikazes in the Okinawa campaign.

Kamikaze Attacks on Iwo Jima

In the lead-up to Operation Detachment, the invasion of Iwo Jima, Task Force 58 raided airfields in the Japanese Home Islands. Between 16–17 February 1945, 11 fleet and 5 light aircraft carriers flew 2,761 sorties that claimed the destruction of 500 enemy aircraft on the ground and in the air. The Japanese managed only one kamikaze raid on American forces supporting the subsequent Iwo Jima landings. On 21 February 1945, 50 kamikazes from the 601st Air Group struck 6 ships, sinking the escort carrier *Bismarck Sea* (CVE-95), killing 318 sailors; and badly damaging fleet carrier *Saratoga* (CV-3), leaving 123 dead. They also inflicted minor damage on the escort carrier *Lunga Point* (CVE-94) and three smaller vessels.

On 21 February 1945, while supporting the US invasion of Iwo Jima, the seventeen-year veteran carrier USS *Saratoga* (CV-3) was struck by 3 kamikazes and also by 5 aerial bombs, suffering 123 men dead and 192 wounded. Thirty-six of its seventy aircraft were destroyed, causing a return to the US where the ship was converted into a training carrier. (*USN*)

Kamikaze Attacks on Okinawa

The zenith of the kamikaze attacks would occur during the ten large-scale attacks launched against US Navy vessels surrounding Okinawa. These attacks, called kikusui by V Adm. Matome Ugaki, C-in-C, Fifth Air Fleet, translated to 'chrysanthemums floating on water'. The chrysanthemum is probably the most revered of all flowers by the Japanese as they are woven into wreaths for weddings and funerals and decorated graves or were dropped by mourning Japanese pilots on to the waters into which their fellow pilots had plummeted to their deaths. Although Ugaki's air capability on Kyushu had been badly weakened by Halsey's carrier strikes during mid-October 1944, and then even more so by Spruance's sweeps of 18–19 March 1945, he nonetheless had more than 3,000 aircraft, conventional and suicide, available when the Americans landed on Okinawa.

V. Adm. Matome Ugaki, C-in-C, Fifth Air Fleet. (*NARA*)

The kamikaze reaction at Okinawa began slowly, with a few attacks beginning in late March. On 31 March a kamikaze hit Adm. Spruance's flagship, the heavy cruiser *Indianapolis* (CA-35), killing nine crewmembers and forcing the ship from combat to return to the US for repairs. After her repair, the *Indianapolis* would secretly transport the two A-bombs to Guam and then on her way to Okinawa on 15 July 1945 was sunk with 1,195 crewmen going down with the ship and 588 of the nearly 900 men set adrift after the sinking vanishing, many falling prey to shark attacks. The first and largest kikusui raid occurred on 6–7 April 1945, consisting of 230 IJNAF and 125 IJAAF kamikazes and 340 conventional attack aircraft and their escorts. They hit thirty-three ships, sinking a destroyer and three smaller ships, and damaging the fleet carrier *Hancock* (CV-19), (sixty-two killed and seventy-one wounded) badly enough to require repair in the US, the light carrier *San Jacinto* (CVL-30) (no casualties), the battleship *Maryland* (BB-46) (ten killed, thirty-seven injured, and six missing); eleven destroyers, and three destroyer escorts. Nine more kikusui raids followed, none as large as the first. Three more occurred in April (12–13, 15–16, 27–28); four in May (3–4, 10–11, 24–25, 27–28), and two in June (3–7, 21–22).

Chapter Four

Ohka Combat Operations

Philippines Ohka Operations: Late 1944

Ohkas on the Carrier *Shinano*

After the successful American landing on the southern Philippine island of Leyte on 18 October 1944, during which General Douglas MacArthur famously waded ashore, proclaiming: 'I have returned', the Japanese reacted by activating Operation Sho. Their plan for Sho included 4 carriers, with a total strength of just over 100 planes, and a fleet of battleships, cruisers, and destroyers that were to converge on Leyte Gulf. However, the Battle of Leyte Gulf became a catastrophe for the Japanese Navy as Operation Sho not only failed to inflict serious losses on the US Navy fleet, but resulted in significant Japanese Navy losses, totalling 3 battleships, 1 large carrier, 3 light carriers, 6 heavy cruisers, 4 light cruisers, and 11 destroyers and approximately 300 land and seaborne aircraft. The IJN was never able to fight a major naval battle after this.

Despite their huge naval losses, the Japanese were determined to hold Leyte, and began sending reinforcements to the island while continuing aerial attacks against Allied shipping in Leyte Gulf. On 26 November, as part of their scheme to supply reinforcements, the Japanese Combined Fleet ordered a special and emergency cargo of the navy's new Ohka rocket-propelled kamikazes to be shipped to Manila by the new aircraft carrier *Shinano* without delay.

Originally constructed as a 68,000-ton, 840ft-long battleship, *Shinano* was converted into the world's largest aircraft carrier at double the tonnage of the USN Essex-class carriers. Although the *Shinano* was not scheduled to be commissioned until the beginning of 1945, her construction was accelerated following the Battle of the Philippine Sea, 19–20 June 1944, during which the Japanese lost two fleet carriers and one light carrier, which precluded the IJN's ability to conduct large-scale carrier actions.

The *Shinano* was to have been equipped as an attack carrier with a large air group on board, but its intended mission was revised during conversion with the bulk of its capacity provided for replacement aircraft for fleet carriers and forward land bases. Later it was to act as a floating airbase that could be used for repairing, transferring, and maintaining the enormous armada of kamikaze aircraft that would be assembled in the Home Islands and launched in last-ditch suicide attacks against the invading American forces.

After spending two weeks fitting out and performing sea trials, *Shinano* was formally commissioned on 19 November 1944 at Yokosuka. On 28 November, *Shinano* was ordered to embark despite Capt. Toshio Abe's request to postpone the cruise for a few days to complete more work and further train its largely inexperienced crew. Working in three shifts, crews had completed the packing and loading of six Shinyo suicide boats and the

Shinano. (*USN*)

first fifty Ohka Type 11 aircraft and their accompanying Ohka personnel from its Yokosuka base, which was under threat of Allied air attack. *Shinano* did not have its air crew assigned yet as they were to arrive and qualify in December or later. Abe's orders were to cruise to Kure, Hiroshima, where the carrier would complete its fitting out, and then continue first to the Philippines and Okinawa to deliver the kamikaze craft. However, there was a last-minute change: after requesting air support on the way to Kure, Abe's request was rejected, and he chose instead to make a night-time run to Kure and then depart for the Philippines and Okinawa to deliver the kamikaze craft. At 2048 on the 29th the USN submarine *Archerfish*, commanded by Cdr Joseph Enright, detected *Shinano* and her escorts on her radar. Finally, at 0315 on the 29th, *Archerfish* fired six torpedoes, four hitting their huge target, which finally capsized and sank stern-first at 1057. Among those lost were 1,435 officers, crew, and civilians including Abe, who chose to go down with the ship (1,080 survivors were rescued). *Shimano*'s sinking marked the first Ohka losses of the war.

Ohka Losses on the Carriers *Unryu* and *Ryuho*

Unryu

The impending autumn 1944 invasion of the Philippines had caused the Japanese to consider using their remaining carriers as aircraft ferries but after the escort carrier *Shinyo* and super carrier *Shinano* were sunk by American submarines in Japanese waters that November, the scheme was abandoned. However, on 13 December 1944, MacArthur's fleets had been sighted off Luzon and the long-awaited invasion was apparently imminent. This action caused the IJN to reconsider the use of carriers as aircraft ferries and thirty Ohkas were transferred to Kure to be loaded and transported to Clark Field, Luzon, via Takao, Taiwan by Capt. Konishi Kaname's newly commissioned (6 August 1944) fleet carrier *Unryu*.

On 13 December 1944 the *Unryu* had thirty Ohkas of the Jinrai Butai crated and loaded aboard and secured in the lower hangar deck for transport to Manila, escorted by the three destroyers. Four days later, *Unryu* departed Kure escorted by three destroyers on

Unryu. (*USN*)

its maiden sea voyage. On 19 December 1944, at 1635, Cdr Louis McGregor's submarine, USS *Redfish* (SS-395), fired four bow torpedoes at *Unryu*. The first torpedo stopped the carrier, but a second torpedo struck the starboard side containing the highly volatile forward aviation fuel tanks. The ensuing explosion caused the warheads of the Ohkas stored on the lower hangar deck to detonate and to essentially blow off the carrier's bow. After only twenty-two minutes the carrier sank with very heavy casualties, including Capt. Konishi. A total of 1,238 officers and crew were lost and only 145 rescued.

Ryuho

The *Ryuho* was launched on 16 November 1933 as the submarine depot ship *Taigei* and until 1940 performed normal operations to support submarine operations off the coast of China from her home port of Kure. *Taigei* served as an aircraft ferry before being ordered back to Kure for conversion into the light aircraft carrier *Ryuho* on 4 December 1941. The

Ryuho. (*USN*)

conversion was completed on 30 November 1942 and *Ryuho* served as an aircraft ferry and survived the Battle of the Philippine Sea but with nearly all its aircraft shot down. On 31 December 1944 *Ryuho* accompanied convoy HI-87, consisting of ten empty oil tankers and nine destroyers. *Ryuho* had a load of fifty-eight Ohkas and their personnel aboard on the first part of its route via Formosa to Hong Kong and Singapore. On 7 January 1945, while approaching Kirun Formosa, the convoy was attacked by a USN submarine wolf pack. The *Ryuho* and a destroyer escort were detached to Kirun and after arriving safely there, the Ohkas were unloaded for their further operational deployment from Formosa during the Okinawa campaign. *Ryuho* returned to Japan with the distinction of being the last carrier to operate outside of Japanese home waters. *Ryuho* was attacked by Task Force 58 aircraft on 19 March at Kure, suffering severe bomb and rocket damage, and was considered to be a total loss, sitting abandoned until being scrapped in 1946.

Ohkas Are Readied for the Okinawa Invasion

On 20 January 1945, the 721st Naval Squadron comprised of twenty-four Ohkas supported by Zero fighters carrying 500lb bombs arrived at Kanoya Airbase on Kyushu, at the south end of Japan's southern-most island. The 721st was activated that same day and the transfer of all equipment and personnel was completed on the 25th. The town of Kanoya is located in a very flat valley surrounded by a wall of mountains bordering the coast. The landscape is quite bare, an ideal site for a naval airbase. Plans to use the Ohka during the Iwo Jima campaign in February 1945 were frustrated by pre-emptive US air attacks against their Konoike base that destroyed all twenty-four modified Betty bombers intended to carry Ohkas to Iwo Jima. It would not be until 8 March 1945 that existence of the Ohka was discovered when an XXI Bomber Command B-29 reconnaissance aircraft overflew Kanoya and photographed the strange-looking aircraft that American Intelligence first code-named 'Viper'.

On 8 March 1945 the existence of the Ohka was discovered when an AAF B-29 reconnaissance aircraft overflew Kanoya. AAF Intelligence first code-named them 'Viper'. (*AAF*)

Prelude to the First Ohka Attack

During the first few weeks of spring 1945, the Thunder Gods Corps was assigned to the newly reorganised Fifth Air Fleet, which was charged with the defence of southern Japan including Okinawa. The fleet's commander was V Adm. Matome Ugaki, a surviving member of Admiral Yamamoto's old staff and previous commander of Battleship Division One, formerly consisting of the super-battleships *Yamato* and *Musashi*. The Thunder Gods were merged with the T-Attack Corps, which was made up of kamikaze pilots flying conventional fighters and fighter-bombers. Besides the conventional aviation, which still accounted for the majority of combat sorties, a total of 162 Ohkas, 108 T-attack fighters, and several dozen medium bombers were available for the first wave of special attacks against any American forces that attempted to approach Okinawa.

In late February 1945 an American task force moved towards Iwo Jima, far to the east of Okinawa, and in conjunction with massive B-29 raids on Tokyo, stormed and took the island in a protracted and bloody fight. By 1 March American aircraft began raiding Okinawa, striking airfields and depots as part of a systematic destruction of the infrastructure.

The First Ohka Mission Disrupted

On 17 March, American aircraft carriers were spotted moving north toward the Japanese mainland and Imperial High Command began mobilising the Fifth Air Fleet for the final battle. V Adm. Matome Ugaki, commander of the Fifth Naval Air Fleet, ordered the execution of 'First Tactics', which entailed a radar scout patrol that night, a torpedo attack on the US Navy fleet at dawn, and an Ohka attack during the day.

The next day, Okamura ordered K708's eighteen Bettys and Ohkas based at the Usa Naval Airbase, on north-eastern Kyushu, to prepare the first Ohka mission scheduled for 1213. Ground crews and those aircrew not scheduled for the mission removed the Bettys out of their revetments and the Ohkas from their tunnels across the runway to the waiting Bettys. Suddenly, at 1000, before the mission could take off, the airfield was attacked by carrier fighters of VF-9 off the USS *Yorktown* (CV-10) and VF-10 off the USS *Intrepid* (CV-11). The Bettys, exposed on the runway and several still in shelters, met flaming destruction but incredibly none of the Ohkas was hit. However, an air raid shelter suffered a direct hit that killed several Ohka pilots.

Not only did the American pre-emptive attack upset the first Ohka attack schedule but many of the fighters held in reserve to fly cover for it were obliged to defend their own airfields. Consequently, more than half of the escorts originally assigned to protect Nonaka's Ohka mission were destroyed. Meanwhile, US bombers also attacked Tomitaka Airbase, were the fighters intended to protect the Ohkas were based. When the bombing finally ended, approximately half of the fighters had been destroyed. Fifth Naval Air Fleet headquarters was unable to fully assess the damage as communications between the bases had been destroyed. Fleet Chief of Staff Toshiyuki Yokoi suggested that Ugaki suspend the Ohka missions to conserve the few forces remaining. However, Ugaki was adamant that the Ohka mission proceed before the remaining Bettys and Ohkas were destroyed on the ground.

For the next two days Ugaki's Fifth Air Fleet attempted to get the situation under control and launch the mission. Ugaki's decision was reinforced by unjustifiably positive intelligence assessments, which included the preposterous assertion that American carriers seemed to have no air cover because Japanese medium and light bomber kamikaze missions of the previous days were thought to have caused massive damage to them and their aircraft. However, the carriers and their aircraft were intact and were cruising south to support the imminent Okinawa landings.

First Ohka Attack: 21 March 1945

At 0830, two long-range Nakajima C6N Myrt reconnaissance aircraft belatedly detected and tracked Task Group 58.1, which had been located 360 miles (580km) south-south-east of Kanoya, 80 miles (130km) further and a more daunting distance than had been anticipated and certain to have robust covering CAP. Task Group 58.1, commanded by R Adm. Joseph 'Jocko' Clark, offered a choice target comprised of fleet carriers *Hornet* (CV-12), *Bennington* (CV-20) and *Wasp* (CV-18) and the light carriers *Belleau Wood* (CVL-24), returning from Philippines kamikaze damage repairs in the US, and USS *Langley* (CVL-27) and their formidable air contingent. The carriers were escorted by the battleships USS *Indiana* (BB-58) and USS *Massachusetts* (BB-59) and a large cruiser and destroyer force. The Myrt's recon reports had to be decoded before transmission, meaning the Betty/Ohka force would leave without this vital information.

Pre-Flight Preparation

Cdr Goro Nonaka, K711 Betty Squadron commander, selected the best Betty and Ohka pilots in his squadron for this auspicious first mission, dividing the eighteen into six groups of three, with fifteen Bettys to carry the Ohkas, leaving three as conventional bombers. These eager volunteers were imbued with the so-called 'kamikaze spirit', based on the ancient warrior/religious precepts of Shintoism, which became the state cult and promoted with growing zeal the military build-up to the Second World War. This warrior/religious implication explains the kamikaze pseudo-ritual feature that going into the final battle took on. The kamikaze volunteers were admired as national heroes and demigods. A pilot whose death caused damage to an enemy aircraft carrier rose in rank posthumously, and his family received a substantial pension.

The night before the mission, the doomed Ohka pilots took their fingernail and hair clippings and placed them in unpainted wooden funeral boxes for delivery to their parents. Some wrote farewell poems and letters to their loved ones and carried prayers from their families. They also composed and read a death poem, a tradition stemming from the samurai, who did so before committing seppuku (ritual suicide by disembowelment).

The next day, readying for the farewell ceremony, they dressed in new uniforms and strapped a sword in a brocade sheath to their waists, before burning their old clothes. Many kamikaze a rmy pilots took their swords along on their mission, while, commonly, the n avy pilots did not. Kamikaze ritual included wearing a white scarf around their necks and under the helmet and hachimaki (headbands) that had been personally inscribed with the words 'Thunder Gods' by Adm. Soemu Toyoda, Commander-in-Chief of the Combined Fleet. The hachimaki was commonly made of white and sometimes red cloth, generally featuring inspirational slogans at the front, and worn as a symbol of effort or courage by the wearer. Another ritual was wearing the One Thousand Person Stitch Sash known as Senninbari Haramaki. This waist sash was made by a woman from the pilot's family or a community group like the Women's Patriotic Association or the National Defence Women's Association, who would stand in a busy location like the entrance to a train station and ask a thousand women passing by to add one stitch each on the belt as a good luck talisman. When 1,000 stitches had been collected, the belt was believed by some to have special power to protect the bearer from the hazards of battle. Five sense coins (a sen is a fifth of the yen) were sewn in their belts. This ritual was based on the term 'death' that is called Shi-sens, literally 'close to death'. A final ritual was the consumption of a holy potion to ensure the mission's success and guide the pilot to his destiny.

The hachimaki was commonly made of red or white cloth, generally featuring inspirational slogans at the front, and worn as a symbol of effort or courage. (*Author's collection*)

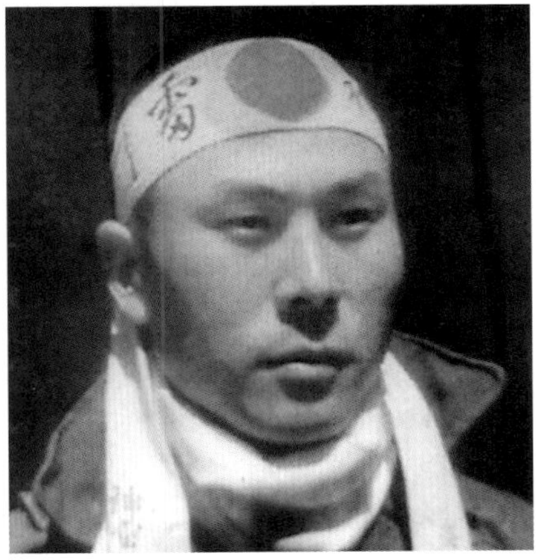

The Betty and Ohka pilots selected for the mission then gathered in front of the headquarters building, to a drum roll waiting for V Adm. Ugaki to appear for this auspicious moment in kamikaze history. After Ugaki took his place in front of the formation, Capt. Motoharu Okamura, the purported kamikaze originator, gave an impassioned, tearful pep talk. To conclude the solemn ceremony, Ugaki, Okamura, and the other officers and non-selected pilots who stayed behind took part in an old Samurai farewell ceremony, partaking of cups of sake or water, known as 'mizu no sakazuki', literally 'glass of water', with the Ohka pilots and Betty crewmen about to leave.

The assemblage then proceeded to the airfield by flatbed trucks festooned with large banners with the sayings '*HI-RI-HO-KEN-TEN*' and '*NAMU-HACHIMAN-DAI-BOSATSU*' emblazoned on them. The first saying was a favourite motto of the famous early thirteenth-century Samurai General Kusunoki Masashige, who had attempted to support Emperor Go Daigo's bid to regain power from the ruling Shogun but committed suicide when he failed. Kusunoki became kind of a patron saint to the kamikaze, who saw themselves as his spiritual heirs in sacrificing their lives for the Emperor. *HI-RI-*

One Thousand Person Stitch Sash known as Senninbari Haramaki being made by a woman from the pilot's family or a community group. (*Author's collection*)

HO-KEN-TEN was an acronym for 'Irrationality can never match reason – Reason can never match law – Law can never match power – Power can never match Heaven'. The inscription on the second banner was a popular Buddhist prayer.

The first Ohka mission seemed doomed even before take-off. While an Ohka was being moved to the Betty, its rocket motor unaccountably ignited, which could have been disastrous if it had happened while attached to the Betty. Since there was no time to replace the spent motor, another Ohka was attached to the waiting Betty. When the group reached the airfield, the escorting fighters had been moved to the taxiways and the ground crews began warming up the Bettys loaded with their Ohkas. Then tragedy struck again as the Ohka pilots were boarding their aircraft. One walked into a whirling Betty propeller, which grotesquely dismembered the victim. Squadron Leader Nonaka made a last passionate address to the departing pilots, then saluted Okamura, and signalled the men to break ranks and man their aircraft. Nonaka's superiors had ordered him to stand down for the mission but after joining the fleet commanders in the traditional farewell ceremony he brusquely joined his men and manned a Betty mothership.

The Attack

At 0945 on 21 March, V Adm. Ugaki gave the order for the 203rd Naval Air Group to launch the first Ohka Floating Chrysanthemum attack, even though the Ohkas would be unsupported by any other conventional kamikaze sorties that day. The Bettys lumbered

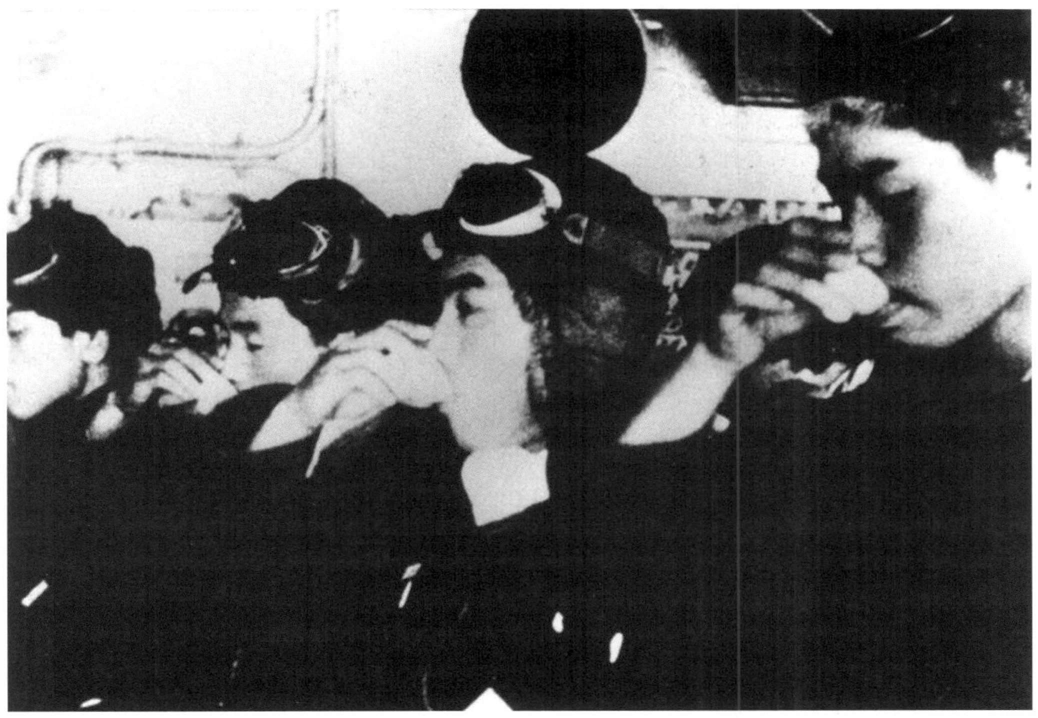

Similar to an old Samurai farewell ceremony, officers and pilots who stayed behind drank cups of sake or water with the Ohka pilots and Betty crewmen about to leave. (*Author's collection*)

Ohka pilots receive their hachimaki head bands. (*Author's collection*)

The Betty and Ohka pilots leave for the airfield by flatbed trucks festooned with large banners with the inspirational saying '*HI-RI-HO-KEN-TEN*' and Buddhist prayers. (*Author's collection*)

Ohka and Betty crews waiting for take-off at Kanoya Airfield, just prior to the departure of Lt Cdr Nonaka's Ohka-carrying Betty bombers on 21 March 1945. Virtually all these bombers were shot down by defending navy fighters. (*Author's collection*)

down the runway with their heavy Ohkas suspended from their bomb bays and were soon followed by the two squadrons of fighter escorts. A third squadron of twenty-three fighters took off from nearby Kasanohara Airbase and joined them, and all headed south-east. Thus, seven months after the Ohka programme was first proposed, the chosen Thunder Gods were heading for their first and last sortie.

At 1120, the 1st and the 2nd flights of the K711 Betty squadron led by Lt Cdr Nonaka Goro with eighteen Bettys, fifteen carrying Ohkas and three others with conventional bombloads took off from Kanoya to attack TG 58.1. However, the mission's misfortunes continued as the eighth Betty to leave briefly lost control on take-off and veered into the crowd of cheering onlookers, badly injuring two, but it continued flying.

Even before take-off, the eighteen Betty/Ohka formation was jeopardised as the recommended mission protocol of four escorts per each Betty/Ohka combination should have meant there was a total of seventy-two escorts. But on take-off the close escort support was reduced to fifty-five, to be partly provided by thirty-two Kanoya-based A6M5 Zeros from the 721st NAG fighter unit led by Lt Urushiyama Mutsuo. Top cover was to be provided by twenty-three Kasanohara-based Zeros of the 203rd NAG led by Lt Cdr Okajima Kiyokuma. However, twelve of the 203rd NAG fighters could not be ready in time and did not escort the mission. During take-off one escort crashed and another immediately returned with engine problems, leaving forty-one of the fifty-five escorts on hand. On assembly two close cover Zeros encountered problems with their drop tanks and returned to base. Added to these problems, both the escort aircraft and their pilots were suffering battle fatigue from long months of combat.

Several Fifth Naval Air Fleet staff suggested that Ugaki abandon the mission and recall Nonaka's Bettys with their Ohkas. But Ugaki refused, claiming that the Ohka pilots were consigned to dying and recalling them would be a disappointment to them! More of a disappointment was that without the latest 1100 morning reconnaissance report, the oncoming Japanese formation had no idea of TG 58.1's accurate position. When the Japanese arrived at the previously reported position, they found an empty ocean below. Since the lead Betty's on-board radar only scanned to 70 miles (113km), the Betty formation began to circle, waiting for its commander to continue. Nonaka's bombers then flew south and approached the USN Task Force at 13,000ft (3,962m), flying in a V of Vs formation with their close escort staggered at 14,000ft (4,762m) and their top cover at 16,000ft (4,877m).

The attack was not coordinated with any others and was revealed on the cruiser *Vincennes* (CA-44) radar as a single large raid at over 100 miles (161km) out. *Vincennes'* FDO notified the Task Group 58.1 fighter director, who immediately vectored airborne CAP to intercept the incoming bogies, launched back-up TG 58.1 fighters, and requested the other three task groups to launch fighters in support. Soon there were 150 Corsairs and Hellcats vectored out to intercept the Japanese and provide CAP.

At 1350 *Hornet* radar observers detected the Betty formation that had closed to 70 miles (113km) and the carrier retreated from the incoming threat and ordered its sixteen combat air patrol F6F Hellcats to intercept but leaving eight to defend over the carrier.

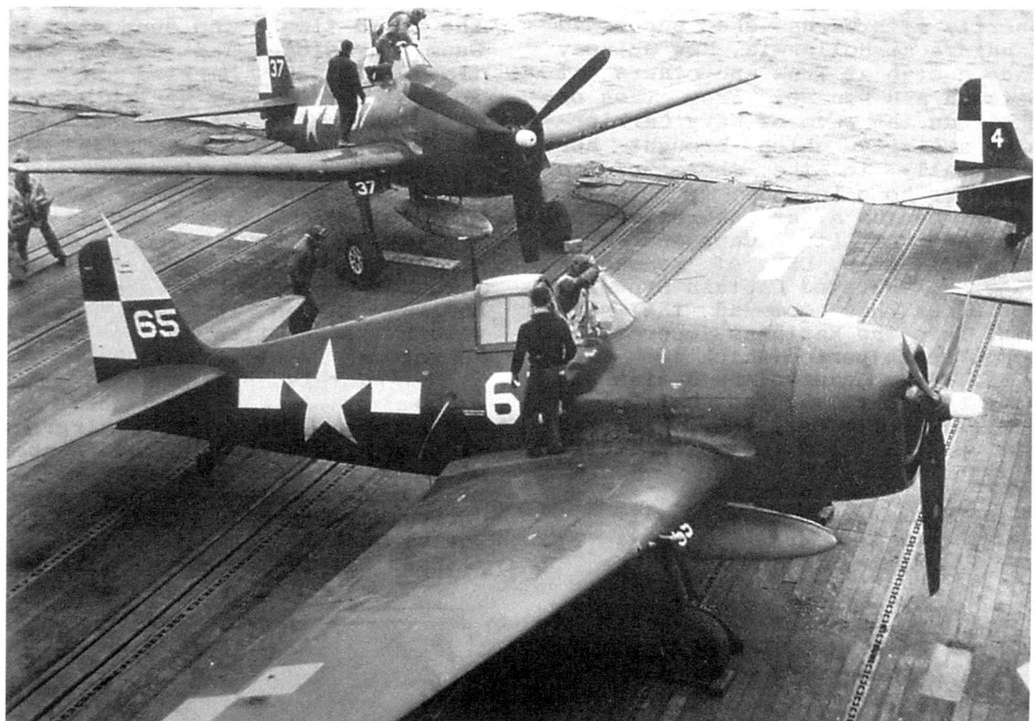

US Navy Grumman F6F Hellcats of VF-17 on the flight deck of the Essex-class fleet aircraft carrier USS *Hornet* (CV-12). (*USN*)

Lt James Pearce was in command of four VF-17 *Jolly Rogers* Hellcats while Lt (jg) Henry Mitchell led four VBF-17 *Gladiators* F4U Corsairs. At 1414, flying at a height advantage at 18,000ft (5,486m), they approached the Japanese at a distance of 10 miles (16km), flying directly towards them. Pearce split his force and closed to 3 miles (4.8km) and recognised they were confronting eighteen bombers and at least thirty Zeros. The Japanese bombers were flying unusually slowly in a V of Vs formation and, even so, would be over the Navy Task Force in about twenty minutes. At 1418, Pearce quickly decided to attack.

Betty commander Nonaka realised that the arrival of the Hellcats meant he would have to launch his Ohkas soon but needed more time to close the distance to their targets. He depended on his Zero escorts and the Betty's gunners to defend long enough to accurately launch the Ohkas. However, the Japanese plan immediately failed as, unable to match the US Navy fighters in number or firepower, the eleven remaining Japanese top cover escorts quickly dispersed. Left unprotected, the mother Bettys jettisoned their unmanned Ohkas, dispersed, and began their life and death evasion from the eight Hellcats. The Navy fighters dived in succession firing their six .50 calibre wing machine guns at their slow-moving easy targets that were desperately attempting to escape northward, diving to sea level and ineffectively dropping radar-deflecting chaff. Within ten minutes, the only Bettys surviving were Nonaka's and three others, which were last seen diving together to escape at wave-top altitude, but were never seen again.

Although some Bettys carrying their Ohkas did close to within 30 miles of the carriers, not one Ohka was launched at them. The close escort 721st NAG formation was chased down and destroyed by TG 58.1 CAP, losing ten Zeros, including one flown by commander Matsuo. The top cover 203rd NAG was relatively unscathed, losing two Zeros, which force-landed after receiving combat damage. The loss of all 15 Ohkas and 3 bomb-carrying Bettys and their 137 crewmen that day became known as the 'Betty Turkey Shoot'. Most of the Bettys shot down had already abandoned their unmanned Ohkas and so the Navy found that the best defence against the new Cherry Blossom threat was the destruction of their motherships before they got to their launching point.

The US Navy scoreboard for the day included:

> VBF-17 (*Hornet*): Lt (jg) Henry Mitchell was credited with destroying five Bettys, making him an ace in a day, and was awarded the Navy Cross; only to be KIA two weeks later. Lt (jg) Carl van Stone shot down two Bettys and a Zeke for VBF-17 that day.
>
> VF-17 (*Hornet*): Lt (jg) Murray Winfield was credited with 4½ Bettys (with one shared with a F4U pilot), while squadron mates Lt (jg) George Johnson downed three Bettys; Lt James Pearce downed two Bettys; and Lt (jg). Jack Crawford was credited with a single Betty.

Following the 21 March air battle, US Navy fighter gun camera footage and pilot debriefings revealed the existence of the Ohka as a new weapon, but its true nature remained unknown until a secret cache of Ohkas was discovered in the caves near Kadena Airfield after the 1 April invasion of Okinawa.

The 21 March Disaster Causes a Change in Ohka Tactics

Even before the shocking Ohka losses during the 21 March mission, the vulnerability of the Ohka/Betty composite when confronted by enemy fighters was well known. Imperial Japanese Navy commanders had been warned that the Ohka concept was only feasible if unopposed by enemy interceptors or accompanied by heavy fighter escort. To remedy the situation, the IJN changed tactics so that a Ohka/Betty composite was flown singly or in small groups to avoid detection and intercept by USN air patrols. Meanwhile, new Ohka versions, the Model 21 and Model 22, were in progress.

Second Ohka Attack: 1 April 1945

The Ohka's first attack off Okinawa that day took place when six Ohka-carrying G4M2es of the 1st and the 2nd flights of K708 took off in three-minute intervals from Kanoya at 0220 for a dawn attack against TF 54 battleships discovered off Okinawa's main island. The Betty/Ohkas were to be unescorted, and each would take a different route to the targets, hoping to avoid detection and the mass decimation of the first Ohka attack.

Immediately after take-off, one Betty/Ohka aborted due to engine problems. At about 0245, the lead Betty bomber, piloted by Lt (jg) Yoshio Sawamoto with Ohka pilot FPO

Keisuke Yamamura waiting on the 'Devil's Gate', was intercepted at 12,000ft (3,658m) and damaged by an American night fighter. After dropping its unmanned Ohka, it ditched off the Kyushu coast with two crew succumbing to injuries. The two pilots and three of the Betty crew were rescued the following morning. From that point on, the mission further deteriorated when a Betty crashed into a mountain in the darkness en route to Okinawa, while another lost its way in bad weather and jettisoned its unmanned Ohka and returned to base. Another bomber floundered on making an emergency landing on Formosa (Taiwan) but then crashed during the return flight to base. As a final indignation, two more bombers, one from each flight, disappeared without a trace. Some sources state that an Ohka was thought to be successful in partially damaging a gun turret on the USS *West Virginia* (BB-48) off Okinawa during a mass kamikaze attack. However, from the combat report the hit was inflicted by a dropped bomb.

1 April 1945: Capture of Ohkas on Okinawa

On 1 April 1945, the first day of the invasion of Okinawa, 'L-Day', the 6th Marine Division captured several abandoned intact Ohkas that they called Bakas on Okinawa's Yonton and Kadena Airfields. The aircraft were concealed in bunkers or covered with camouflage netting. An American Air Technical Intelligence Unit (ATIU) examined the Ohka 11s. One was shipped to the United States for further evaluation and study in Philadelphia by a US Navy Air Material Unit. After their examinations were completed, the Ohka became part of a mobile exhibit of captured enemy weapons.

SECT.

I-13

I-10

Third Ohka Attack: 12 April 1945

Ohka Attack on the *Mannert L. Abele* (DD-733)

The *Mannert L. Abele* was a Sumner-class destroyer launched on 23 April 1944; and commissioned on 4 July 1944. The ship was named in honour of Mannert L. Abele, the CO of the USN submarine USS *Grunion* lost during July 1942.

Under her captain, Lt Cdr Alton Parker, the *Mannert L. Abele* undertook a shakedown cruise off Bermuda, and then served as a training ship for destroyer crews in Chesapeake Bay before departing Norfolk, Virginia, on 16 October for duty in the Pacific. It arrived at Pearl Harbor on 17 November for two weeks of rigorous training and then left for the western Pacific on convoy duty on 3 December. It returned to Pearl Harbor two weeks later for transformation to a fighter director ship, receiving special radio and radar equipment. After finishing radar picket training, the *Abele* left on 27 January 1945 to participate in the Iwo Jima invasion during early March 1945 where it contributed to the bombardment of the island. It then sailed for radar picket duty off Ulithi Atoll, the large navy staging base in the Caroline Islands in the western Pacific.

On 21 March the *Abele* departed the Atoll with TF 54, Gunfire and Covering Force, for the invasion of Okinawa where the destroyer screened heavy shore bombardment ships during pre-invasion operations from Kerama Ketto to Ie Shima. On 1 April, *Abele* provided close fire support for the invasion beaches before beginning radar picket patrols north-east of Okinawa later that day. On 3 April three Japanese planes attacked, but the destroyer shot down two with intensive accurate gunfire. Released from picket duty on 5 April, *Abele* resumed screening patrols off the beaches and on the next day joined TF 54 to protect the transports off Okinawa from the threat of the super battleship *Yamato*, proceeding south from Japan to destroy the US Fleet off Okinawa. When the *Yamato* was sunk, *Abele* resumed radar picket duty on 8 April, patrolling station No. 14 about 80 miles (129km) north-west of Okinawa, accompanied by Landing Ships Medium (Rocket), LSM(R)-189 and LSM(R)-190. For its defence the *Abele* was armed with 6 × 5in (130mm)/38-calibre guns (3 × 2), 12 × 40mm AA guns, and 11 × 20mm AA guns.

On 12 April, the same day as President Roosevelt passed away, midway through the afternoon watch at 1345, three Aichi D3A Val dive bombers initially attacked picket Station 14, but the picket's gunfire drove off two and set fire to the third, which then failed in its attempt to crash into LSM(R)-189. By 1400, nine conventional Bettys and ten to twelve Zero kamikazes and escorts swarmed around the pickets. Except for one Betty, which attacked but was damaged by the destroyer's fire, the other enemy aircraft remained outside gun range. At about 1440, three Zeroes left orbit and closed to attack. *Abele* AA drove off one and destroyed another at about 4,000 yards (3,658m). Despite numerous hits from 5in bursts and light anti-aircraft fire, the third kamikaze flew through spewing smoke and flame and crashed into the starboard side, penetrating the after-engine room, where it exploded. Immediately, *Abele* began to lose headway. The downward force of the blast wiped out the after-engineering spaces and broke the destroyer's keel abaft the No. 2 stack. The bridge lost control and all guns and directors lost power. One minute later, the *Abele* suffered a second and fatal hit from an Ohka that exploded at the starboard waterline beside the forward fireroom. The attack was described by Capt. James Stewart, observed from nearby LSM(R)-189:

> It is difficult to say what it was that hit the DD 733. This officer personally saw what appeared to be two (2) planes orbiting in a northerly direction from the DD 733, and then suddenly, what appeared to be, one plane, accelerated at a terrific rate, too fast for us to fire at. This plane dove at an angle of approximately 30 degrees, starting at about four miles (7.5km) away. Since we had no air search radar, the above statements are merely my own conclusions.

Later, Japanese records would later confirm that Lt Saburo Dohi, launched by Ens. Kitaro Miura's Betty attached to the third flight, were credited with the Ohka's first success, With its midship section shattered, the *Abele* immediately broke in two; her bow and stern

Mannert L. Abele (DD-733). (*USN*)

sections sinking quickly. *Abele*'s survivors were then bombed and strafed by Japanese fighters until the LSM(R)-189 and LSM(R)-190 arrived and shot down two of the attackers, repelled further attacks, and rescued the survivors. The casualty totals of the *Mannert L. Abele*'s crew complement of 358 (26 officers and 332 enlisted men) was:

Killed in Action: One officer and five enlisted men
Died of Wounds: Five enlisted men
Wounded in Action: Three officers and 35 enlisted men
Missing in Action: Two officers and 71 enlisted men
Survivors: 20 officers and 216 enlisted men

Lt Cdr Alton Parker, *Abele* captain, as a midshipman. (*USN*)

During December 2022 veteran ocean explorer/CEO of Tiburon Subsea Tim Taylor and his Lost 52 Project team discovered the wreck of the USS *Mannert L. Abele* about 75 miles (121km) off the northern coast in 4,500ft (1,380m) of water. Lost 52 Project is an exploration and underwater archaeological project that concentrates on 'documenting and preserving the story of the US Navy's 52 lost WWII Submarines' and has found twelve.

Roy Anderson, a survivor of the sinking, wrote a detailed history, *Three Minutes off Okinawa: The Sinking of the Radar Picket Destroyer the U.S.S. Mannert L. Abele by Japanese Kamikaze Aircraft*, published in 2007 by Jana Press.

Ohka Attack on the USS *Jeffers* (DMS-27)

USS *Jeffers* (DD-621) was commissioned on 5 November 1942 as a Gleaves-class destroyer. It was reclassified and converted to a highspeed minesweeper (DMS-27) on 15 November 1944. On 12 April, at 1435, north-west of Okinawa, *Jeffers* under Cdr Hugh Murray was

USS *Jeffers* (DMS-27). (*USN*)

attacked by a Betty (misidentified as a Ki-49 Helen in USN reports) that released its Ohka at close range off Radar Picket Station No. 12. As the Ohka was closing from 14,000 yards (12,800m) and at 4,000ft (1,220m) altitude, *Jeffers'* AA gunners shot it down at only 50 yards (46m) from the ship, but the explosion of its warhead caused extensive damage forcing the *Jeffers* to withdraw. It aided *Abele's* survivors before retreating into Kerama Retto, called 'Busted Ship Bay', to repair its battle damage later that afternoon. This island group, 20 miles (32km) south-west of Okinawa, would prove to be an important temporary repair haven for Allied ships damaged by kamikazes. On 16 April the repaired *Jeffers* joined a carrier group operating off Okinawa in support of ground forces. *Jeffers* would continue on a long career, being decommissioned on 23 May 1955 and reclassified back to a destroyer, DD-621, on 15 June 1955. *Jeffers* was finally struck from the navy register on 1 July 1971 and sold for scrap on 1 May 1973.

Ohka Attack on the USS *Stanly* (DD-478)

The Fletcher-class destroyer USS *Stanly* (DD-478) was named for R. Adm. Fabius Stanly, a forty-three-year career navy officer (1831–1874). She was laid down on 15 September 1941, launched on 2 May 1942, and commissioned on 15 October 1942. *Stanly* spent her early career in the Pacific escorting convoys and screening battleships and aircraft carriers in the Solomons-Bismarcks area until late February 1944. As the Pacific War moved from the South Pacific to the Central Pacific in early 1944, so did the need for destroyers and *Stanly* joined the sea battles around Palau, Kwajalein to Eniwetok, the assault on the Marianas, and the Philippines. After a patrol off Iwo Jima from mid-February to mid-March 1945, on 25 March 1945 Lt Cdr Richard Harlan took command of the *Stanly* and sailed to support the Okinawa invasion. Previously, Harlan was in command of the USS *Caldwell* (DD-605) from 7 to 30 January 1945.

For the first eleven days of April 1945, *Stanly* moved from station to station around Okinawa on radar picket duty. On the 12th, while stationed at Radar Picket Station No. 2, *Stanly* was ordered to Radar Picket Station No. 1 to assist the picket destroyer *Cassin Young* (DD-793) that had just been hit by a kamikaze. Upon arrival, the *Stanly* was attacked by several Aichi D3A Val IJN dive bombers, but USN combat air patrol fighters arrived and quickly shot down six. At 1449, while manoeuvring radically at 30 knots (34.5mph/55.5kmph), an unidentified bogie outran the CAP, dived on *Stanly's* starboard beam and was fired on by the 40mm Bofors and automatic weapons as it closed rapidly on a collision course. The aircraft, although hit by automatic fire, crashed into the starboard bow about 5ft above the water line, with parts of it passing through the ship and continuing through the port side, but not detonating. There was a large explosion in the water off the port bow as the warhead exploded, thereafter passing through the ship. The *Stanly's* post-combat report described the aircraft as a '"Baka" being approximately 20ft long, had a 15ft wingspan and no engine or propeller was observed'. The remains of a pilot were later found in a compartment with the wreckage.

At 1458, *Stanly* continued high-speed manoeuvres when another bogie suddenly appeared unseen low on the starboard beam. It closed so rapidly that it was fired on

USS *Stanly* (DD-478). (*USN*)

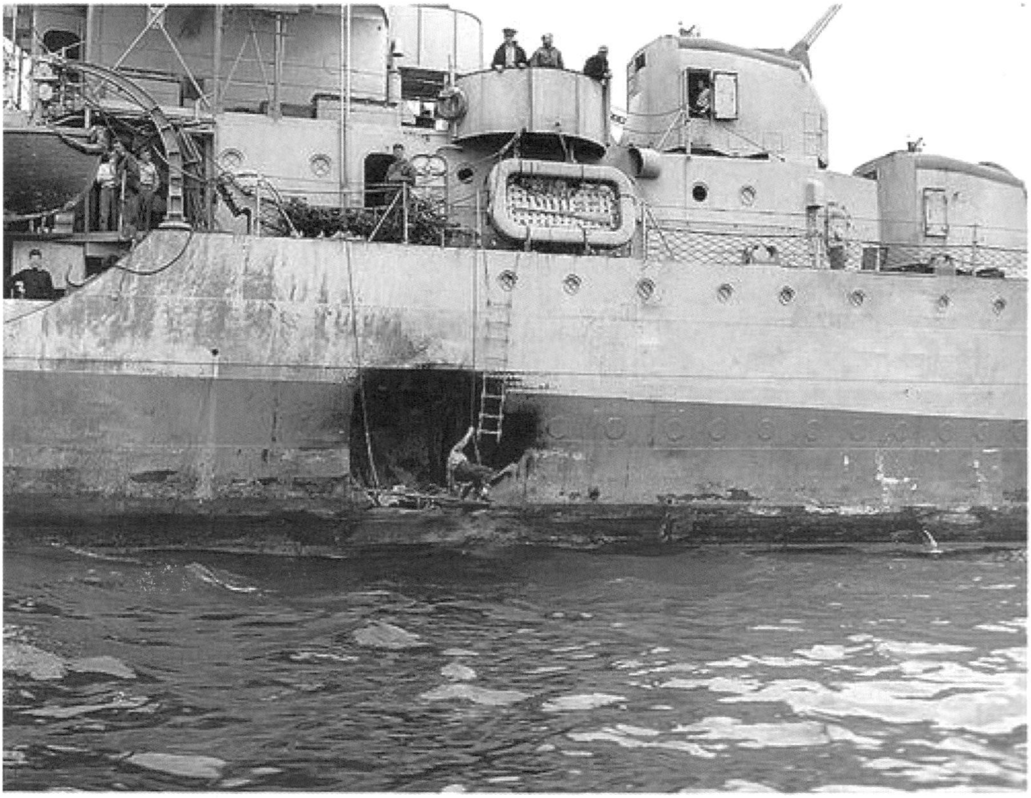

An aircraft described as an 'Baka' in the *Stanly*'s after-action report hit 5ft above the starboard bow water line. *Stanly* was without its earlier dazzle camouflage. (*USN*)

only by automatic weapons. Many hits were observed, and a small wing section was shot away as it passed over just aft of #2 stack; it 'snatched the ensign from its gaff in passing'. It took continued fire as it passed over to port and then attempted to bank but hit the water 2,000 to 3,000 yards (6,000–9,000ft/600–900m) off the port bow, bouncing once, hitting the water again, and then disintegrating. The combat report confirmed the bogie was another Baka: 'This was another engineless, propellerless plane similar to the one that crashed into the ship. The speed of both planes was estimated to be in excess of 500 knots and only "swishing" was heard.'

As the *Stanly* continued manoeuvring, it endured its third near-fatal encounter of the day when a Zero tried to bomb and then crash into it during a single pass. *Stanly*'s luck continued as the bomb fell short and the Zero overshot. During these various attacks the CAP, controlled by *Stanly*'s fighter directors, shot down seven enemy attackers. Amazingly, the day's combat resulted in only three crew injuries, and captain Lt Cdr Richard Harlan headed for Kerama Retto for repairs.

Harlan later commented:

> Ship handling while under attack by Japanese suicide 'buzz bombs' affords the conning officer an occupation but, due to the comparative speeds involved, fails to produce the desired result, i.e. a complete miss or a near miss by the attacking plane. Only major structural damage to the plane will stop or deflect it from its course. Once it is inside the range of automatic weapons it is almost too late. From there on pilot error is the only escape. It is recommended that the Combat Air Patrol while attacking these planes concentrate on killing the pilot rather than setting the plane on fire.

After ten days at Kerama, the picket returned to Okinawa for an anticlimactic period of radar picket duty. *Stanly* departed with an Ulithi-bound convoy on 5 May and underwent further repairs, then taking part in gunnery exercises. During these drills, the barrel of its No. 5 gun exploded, killing two coxswains. Ironically, *Stanly*'s only mortal casualties of the war occurred during training.

Stanly was decommissioned in October 1946 and remained in the Pacific Reserve Fleet until 1 December 1970, when its name was struck from the Navy list and it was sold for scrap in February 1972.

14 April 1945: The Fourth Ohka Attack

Between 1130 and 1153, seven Ohka-carrying G4M2es Bettys, led by Lt Hikoshi Sawayanagi of the K708, took-off from Kanoya to attack a task force sighted 85 miles east of Tokunoshima Island. At about 1300 Lt (jg) Charles Watts of VF-17 (USS *Hornet*) was escorting a photo recon aircraft west of Kikaigashima in his F6F-5 Hellcat when he identified an unescorted Betty bomber carrying an Ohka at 11,000ft (3,353m). Watts dived and opened fire, hitting the bomber's starboard engine and causing the Betty to jettison its Ohka while attempting to escape. On Watts' third attack, his .50s collapsed the Betty's starboard wing and it spiralled into the sea. Shortly after, a second VF-17 pilot shot down another Betty/Ohka composite. All seven Bettys and their Ohkas were lost.

At 1410, the USS *Hudson* (DD-475), patrolling at Radar Picket Station No. 3, identified incoming bogeys 20 miles to the north-west. A division of F6F-5 Hellcats, led by Ens. James Noel from VC-30 (USS *Belleau Wood*), was also patrolling over Picket Station No. 3, and was vectored to intercept them. The Hellcats sighted two incoming Bettys carrying Ohkas at 8,000ft (2,438m) and another at 4,000ft (1,219m), escorted by a single Zero at 19,000ft (5,791m). Ensign H.A. Lee attacked the Zero, hitting its engine multiple times and causing the pilot to bail out. Noel then damaged the starboard wing and engine of one of the higher-flying Bettys, which spiralled towards the sea, taking its Ohka with it. Ens. K.W. Curry attacked a second Betty, hitting its wing root and fuselage. Before going down it jettisoned its Ohka, which hit the water without attempting to fire its rockets to escape. Ens. R.L. Rhodes, flying at 4,000ft (1,219m), intercepted the third Ohka-carrying Betty, hitting it in both engines before it plunged into the sea.

16 April 1945: The Fifth Ohka Attack

Between 0605 and 0708, six Ohka-carrying Betty bombers from K708 (the 1st and the 2nd flights) took off from Kanoya to attack shipping off Okinawa. Lt (jg) Masao Sawai, leading the 1st flight, reported a successful launch of his Ohka, after which a pillar of smoke was sighted rising from the target area. Only two Bettys returned, one of them still carrying its Ohka. The known fates of two Bettys and their Ohkas were included in navy CAP after action reports described below:

Near Radar Picket Station No. 1, 8 miles (12.9km) north-west of Iheya Shima Island, two F6F-5 Hellcats (USS *San Jacinto* CVL-30) and two F4U Corsairs intercepted an Ohka-carrying Betty that was approaching the already severely damaged destroyer USS *Laffey* (DD-724). The Betty released its Ohka, but its rocket failed to ignite and it spiralled into the water. Meanwhile, its Betty carrier was attacked by Lt (jg) L. Grossman from VF-45 (USS *San Jacinto*), who scored multiple hits to finally destroy it.

Another Ohka-carrying bomber, misidentified as a Ki-49 Helen, was intercepted over Radar Picket Station No. 14, north-west of Okinawa by two VMF-323 Death Rattler F4U Corsairs from Kadena, Okinawa. Flying at 8,000ft (2,438m), the Betty took violent evasive action and jettisoned its Ohka but was chased and then downed by 2Lt Dewey Durnford. As Durnford began firing on the enemy aircraft it released a smaller aircraft, causing him to radio 'It's carrying a papoose!'

28 April 1945: The Sixth Ohka Attack

After 1625, four Ohka-carrying Bettys from K708 took-off from Kanoya for a dusk attack against Allied shipping off Okinawa. Only one Betty/Ohka composite reached the target area, and its Ohka was hastily launched in the dark at 1935, with AA fire then hitting the Ohka, exploding its warhead. The Betty ditched at sea off the west coast of Kyushu because of combat damage. Another returning Betty was intercepted off Amakusa Island by the US fighters and ditched still carrying its Ohka. The two other Betty mothers returned to base, with one still carrying its Ohka.

4 May 1945: The Seventh Ohka Attack

Ohka Attack on the Destroyer-Minelayer *Shea* (DM-30)

The USS *Shea* was launched on 20 May 1944 as DD-750, a Sumner-class destroyer, but was modified to be a destroyer-minelayer, redesignated DM-30 in late 1944 and commissioned on 30 September 1944. On 19 March 1945, it sailed from Ulithi with TG 52.3 and arrived off Okinawa on 24 March to join the preparations for the 1 April invasion. Although its mission was to protect and assist the minesweepers clearing the area of mines, it was also to serve picket duty around Okinawa. From 24 March to 4 May, *Shea* constantly protected against Japanese air attacks and secured the area against enemy submarines; reportedly sinking or severely damaging at least one. On 16 April, during a ten-minute engagement, *Shea* downed six enemy attackers.

At 0522, on 4 May, seven Ohka-carrying Betty bombers from K708 and K711 took-off from Kanoya as part of a large mixed Japanese conventional and kamikaze formation to attack Allied shipping off Okinawa. Meanwhile, just after 0600 on 4 May, *Shea* arrived at station for picket duty 20 miles north-east of Zampa Misaki, Okinawa. Along the way, it encountered two patrolling Japanese aircraft, firing on both and possibly downing one. *Shea*'s captain, Cdr Charles Kirkpatrick, called general quarters upon receiving the report of the approach of large Japanese formations and began full-speed manoeuvring. Soon a considerable onshore smoke haze covered *Shea*, reducing visibility to 5,000 yards (4,572m) maximum. At 0854 a lone Betty was sighted at 6 miles and, four minutes later, one was shot down by *Shea*-directed overhead CAP. Five minutes later a lookout spotted an Ohka on *Shea*'s starboard beam, closing rapidly at more than 500mph (800kmph). Almost instantaneously, the Ohka crashed into *Shea* and caused a 4 × 5ft hole in the starboard side of the bridge structure. The craft entered the sonar room, traversed the chart house, just missing two men in the sound hut adjoining the chart room, went through a passageway on the port side of the chart room, deflected off a fire director shaft, smashed through a door and exploded on the ocean's surface just beyond *Shea*'s port side. F4U pilot, Maj. Edwin Roberts, squadron commander of VMF-221 off the *Bunker Hill* (CV-17), who was flying patrol over *Shea*, described the incident as a 'minor miracle' in his after-action report:

> I was too high to catch him [Ohka], so all I could do was watch and it looked like a certain hit. Into the side of the ship he went and I waited for the explosion, but none came. A second later he emerged from the other side of the ship minus his wings. The ship continued on course, a hole straight through her! It was a miracle, but it happened.

(Note: Roberts would survive the devastating kamikaze crash on the carrier *Bunker Hill* a week later on 11 May.)

Fire broke out on the mess deck, and in the CIC, the chart house, division commander's stateroom, No. 2 upper handling room, and compartment A-304-L. *Shea* lost all ship's communications, 5in gun mounts Nos. 1 and 2 were inoperative and mount No. 3 was

USS *Shea* (DM-30). (*USN*)

operative only in local control. The forward six port 20mm guns were damaged, the two twin 40mm Bofors were only operable in local control, and two quad 40mm only operable in automatic. The main gun director was inoperable, and the gyro and computer were rendered unserviceable. One officer and thirty-four men were killed by concussion, shrapnel, flash, or shock; and eleven officers and eighty crewmen suffered wounds of varying degrees. *Shea*'s damage control parties quickly controlled the flooding that caused a 5-degree list to port and successfully fought fires, while survivors aided the wounded. The engineering section got the engines ready for full power and finally *Shea* struggled toward Hagushi Bay, Yontan, for medical assistance.

Cdr Charles Kirkpatrick, *Shea*'s captain. (*USN*)

It arrived at 1052 and transferred the most seriously wounded and the thirty-five dead to the USS *Cresent City* (APA-21) for transport to Okinawa. *Shea* then turned towards Kerama Retto anchorage for repairs, where most of its ammunition and gear, particularly radar and fighter-direction equipment, was transferred to DesRon 2 for distribution to less severely damaged ships. After a memorial service on 11 May, *Shea* was under way on 15 May to join convoy OKU 4 heading for Ulithi Atoll for more repairs and from there eventually arrived at the Philadelphia Navy Yard and underwent extensive repairs to prepare it for sea duty. From 1946 to late 1953 *Shea* was engaged in operations with the Atlantic Fleet and then spent the remainder of its active service in the Pacific, based at Long Beach, California. In September 1973 it was decommissioned and sold for scrap in September 1974.

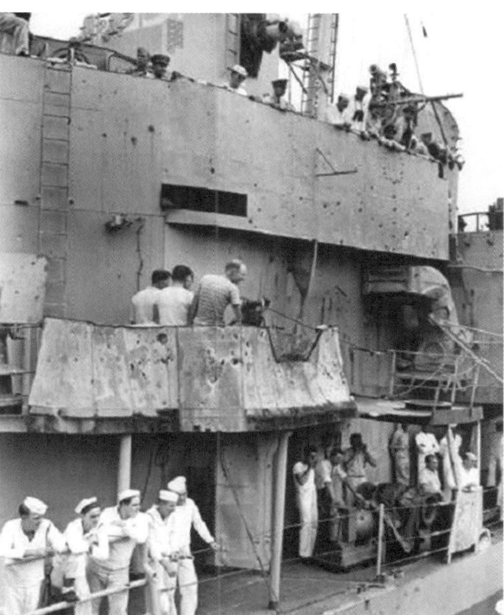

After suffering thirty-four killed and ninety-one wounded, *Shea* arrived at Kerama Retto anchorage for repairs. (*USN*)

Ohka Attack on the Minelayer *Henry A. Wiley* (DM-12)

The *Henry A. Wiley* was launched on 21 April 1944 as the destroyer DD-749 but was reclassified as the Smith-class minelayer DM-29 on 20 July 1944 and commissioned on 31 August 1944. The minelayer was named after forty-year navy veteran Adm. Henry A. Wiley (1888–1929). After screening battleships and cruisers for the three-day preliminary bombardment for the Iwo Jima invasion and then providing fire support, *Henry A. Wiley* (DM-12) arrived at Okinawa on 23 March, D-Day minus eight, to begin screening minesweepers as they cleared channels for invasion transports and support ships. On 28 March, *Wiley* downed two kamikazes, and the next morning during a frantic, fifteen-minute attack, had a bomb explode only 50 yards astern, downed two more kamikazes, and rescued a fighter pilot. While screening transports on 1 April, D-Day at Okinawa, *Henry A. Wiley* destroyed its fifth kamikaze.

There was no respite after the *Wiley* was assigned picket duty, as during the next thirty-four days it fired on sixty-four attacking enemy aircraft, destroying several. During the night of 4 May, while patrolling at Radar Picket Station No. 12, *Wiley*'s battle experience off Okinawa reached a crescendo as it underwent its first attacks at 0215 and forced three attackers to turn away. Soon another three attackers closed to within 10,000 yards (9,144m) and *Wiley*'s AA fire turned two away and shot down the third, a Betty, in flames at 0307. Meanwhile, the destroyer *Luce* (DD-522) had suffered a damaging near miss before taking a direct hit from astern, exploded and sunk in 3 minutes, losing 126 of her 312-man crew. The *Wiley* headed for the stricken *Luce* at 25 knots and during the rescue effort it was engaged by five enemy attackers, forcing away two Jills. While fighting off an attacking Betty, lookouts sighted an Ohka approaching from the starboard quarter. While

USS *Henry A. Wiley* (DM-12). (*USN*)

other guns continued to fire at the Betty, destroying it, the 20mm guns reallocated their continuous quarter minute of fire at the Ohka, which received several hits, struck the water, bounced over *Wiley*'s fantail, and exploded just off its port quarter only 75 yards (69m) away. Soon a second Ohka approached on the starboard beam at 4,000 yards (3,657m). The fire-control director computed, and all guns opened fire but were unable to establish its high speed. Finally, VT proximity-fused projectiles and their blast effect drove it down into the water at 1,200 yards (3,937m), where it disintegrated and the warhead ricocheted across the fantail and exploded harmlessly. *Wiley* then proceeded to rescue *Luce*'s survivors.

Cdr Paul Bjarnason, *Wiley* captain. (*USN*)

For its heroic actions off Okinawa, which 'resulted in the destruction of 15 Japanese planes', *Henry A. Wiley* received the Presidential Unit Citation, and its captain, Cdr Paul Henrik Bjarnason, the Navy Cross and Legion of Merit. From Okinawa, *Henry A. Wiley* sailed for the East China Sea on 12 June to screen minesweepers attempting to clear that vast area until the end of the war. *Wiley* was decommissioned at San Francisco on 29 January 1947, went into reserve at San Diego, was struck from the Naval Vessel Register on 15 October 1970, and sold for scrapping on 30 May 1972.

Ohka Attack on the Minesweeper USS *Gayety* (AM-239)

After arriving in time for the 1 April invasion of Okinawa, the newly commissioned (23 September 1944) Admirable-class minesweeper USS *Gayety* (AM-239), commanded by Lt Cdr Robert Harrell, swept minefields and took part in ASW patrols off the island before being assigned to picket duty. On 4 May, following a kamikaze attack on nearby USS

USS *Gayety*. (USN)

Hopkins (DD-249), another kamikaze began its suicide run on the *Gayety*'s starboard, where its automatic AA weapons peppered the attacker as passed close over the fantail before crashing into the sea only 30 yards (27.4m) off the port quarter. Later an Ohka made a low-altitude run over several smaller minesweepers, then turned towards the *Gayety*. The ship's AA gunners hit the Ohka's cowling and it disintegrated, tumbling end over end into the sea only 15 yards (14m) off *Gayety*'s port bow. The pieces of the Ohka's wreckage destroyed the port 40mm gun, wounding three, but *Gayety* continued on station. On 27 May 1945 *Gayety* suffered a near miss from a 500lb, which caused damage, killed five and wounded two.

After the war the minesweeper was decommissioned on 7 June 1946 and entered the Atlantic Reserve Fleet. *Gayety* recommissioned 11 May 1951, and until 1954 it was based on the US east coast, serving as a training ship, and was decommissioned 1 March 1954, again re-entering the Atlantic Reserve Fleet. *Gayety* was reclassified MSF-239 on 7 February 1955, was transferred to the Republic of Vietnam Navy on 17 April 1962 and renamed *Chi Lang II* (HQ_08). It escaped to the Philippines after the fall of South Vietnam, was acquired by the Philippine Navy and renamed RPS *Magat Salamat* (PS-20). It was decommissioned on 10 December 2021.

Note: The next day, 5 May, following continued heavy losses, particularly during the previous day, the veteran Ohka-carrying K711 Betty squadron was disbanded, leaving K708 to carry them from Kanoya.

11 May 1945: The Eighth Ohka Attack

Ohka Attack on the USS *Hugh W. Hadley* (DD-774)

The Sumner-class *Hugh W. Hadley* (DD-774) was launched 16 July 1944 and commissioned on 25 November 1944. *Hadley* was named after Lt Cdr Hugh Hadley, who was KIA as captain of the destroyer USS *Little*, which was sunk in 'valiant action' off Guadalcanal. Since radar-equipped destroyers were in short supply, the *Hadley*, commanded by Cdr Baron Mullaney, was allocated picket duty during the afternoon of 10 May. *Hadley* joined the destroyer USS *Evans* (DD-552) and four smaller landing ships at Picket Station No. 15 west of Okinawa.

During the early morning of 11 May, *Hugh W. Hadley*'s fighter controller vectored sixteen VF-85 F6F Hellcats off the newly arrived, newly commissioned *Essex*-class carrier *Shangri-La* (CV-38). *Hadley* also had control of two VMF-323 'Death Rattler' Marines F4U Corsairs flying from airfields on Okinawa, who were record kamikaze killers over Okinawa. By this time CAP tactics over the radar picket stations had become more regimented, with navy aircraft from the Fast Carrier Task Force (TF 58) vectored to intercept incoming Japanese raids between 25 and 50 nautical miles out, while the Marines Corsairs would remain close to the pickets to intercept any enemy aircraft escaping the outer naval perimeter.

At approximately 0730, *Hadley* and *Evans* radar scopes began indicating a massive fleet of an estimated 160 enemy aircraft approaching from the north in 5 main groups. The navy CAP was vectored to intercept with other TF 58 fighters to join the largest air-to-air action of the Okinawa campaign. By 0800, an estimated 40 to 50 Japanese aircraft had been shot down by navy fighters, but about 100 continued their approach.

Without their CAP, *Hadley* and *Evans* were continuously attacked by numerous enemy aircraft coming in groups of four to six on each picket. *Evans* was about 3 miles to the north, fighting off attackers until 0900 when it was hit by four kamikazes and put out of action. From 0830 to 0900 *Hadley* was attacked by groups of aircraft coming in on both bows; many on kamikaze attack runs with some crashing in near misses. To this point, *Hadley* was not seriously damaged, but was urgently calling for its CAP to return for support.

Cdr Mullaney reported on this heroic air defence later:

> For 20 minutes, the *Hadley* had fought off the enemy singlehanded, being separated from the *Evans*, which was out of action, by three miles and the four small support ships by two miles. Finally, at 0920, ten aircraft which had surrounded the *Hadley*, four on the starboard bow under fire by the main battery and machine guns, four on the port bow under fire by the forward machine guns, and two astern under fire by the aft machine guns, attacked the ship simultaneously. All ten planes were destroyed in a remarkable fight and each plane was definitely accounted for …

Astonishingly, all ten enemy attackers were indeed destroyed but during the battle *Hadley* suffered four hits. The first bomb exploded topside aft, causing deaths and casualties. A 'fast-moving plane identified as a Baka' hit the starboard side at the waterline at the after fireroom aft number two stack and plunged through the ship, resulting in 'extremely severe flexural vibrations running through the ship'. It continued into the deck below, with an enormous explosion resulting in an intense fire with exploding ammunition. The three after engineering spaces flooded to the waterline immediately and the ship lost headway, taking on a 5-degree starboard list and starting to settle by the stern.

Cdr Mullaney described the Ohka attack:

> The ship was put out of action by a Baka Bomb. It was released from a large lumbering Betty which came in from astern during the final attack, altitude about 600ft. The bomb appeared to be about one-and-one-half times as large as a 21-inch torpedo. On each side were very short stubby wings about one-third the usual normal wing length of a plane. There was no engine. The bomb struck the ship on the starboard side at frame number 105, which is the bulkhead between the after engine room and forward fireroom. The explosion from this bomb was terrific and some decks were lifted about 20in causing ankles and knees to be broken or strained. Three large engineering spaces were immediately flooded and the ship settled in the water rapidly.

A fourth kamikaze of an 'unconfirmed' type passed through the rigging, tearing away wires and antenna, and then crashing close aboard to port (classified as not a hit but a near miss). By this time the destroyer was 'badly holed' with both engine rooms and one fireroom flooding as the ship listed rapidly to 7 degrees. Fires were becoming uncontrollable, ammunition was exploding, and the entire ship was engulfed in thick black smoke. With the ship unable to defend itself, fortunately, the CAP arrived just in time to shoot down and drive off circling Japanese aircraft.

The *Hadley* was in an extremely vulnerable state, dead in the water with a fire raging amidships setting off munitions, listing to starboard with the fantail awash, and with the risk looming that the Torpex explosive in the torpedoes might explode. At this point, Commander Mullaney gave a 'prepare to abandon ship order' and to hoist all available colours, exclaiming, 'If this ship is going down, she's going with all flags flying.' Mullaney ordered most of the crew and the wounded over the side into life rafts, while fifty officers and men remained on board to make a last attempt to save the ship. Torpedoes, depth charges, and unexploded ammunition were jettisoned overboard while available topside weight was also jettisoned from the starboard side to try to correct the list. The forward boilers were secured so that they would not explode. These men performed a heroic and incredible mission to save their ship 'with utter disregard for their personal safety'. The fires were extinguished, and the list and flooding were controlled until the fast transport USS *Barber* (APD-57), auxiliary fleet tug ATR-114, and destroyer USS *Wadsworth* (DD-516) arrived to assist and to fend off any renewed Japanese threats, with the LCS 82 and LCS(L) 84 aiding the heavily damaged *Evans*. About noon, after the situation became settled on the *Hadley*, LSM(R) 193 and LCS(L) 83 began towing the wounded destroyer to the nearest relative safe temporary anchorage at Ie Shima, a small island north-west of Okinawa.

Cdr Mullaney later described the valiant mission to save his ship:

> The ship was badly holed and immediately both engine rooms and one fireroom were flooded and the ship settled down and listed rapidly. All five inch guns were out of action, a fire was raging aft of number two stack, ammunition was exploding, and the entire ship was engulfed in a thick black smoke which forced the crew to seek safety, some by jumping over the side, others by crowding forward and awaiting orders. The ship was helpless to defend herself and at this time the situation appeared hopeless. The Commanding Officer received reports from the Chief Engineer and the Damage Control Officer which indicated that the main spaces were flooded ... The engineers were securing the forward boilers to prevent them from blowing up ... The order to 'prepare to abandon Ship' was given and life rafts and floats were put over the side. A party of about 50 men and officers were being organised to make a last fight to save the ship and the remainder of the crew and the wounded were put over into the water.

Credited with shooting down twenty-three Japanese aircraft during the 11 May epic duel on the picket line, the USS *Hadley* established a US Navy record for enemy aircraft destroyed in a single engagement. Its guns fired 801 rounds of 5in ammunition, 8,950 rounds of 40mm, 5,990 rounds of 20mm, and 801 charges of smokeless gunpowder. Incredibly, the *Hadley* had survived but twenty-eight crew were killed in action, two more later died of their injuries, and sixty-eight were wounded. Including the enemy aircraft that struck it, the *Evans* was credited with nineteen aircraft plus four more shared with the *Hadley*. Together, the two heroic destroyers accounted for a record forty-two enemy

USS *Hugh W. Hadley* (DD-774). (*USN*)

aircraft and both ships were awarded the Presidential Unit Citation for this action. Their captains, Commander Baron Mullaney and Commander Robert Archer, were each awarded a Navy Cross. The *Hadley* gunnery officer, Lt Patrick McGann, was also awarded a Navy Cross. The *Hadley* crew received 7 Silver Stars and 8 Bronze Stars and more than 100 Purple Hearts were awarded.

After the battle, Cdr Mullaney paid tribute to the extraordinary effort of his crew:

Cdr Byron Mullaney, *Hadley* captain. (*USN*)

> No Captain of a man of war ever had a crew who fought more valiantly against such overwhelming odds. Who can measure the degree of courage of men, who stand up to their guns in the face of diving planes that destroy them? Who can measure the loyalty of a crew who risked death to save the ship from sinking when all seemed lost? I desire to record that the history of our Navy was enhanced on 11 May 1945. I am proud to record that I know no record of a Destroyer's crew fighting for one hour and thirty-five minutes against overwhelming enemy aircraft attacks and destroying twenty-three planes. My crew accomplished their mission and displayed outstanding fighting abilities. I am recommending awards for the few men who displayed outstanding bravery above the deeds of their shipmates in separate correspondence. Destroyer men are good men, and my officers and crew were good destroyer men.

After temporary repairs, the destroyer was towed to Kerama Retto on 14 May, where the crew of the repair ship *Zaniah* (AK-120) repaired the damaged hull. On 15 July 1945 *Hadley* was transported in a floating drydock to Buckner Bay, Okinawa, towed by fleet tug *Avoyel* (ATF-150). After twenty days there, it came under tow of the USN tug *Undaunted* (ATA 199) back to the US and after encountering heavy weather the ship arrived on 26 September 1945 at Hunter's Point, California, via Pearl Harbor. However, the *Hadley* was deemed as being too damaged to be repaired and was decommissioned on 15 December 1945, sold, and scrapped in September 1947. The *Evans* was also towed across the Pacific and met the same unfortunate news that it was also too damaged to be repaired.

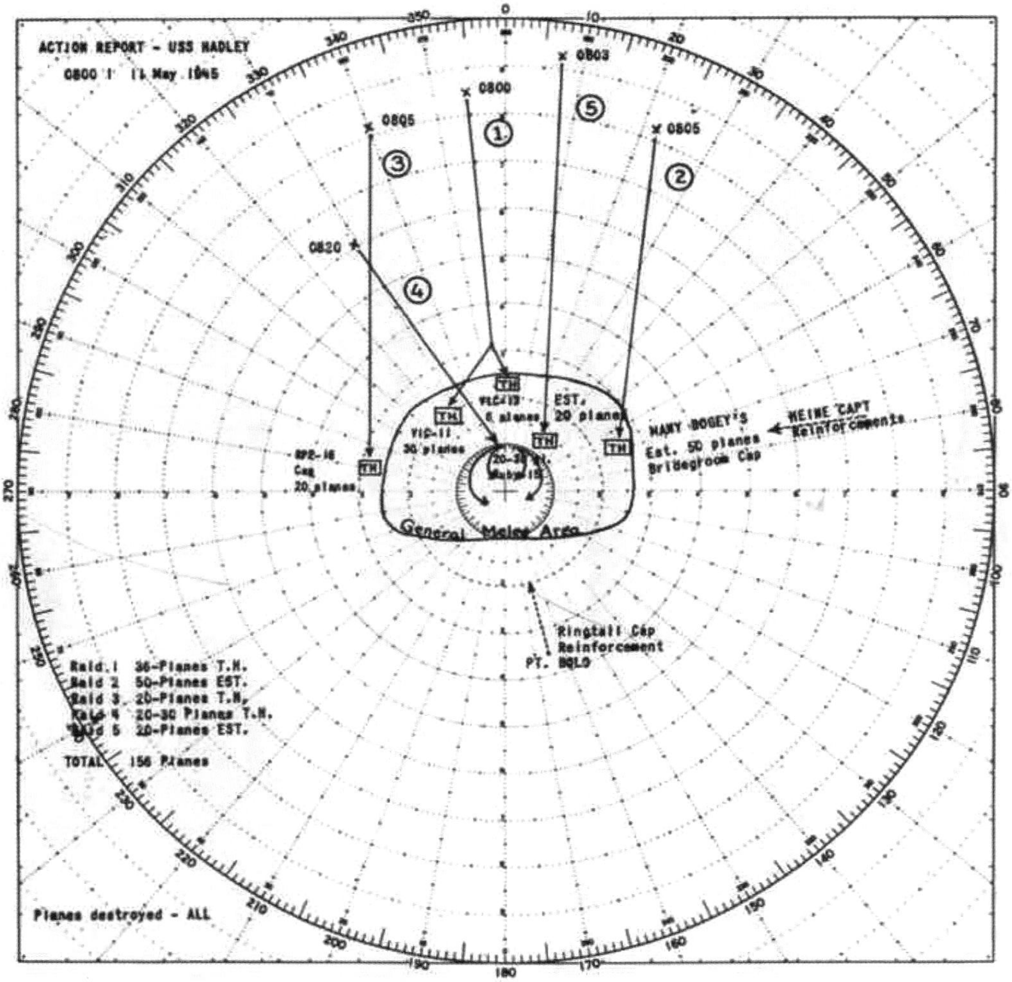

From the *Hadley*'s after-action report. *(USN)*

After suffering thirty KIA and sixty-eight WIA, the *Hadley* was towed back to the US but was beyond economical repair and was scrapped. (*USN*)

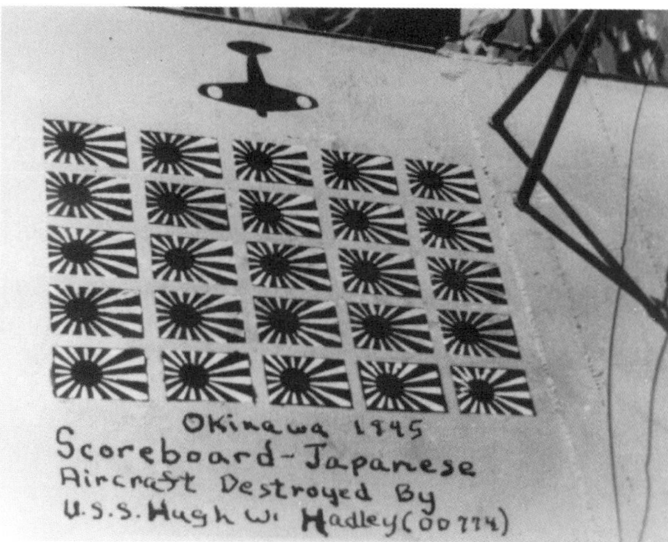

Hadley's proud scoreboard shows its US Navy record for twenty-three enemy aircraft destroyed in a single engagement. (*USN*)

25 May 1945: The Ninth Ohka Attack

Shortly after 0500, eleven Ohka-carrying Betty bombers from K708 took off from Kanoya for a dawn attack against Allied shipping off Okinawa. In a morale-boosting gesture, Adm. Soemu Toyoda was on hand to send off the mission to their fate, which was to be an early return to base after the Bettys carrying their Ohkas encountered a heavy rain squall without locating their targets. However, poor navigation training was taking its toll as three of the mothership/parasite composites disappeared without a trace. Four days later, Toyoda would replace Koshiro Oikawa as Chief of the Navy General Staff after the latter resigned, and Toyoda became the final Supreme Commander of the Imperial Japanese Navy from 29 May 1945 onward.

22 June 1945: The Tenth and Final Ohka Attack

After 0525, six Betty/Ohka bombers, led by Lt (jg) Ito Shoichi, took off from Kanoya on a mission against Allied shipping south of Okinawa. During this, the 721st NAG's final combat sortie, they were accompanied by eight bomb-carrying A6M5 Zeros from No. 1 Jinrai Unit. The six 721st NAG composites rendezvoused with sixty-six escort fighters over Kasanohara airfield, but an incredible twenty-five of these escorts soon returned with alleged 'mechanical problems!' The Japanese approached Okinawa from the north-west in a loose formation but were soon detected by USN radar picket ships and were intercepted north-west of the Okinawa main island. Near Radar Picket Station No. 15A, a VMF-224 F4U-1D Corsair piloted by 2Lt Harry Triece shot down a Betty that released its Ohka before crashing. Another Betty, carrying an Ohka,

Gen. Mitsuru Ushijima, Commander of the Japanese 32nd Army. (*NARA*)

was shot down near Radar Picket Station No. 16, by VMF-314 F4U-1D Corsairs based on Ie Shima. Four Bettys (twenty-eight crewmen) and four Ohkas were lost, while two Bettys returned without launching their missiles.

On this day Gen. Mitsuru Ushijima, commander of the Japanese 32nd Army, committed ritual suicide, effectively ending the Battle of Okinawa after an estimated 110,000 Japanese troops and conscripted Okinawan defenders were killed and the civilian population was reduced by possibly a quarter as 100,000 men, women, and children perished in the fighting or committed suicide under orders from the Japanese military.

23 August 1945: Komatsu Airfield, Honshu

After the 15 August armistice, to prevent further losses and unauthorised attacks on the Allied fleet, the 721st NAG was disbanded, its airworthy fighters were dispersed from Kanoya to various airfields and their crews were ordered to return to their homes.

Immediate post-war photo of Kanoya showing the abandonment of the airfield in the face of destruction by USN fighter-bomber attacks. (*USN*)

Japanese Air Effort Over Okinawa: A Summary

The total Japanese air effort over Okinawa was far greater than that encountered in any other Pacific operation. The proximity of airfields in Kyushu and Formosa permitted the enemy's employment of all types of aircraft and pilots. Altogether, there were 896 air raids against Okinawa, during which approximately 4,000 Japanese aircraft were destroyed in combat, 1,900 of which were kamikazes. The intensity and scale of the Japanese suicide air attacks on naval forces and shipping were the most incredible and remembered aspects of the Okinawa campaign. Between 6 April and 22 June there were 10 organised kamikaze attacks, employing a total of 1,465 planes as shown opposite:

Date of Attack	Total	IJN Planes	IJA Planes
6–7 April	355	230	125
12–13 April	185	125	60
15–16 April	165	120	45
27–28 April	115	65	50
3–4 May	125	75	50
10–11 May	150	70	80
24–25 May	165	65	100
27–28 May	110	60	50
3–7 June	50	20	30
21–22 June	45	30	15
TOTAL	1465	860	605

During the war, approximately 2,800 kamikaze attackers sank 36 navy ships, damaged 368 others, killed 4,907 sailors, and wounded 4,874 more. During the Okinawa campaign, kamikaze pilots sank 26 USN and Allied ships and damaged 225 others, killing at least 3,389 Americans. Despite radar detection, airborne interception, attrition, and massive anti-aircraft barrages, of 793 kamikazes that attacked USN and Allied ships, 181 hit (23 per cent) and 95 achieved damaging near misses (12 per cent) while 517 missed completely. Kamikazes damaged eight fleet and light carriers, four escort carriers, ten battleships, five cruisers, and sixty-three destroyers. Several were knocked out for the remainder of the war.

Chapter Five

Ohka Further Design and Development

Production of the Ohka Model 11 ceased during March 1945 with the Dai-Ichi Kaigui Gijutsu-sho having built 155, the Dai-Ichi Kaigun Kokusho 600, and for unknown reasons Nakajima equipped only one Model 11 with wings. The Model 11 was followed by the improved Model 22 designed to overcome the Model 11's short range.

Ohka Model 21

Several sources distinguish a design as the Model 21 in which Kugisho was reported to have fabricated an experimental test airframe combining the airframe of the Ohka Model 22 with the Model 11's three-rocket arrangement for use with the projected faster Yokosuka P1Y Ginga (Allied code: Frances) mothership design. It was a smaller version of the basic Model 11, with the warhead reduced to 1,320lb (600kg) and the wingspan shortened so that it could be carried by the P1Y1. However, there are no records of this test model ever being flown.

Kugisho Ohka Model 22

During April 1945, the Kugisho design department completed the Ohka Model 22 design proposal within a month of design initiation. Outwardly, the Model 22 was similar to the Model 11, being a cantilever low-wing monoplane with twin tails. The aircraft was of mixed construction; the wings and the tail were wooden, and the fuselage was monocoque, all metal, divided into three sections, similar to the Model 11 (nose, centre, and tail). The nose section contained the reduced 1,323lb (600kg) explosive charge, the centre section included the wings and cockpit, equipped with instruments like those in the Model 11, and the tail section included the empennage and three Toku-Ro.1 rockets, to be replaced later by the proposed Tsu-11 turbojet engine for carriage on the Frances mothership.

The Model 22 was to be launched by the faster and more responsive P1Y3 Frances. Because the PlY3 was smaller than the standard G4M2e Betty mothership, it was necessary to redesign the carrying apparatus and the Model 22 by reducing the wingspan 3.2ft (1.0m), while increasing the length by 2.6ft (0.8m). These changes, using the prevailing three Toku-Ro.1 rockets, improved its range up to 80 miles (129km), although 40 miles (65km) or less was considered safer for the Model 22 (not the mothership!) under most combat conditions.

Although the Ohka's three solid fuel Toku-Ro.1 rockets provided great acceleration, they had a very short burn time and thus a very short range, causing the Ohka's mother Betty bomber to have to carry it very close (40 to 80 miles) to the target. This made it vulnerable to enemy fighter CAP interception and the AA fire from ships surrounding

Kugisho Ohka Model 22 at the Kugisho factory post-war. Kugisho was able to fabricate only thirty-five complete Ohka Model 22s and fifteen airframes by the end of the war. (*USAGF*)

Distinctive view of a Model 22 with its bulbous Tsu-11 motor's exhaust nozzle extending from the rear. Note the engine intakes located just above the trolley wheel. (*USAGF*)

the larger, more enticing targets. Kugisho believed that a turbojet engine would provide high speed as well as enough range to keep the mother bomber safe long enough to release its Ohka and retreat safely from the launch area. Thus, to improve the glide range of the Model 22, Kugisho replaced the short-burn rocket thrusts with the continuous thrust of the then emerging turbojet propulsion of the Tsu-11 engine. The shortening of the fuselage, the wingspan redesign and the installation of the Tsu-11 cruising turbojet engine would result in the reduction of the nose-mounted explosive from the Ohka 11's 2,640lb (1,200kg) to the Model 22's 1,323lb (600kg), which was nevertheless considered to be adequate.

Ishikawajima Tsu-11 Hatsukaze (First Wind) Turbojet

The major change in the Ohka Model 22 was to be the installation of the Tsu-11 turbojet in place of the three Toku-Ro.1 rocket boosters. The Tsu-11 was a Campini-type (partial jet) engine to be an interim development between the solid rocket-powered Ohka Model 11 and the Ne-20 turbojet-powered Ohka Model 43. Although termed a turbojet, the Tsu-11 was an air-cooled, petrol-engine-driven fan-jet (called an 'engine-jet' by the Japanese), that was essentially a ducted fan with an afterburner.

The Tsu-11 was licence built by the First Navy Air Technical Arsenal as a version of the German Hirth HM 504, which was a common engine for light aircraft of the 1930s and 1940s and powered several Luftwaffe training aircraft during the war. It consisted of a 100hp Hitachi Hatsukaze 11 (Ha-11-11) 4-cylinder, inverted inline Toku Model 13 piston engine driving a single-stage compressor and a large nozzle that extended some distance out from the fuselage. The Model 13 designation specified its modification to drive a single-stage compressor. Fuel was injected into the compressed air, which was then ignited, producing up to 440lb (200kg) of thrust. The Ohka 22 was adapted to accommodate this engine by further lengthening the fuselage, adding jet intakes at the sides, with the single exhaust of the piston engine protruding under the fuselage. To compensate for the added weight of the new engine and fuel, the warhead also had to be reduced to 1,323lb (600kg) to extend the Ohka's range to about 80 miles. Because the Ohka 22 lacked emergency acceleration capability while under enemy fighter attack, one rocket was externally mounted under the fuselage of the redesigned airframe for that intent.

In February 1945, before the Tsu-11s were available, a Model 22 made a single test flight propelled by two Type 4-1 Model 10 auxiliary rocket engines under the fuselage. The flight was unsuccessful, as during the climb under high acceleration the pilot lost consciousness, and after the engine stopped functioning the aircraft entered a dive and crashed.

The Tsu-11 was successfully tested attached to a Yokosuka P1Y during late 1944 and Hitachi was given a production order. However, because Hitachi's initial delivery of the completed Tsu-11 turbojet engines was late, the Model 22's completion for the flight tests was delayed until July 1945.

Only approximately twenty of the experimental Tsu-11 engines are known to have been produced. A single Tsu-11 engine survives, conserved at the National Air and Space Museum in Washington, DC. During its 1997 restoration, it was mounted in the museum's

Ishikawajima Tsu-11 Hatsukaze (First Wind) turbojet. (*AFSHRC*)

Installation of the Tsu-11 with the attachment of the very large nozzle installation to follow. (*AFSHRC*)

Ohka 22. During the restoration an engineering evaluation of the engine indicated that the fuel injection and combustion most likely added little to the engine's power, with the main thrust largely being supplied by the compressor.

Ohka 22 Testing

The 722nd Air Wing at Konoike Airbase on Tokyo's east coast was assigned as the Ohka 22 Tokko Corps and was to conduct its testing. The initial Ohka 22/Frances mothership flight tests were conducted without launching the Ohka 22 but were plagued by problems. On 22 July 1945, the first test flight to evaluate the Tsu-11 engine operation at altitude failed when Ohka 22 No. 1 was accidentally dropped from the Frances mothership on the take-off run and destroyed. In the following tests using Ohka No. 2, the Tsu-11's engine oil overheated, which necessitated redesign of the oil cooler and air-cooling intake. After the redesign, problems continued during the Tsu-11's inflight ignition, which was a convoluted process needing the Toku Model 13 petrol-engine to warm up while still on the ground with fuel being fed from the mothership, which was followed by a fuel tank change and turbojet ignition in flight. The Model 22's reduced wingspan made it very difficult to fly and to land, with the pilot ready to bail out and land by parachute!

It would not be until 12 August 1945 that Kugisho was ready for the first Ohka 22 free-flight test. Chief Petty Officer Kazutoshi Nagano had been Kugisho's Ohka project test pilot since the successful MXY7 K-1 test flight. At separation from the mothership, Nagano accidentally fired the under-fuselage auxiliary boost rocket, causing the Ohka to scrape along the bottom of the Frances, severing the Ohka's tail and triggering a spin. Nagano was able to bail out but he was too low and his parachute failed to open. Nagano lost his life only three days before the war ended.

Model 22s were projected to be mass produced at a rate of 200 per month by Kugisho, with follow-on production assigned to Aichi and Murakami Hikoki with Miguro Hikoki and Fuji Hikoki as subcontractors. Aichi's inability to establish production due to frequent USAAF B-29 bomber raids led to the decision to concentrate production of the Ohka Model 22 in underground factories managed by the Dai-Ichi Kaigun Kokusho, but the war ended before these were completed. Kugisho was able to fabricate only thirty-five complete Ohka Model 22s and fifteen airframes by the end of the war. None appear to have been used operationally.

In combat, most Ohka-carrying bombers were shot down before they ever had the opportunity to launch their weapons or they launched their Ohkas prematurely before Allied interceptors arrived. Originally, it was planned that the Ohka Model 22 would be released as far as 80 miles (130km) from the target, thus significantly reducing the risk of interception and loss of the mother aircraft. It was also estimated that the Model 22's cruising speed in a glide would be 265mph (427kmph), which was inadequate when compared with the much higher speeds of Allied interceptors.

The only Ohka 22 example remaining, captured by US occupation forces after the war, has been restored and is exhibited in the Smithsonian National Air and Space Museums Udvar-Hazy centre in Chantilly, Virginia.

Ohka Model 33

Despite the Ohka's numerous operational failures, Kugisho designers continued a more concerted evolution of the Ohka series as the Ohka Model 33 (third airframe model; third engine type, i.e., turbojet). The new Ohka Model 33 was to be an enlarged Ohka Model 22, to accommodate an increased 1,764lb (800kg) warhead and the Ne-20 engine. The Model 33 was to upgrade the Ohka rocket cruise engine to Japan's first turbojet, the 1,050lb (475kg) thrust Ishikawajima Ne-20 turbojet engine, which was still at the prototype stage. The Ne-20 was being developed in parallel with Japan's first jet fighter, the Nakajima J9N1 Kikka, which bore a similar outward resemblance to the German Me 262 jet fighter but was smaller. IJN Technical Commander Eichi Iwaya developed the Ne-20 using only photographs and a single cutaway drawing of the German BMW 003 engine. It is thought only a few of these engines, possibly fifty, were fabricated before the war's end, with two used to power the Kikka on its only flight on 7 August 1945, the day after the Hiroshima A-bomb detonation, marking the Imperial Navy's technological advance into the jet age.

The Imperial Navy, dissatisfied with the progress of the Ohka 22/Tsu-11 turbojet operation and Frances carriage apparatus, then contemplated yet another mothership option operating from the four-engine, long-range attack bomber, the Nakajima G8N1 Renzan (Rita) Model 11, then still in the prototype stage. The Rita was intended to carry two, or even three Model 33s. The Ohka Model 33 conversion was also planned to be carried in watertight capsules fastened to the deck of a I-400 Class aircraft carrier submarine and to be launched from catapults. The existing Aichi M6A1 Seiran special attack aircraft operated from an I-400 and were scheduled to attack the Panama Canal locks before the war ended.

Due to Nakajima's delays in the Renzan production programme and then its cancellation, the Kaigun Koku Hombu ceased further development of the Ohka Model 33, which would mark the last MXY7/Ohka mothership/parasite air-launched series. It was decided to proceed instead to a more radical solution, the Model 43, 43A, and 43B series. The Model 33 would have been a true turbojet aircraft to follow the Kikka fighter.

Kugisho Ohka Model 43 Series

As early as 26 March 1945, immediately after the disastrous first combat mission of the original Ohka, Kugisho considered the Ne-20 turbojet engine and began an investigation of a relatively uncomplicated ship- or shore-based catapult-launch system of the proposed Models 43A and 43B.

Ohka Model 43A *Ko*

Larger in dimensions in comparison to the Ohka Model 22, the Ohka Model 43A powered by a Ne-20 turbojet engine, was designed with folding wings to be launched by a catapult from IJN submarines or alternatively via an air launch. Being inserted or removed from their watertight deck container, the wings could fold backwards and quickly return to the flying position through a hydraulic mechanism connected to the submarine. It had no landing gear as it was intended for submarine catapult launch to be used to defend the Home Islands by being launched into the air towards offshore invasion shipping. During the war Japan inventoried forty-six submarine aircraft carriers capable of transporting aircraft in on-deck watertight hangars. But with the Allies in complete control of the seas, the Ohka Model 43A was soon abandoned and work began on the Model 43B.

Ohka 43B *Otsu*

The Ohka 43B, also powered by a Ne-20 turbojet engine, was basically similar to the 43A but was designed for the defence of the Japanese homeland, where it was to have been launched against an invasion fleet from protective caves so that the launch direction could be changed freely through various cave entrances. The all-metal 43B was to be launched from a small rail car equipped with a booster rocket. Its design entailed a larger wingspan required for catapulting speeds, and folding wings to fit inside an underground bunker. The design also included the inflight release of wing tips for the final suicide dive. A removable and retractable landing skid was to be incorporated for movement between bases and possible training. Kugisho and Aichi Aircraft factories were preparing for production with the objective for deployment during September 1945. However, with Ohka 22 production behind schedule and Ne-20 endurance difficulties being encountered, the Kugisho-Aichi design only attained the mock-up evaluation stage by the end of June and required another month to complete detailed design drawings. Consequently, the Ohka 43B remained on the drawing board when the war ended in August.

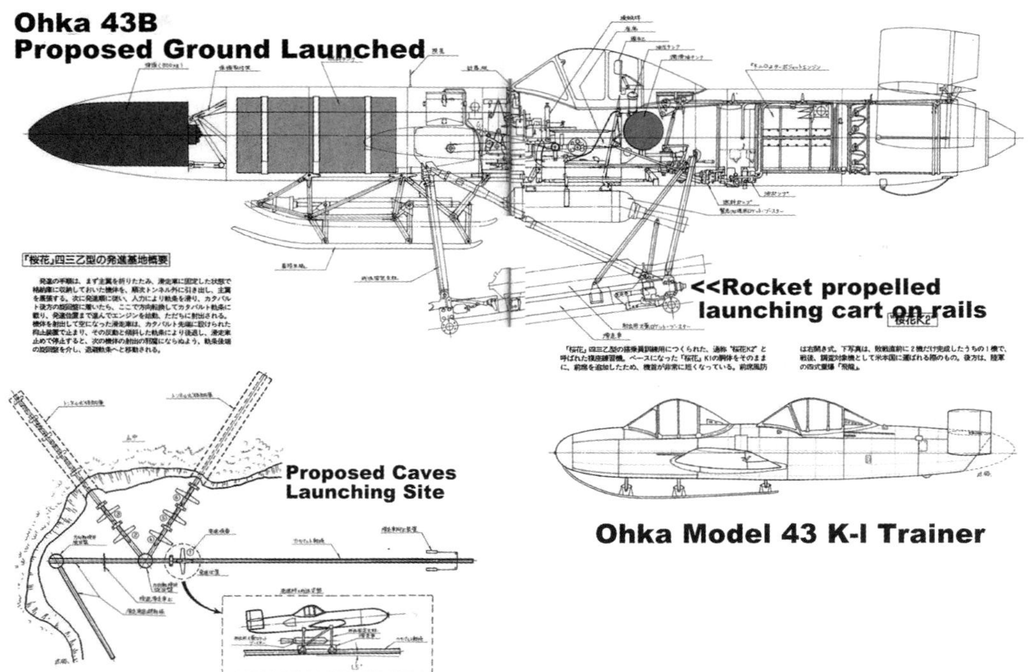

Kugisho Model 43K-2 (Young Cherry) Ohka Trainer

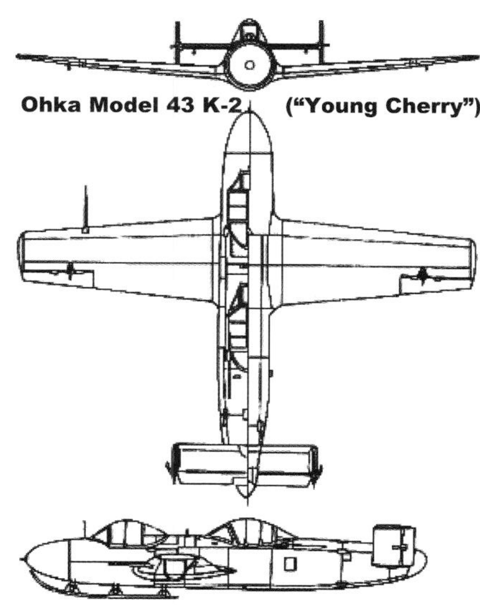

When Kugisho envisaged the Model 43B, the company realised that a catapult-based launch would be necessary to ensure a successful take-off even for the one-way mission. In parallel with the Model 43A and B, Kugisho decided to develop the Model 43K-2, a catapult-launch trainer, the MXY7 K-2 Kai Wakazakura (Young Cherry), intended to be the definitive trainer for pilots destined for operational Ohka models. The Model 43K-2 was to be developed by modifying the Ohka 11 combat version with a second cockpit to accommodate the instructor installed in the nose in place of the warhead. The K-2s was equipped with a longer, low-speed wing to launch the aircraft off the catapult rail. The wings were also mounted with new larger flaps and half-circle metal skids on the ends to protect them during the landing on a single, central, under-fuselage landing skid. The aircraft was to be mounted on the catapult launching cradle strapped with two solid-fuel rockets each with 3,300lb (1,500kg)

The Ohka Model 43 K-2 Kai Wakazakura ('Young Cherry') was to be the definitive trainer for pilots destined for operational Ohka models but only two prototypes were completed before the end of the war. (*TAIU*)

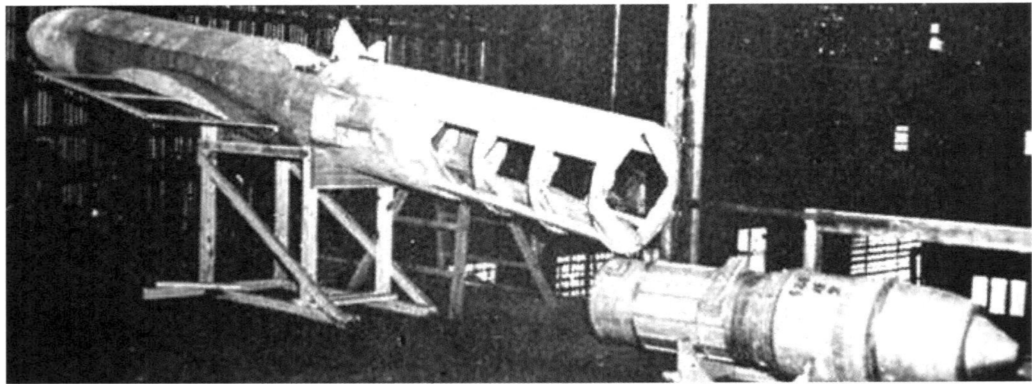

To complement the solid-fuel rockets mounted on the catapult, a single Type 4 Mk I Model 20 booster rocket motor was installed. Later a Model 43B mock-up with Ne-20 turbojet was contemplated (shown on this post-war photo of a captured engine.) (*TAIU*)

thrust during a four-second-burn launch along the 328ft (100m) track. To complement the solid-fuel rockets mounted on the catapult, a single Type 4 Mk I Model 20 booster rocket motor of the kind used in early combat versions of the Ohka 11 was added to the K-2's tail to augment catapult acceleration, to extend take-off training time in the air, and to allow student pilots to practise flying the bomb with power. Later, the Ne-20 turbojet was preliminarily installed but this plan was terminated with the ending of the war. During late June 1945, a prototype MXY7 K-2 made a successful catapult-launch test flight at the Takeyama Marine Corps Airfield located west of Yokosuka with navy pilot Capt. Hiromitsu Ito at the controls and the Ohka project chief designer Tadanao Miki in the trainee observer seat. Ten Model 43Bs were scheduled to be built in Yokosuka during May–June 1945 for preliminary training but near the end of the war only two prototypes of the Kai Wakazakura trainers had been completed. One of these is stored at the National Air and Space Museum in Washington, DC.

Ohka Model 53

Whereas all previous Ohkas, with the exception of the Models 43A and 43B, required modified bombers – Betty, Ginga (Frances), and Renzan motherships – to carry them aloft for launch, the Ne-20 turbojet-equipped Ohka Model 53 was designed to be towed into the air for release. This variant never proceeded beyond the preliminary design stage due to the end of the war.

Ishikawajima Ne-20 Turbojet

The Ishikawajima Ne-20 was Japan's first turbojet engine, developed during the Second World War in parallel with the Nakajima Kikka (Orange Blossom), Japan's first jet aircraft capable of taking off under its own power, and was also planned to power the Ohka Model 33 and 43 versions. The earlier Tsu-11 'pseudo turbojet' (essentially a ducted fan with an afterburner) licence-built by the First Navy Air Technical Arsenal was found unsuitable for powering the Nakajima Kikka. Subsequent Kikka designs were projected to use the Ne-

Ishikawajima Ne-20 turbojet. (*TAIU*)

10 (TR-10) centrifugal-flow turbojet, and the Ne-12 developed by Kugisho (Naval Air Technical Arsenal), which added a four-stage axial compressor to the front of the Ne-10. Tests soon revealed that these engines would not produce nearly enough power required to propel the aircraft, temporarily delaying the project. It was then decided to produce a new axial-flow turbojet based on the German BMW 003. Imperial Japanese Navy engineer Eichi Iwaya, using photographs and a single cutaway drawing of the German BMW 003, re-engineered this engine. The BMW 003 was the world's second successful axial-flow turbojet engine and powered the Heinkel He 162 Salamander and four-engine versions of the Arado Ar 234 Blitz. The Naval Air Technical Arsenal, Kugisho, manufactured the Ne-20 in two variants: the Ne-20 standard production engine and the uprated Ne-20-Kai version. The engine, which weighed 1,034lb (470kg), was 8ft 11in (270cm) long and 2ft (670cm) in diameter. It is estimated that only fifty were produced before the end of the war. Two would power the Kikka on its only flights on 7 and 15 August 1945. Only a few of the engines under manufacture survived, with one removed from the second Kikka and confiscated by American forces at the end of the war.

Ohka Model 11 Floatplanes

Possibly one of the more unusual unsubstantiated uses for the Ohka occurred in Formosa when a few Ohka Model 11s delivered by the carrier *Ryuho* were grounded there without any G4M2e Bettys available to carry them. To somehow utilise these Ohkas, it was somewhat bizarrely suggested to somehow install floats on them, using cannibalised floats from unserviceable or available floatplanes. Where and how these floats were to be installed is questionable as the Ohka's stubby wings surely presented a structural problem. Also, the rocket booster's short burn time, giving a rapid acceleration of the probably unseaworthy Ohka over anything but calm seas without capsizing is a moot point as trials were never held.

Suzuka 24 Ohka-Based Interceptor

This aircraft was first discovered by Technical Air Intelligence Units (TAIU) aerial photos of Suzuka Airfield, which gave it its temporary Suzuka 24 designation. Four additional aircraft of this type were later discovered by the XXI Bomber Command on the Kanoya Airfield, which was a base for kamikaze aircraft. It was a rocket-powered interceptor only based on the Ohka design and not a true Ohka. Unlike the Ohka, this new rocket aircraft was not a composite carried by a mothership or intended as a kamikaze suicide aircraft, but instead was to be launched on a rocket sled and then propelled by its single Toko Ro.2 (KR-10) rocket (a Japanese copy of the Walter HWK 509A rocket) for a complete take-off, combat run against B-29 formations, and landing. There were two combat reports supposedly involving the Suzuka 24 flying against B-29 formations, during which it struggled due to the experimental inadequacies of its KR-10 rockets.

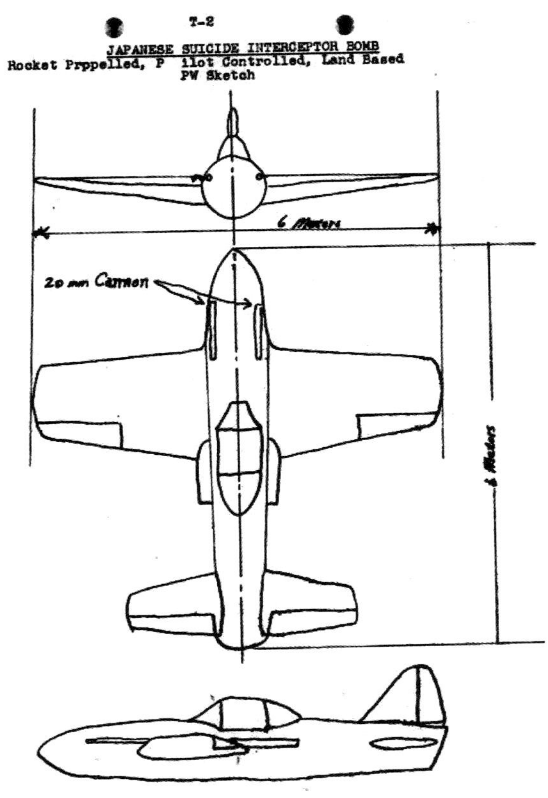

Technical Air Intelligence Unit 3-view drawing of the Suzuka 24 Ohka-based interceptor. (*TAIU*)

General Characteristics
Length: 20.4ft (6.2m)
Height: 6.0ft (1.8m)
Wingspan: 19.8ft (6.0m)
Wing Area: 76.3 sq ft (7.1 sq m)
Wing Loading: 84.6lb/sq ft (413.1kg/sq m)
Empty Weight: 5,631lb (2,554kg)
Loaded Weight: 6,459lb (2,930kg)

Model 11, Model 22, and Model 43B: Specifications and Comparisons
Dimensions:
Length
Model 11: 19.90ft (6.07m)
Model 22: 22.56ft (6.88m)
Model 43B: 26.77ft (8.17m)

Wingspan
Model 11: 16.40ft (5.00m)
Model 22: 13.52ft (4.12m)
Model 43B: 29.53ft (9.01m)

Height
Model 11: 3.94ft (1.20m)
Model 22: 3.94ft (1.20m)
Model 43B: 3.77ft (1.15m)

Wing Area
Model 11: 64.59 sq ft (6.00 sq m)
Model 22: 43.06 sq ft (4.01 sq m)
Model 43B: 139.93 sq ft (13.02 sq m)

Weights:
Empty
Model 11: 970lb (440kg)
Model 22: 1,200lb (545kg)
Model 43B: 2,535lb (1,150kg)

Max Take-Off
Model 11: 4,720lb (2,140kg)
Model 22: 3,200lb (1,450kg)
Model 43B: 5,005lb (2,270kg)

Internal Fuel Capacity: Unknown
Max Payload
Model 11: 2,645lb (1,200kg)
Model 22: 1,325lb (600kg)
Model 43B: 1,745lb (790kg)

Propulsion:
Power plant
Ohka Model 11 and Model 21: Three Type 4 Mark 1 Model 20 solid-propellant rockets, total thrust 1,746lb (800kg)
Ohka Model 22: One 551lb (200kg) thrust Tsu-11 turbojet
Ohka Model 53: One 1,047lb 475kg) thrust Ne-20 axial-flow turbojet
Ohka Model 43 K-1 KAI: One 573lb (260kg) thrust Type 4 Mark 1 Model 20 solid-propellant rocket

Thrust
Model 11: 1,765lb (7.85kg)
Model 22: 550lb (2.45kg)
Model 43B: 1,045lb (4.65kg)

Range
Model 11: 57.5 miles (90km)
Model 22: 80.5 miles (130km)
Model 43B: 172.5 miles (275km)

Performance:
Max level speed at sea level:
Model 11: 535mph (860kmph)
Model 22: 300mph (480kmph)
Model 43B: 345mph (555kmph)

Armament:
Guns: None
Warhead (in nose)
Model 11: one 2,647lb (1,200kg) warhead
Model 22: one 1,323lb (600kg) warhead
Model 43B: one 1,742lb (790kg) warhead

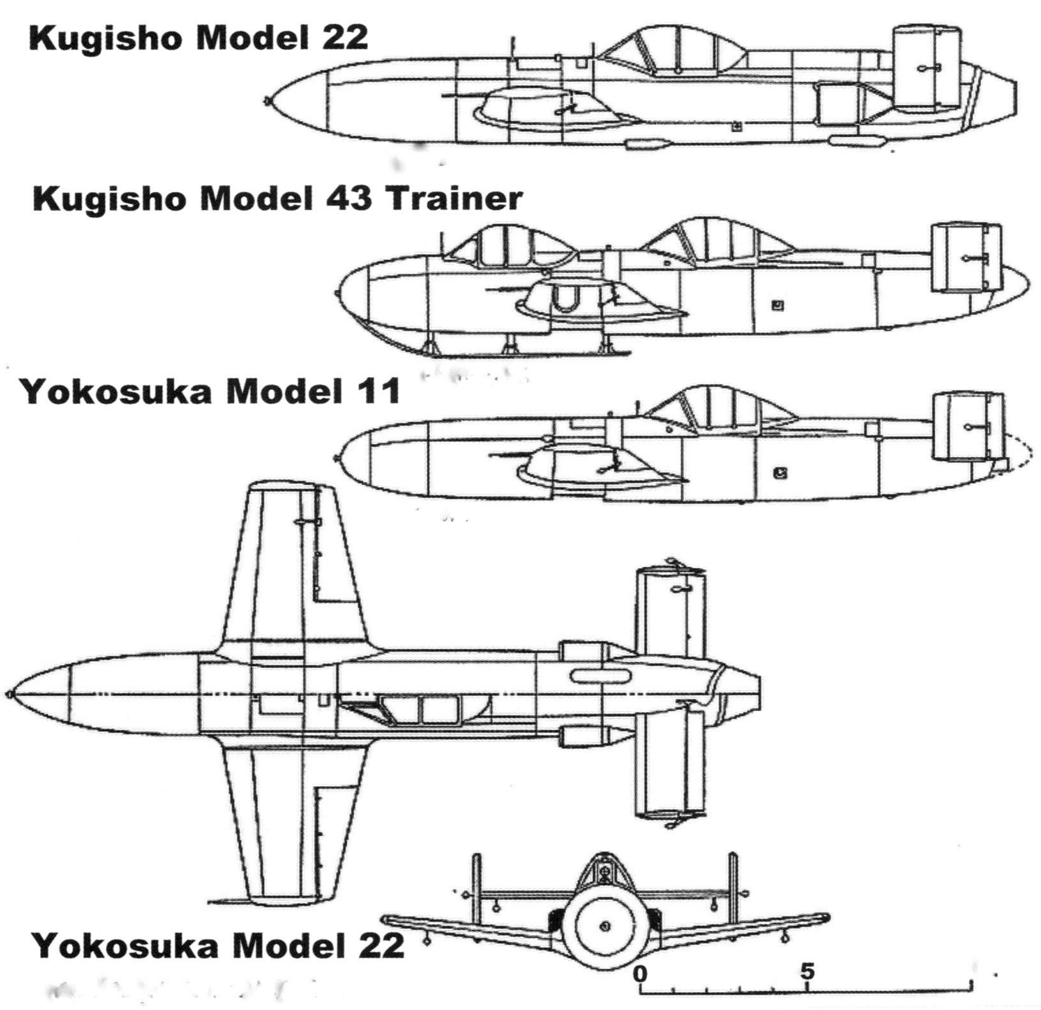

Summary and Conclusions

Impact of Ohka Kamikaze Attacks

Post-war USN analysis concluded that the Ohka's impact was negligible, since no capital ships had been hit during the attacks because of the effective defensive tactics that had been employed. Of the 300 Ohkas available for the Okinawa campaign, 74 embarked on operations, of which 56 were either destroyed while still attached to their carrying Betty aircraft (42) or during their attacks (14). Most kamikaze pilots never survived long enough to reach the target zone, and those who did often attacked the first ships they encountered, which were those on the radar picket lines, far from the main fleet. These small vessels, destroyers and even smaller LCS and LCI support vessels, were extremely vulnerable to aircraft impacts, and suffered attrition rates of almost 30 per cent, which made their role possibly the deadliest naval surface duty in the war. Of the 101 destroyers serving on radar picket duty, 10 were sunk and 32 damaged in kamikaze attacks. But Ohka attacks only sank the destroyer *Mannert L. Abele* and damaged only two other destroyers. Aside from the vulnerability of the Ohka/Betty composite, the Ohka was very difficult to operate in its terminal dive, and there are numerous reports of Ohkas missing their targets. After its combat use in the Okinawa campaign in the spring of 1945, about 230 Ohka Type 11s remained in inventory in July, these being stockpiled for the anticipated final defence of Japan. The Japanese planned to mass produce the Ohka in underground factories, but the war ended before these could be completed.

R Adm. Toshiyuki Yokoi, commander of the 25th Air Flotilla, summarised his thoughts about the Okinawa suicide attacks (*The Japanese Navy in World War II: In the Words of Former Japanese Naval Officers*, Naval Institute Press, 1986):

> The battle for Okinawa proved conclusively the defects of suicide air attacks. Such operations cannot be successful where materiel and trained manpower are limited. It would have been far wiser for the sadly depleted Japanese military to have conserved its manpower instead of squandering it as was done. It is not strange that this unrealistic aerial tactic ended in failure. Even the physical destructive power of the weapon itself was not sufficient for the task for which it had been designed. While it might deal a fatal blow to small warships or transports, the enemy aircraft carriers, which were meant to be primary targets, were sometimes able to survive attacks in which they were hit several times. Setting aside Admiral Ohnishi's original concept of adopting suicide attacks for the limited purpose of inactivating carrier decks for a week, the whole concept of suicide attacks to annihilate enemy task forces was more than unreasonable, it was sheer lunacy. Once the order had been issued by headquarters for these suicide attacks, they lost their voluntary aspect and became, instead, 'murder attacks', and humanity was lost sight of … Japan's suicide air operations mark the Pacific War with two scars that will remain forever in the annals of battle: one, of shame at the mistaken way of command; the other, of valour at the self-sacrificing spirit of young men who died for their beloved country.

Impact of the Kamikaze Attacks on Planning the Invasion of Japan

The *United States Strategic Bombing Survey: Pacific War Summary* concluded that the Japanese military had stockpiled approximately 5,000 tactical aircraft and 5,400 purposely designed kamikaze aircraft for use in the invasion of the Home Islands, with an additional 1,000 kaitens (manned suicide torpedoes). Allied Ultra code-breaking intelligence intercepts determined that the Japanese intended to target slow-moving, lightly armoured Allied troop transports, changing from targeting aircraft carriers. This change in targets was intended to exponentially impose the most possible personnel casualties on Allied forces at the expense of achieving a tactical victory by targeting Allied carriers.

Then, so close to victory, with the Nazi surrender in Europe two months earlier, the large and unexpected kamikaze toll during the Okinawa campaign so alarmed the casualty-conscious Navy leadership that Chief of Naval Operations Adm. Ernest King, and Chief of the Pacific Fleet, Adm. Chester Nimitz, both discontinued their support for an invasion, but instead supported a blockade and the continuation of the devastating aerial bombardment of Japan. Certainly, the costly kamikaze operations a played a role, among other decisive factors, in America's decision to use the two atomic bombs and thus avoid the final costly amphibious invasion of Japan, which was projected to last into 1947. Operation Downfall would kill or wound an estimated 500,000 Allied troops and upwards of 10 million Japanese, with 500,000 Purple Hearts ordered to be struck in anticipation of these massive casualties. The dropping of the atomic bombs led to the Japanese surrender and these Purple Hearts were stored and continued their unfortunate distribution through the Korean War and into Vietnam.

Epilogue

Kamikaze and Ohka Creator Epilogues

After the Japanese defeat in the Philippines, Vice Admiral Takijirō Ōnishi was recalled to Tokyo, and became Vice Chief of the Imperial Japanese Navy General Staff in May 1945. Ōnishi persisted in advocating the continuation of Japan's engagement, maintaining that the sacrifice of millions more lives would make his country victorious.

On 16 August 1945, after Japan's surrender, Ōnishi, commander of the First Fleet, committed seppuku ritual suicide as a penance to the kamikaze pilots and their families. In his suicide note, Ōnishi offered contrition to the 4,000 pilots he ordered to their deaths, and implored all young civilian survivors to work towards rebuilding Japan and encouraged them to find peace among nations. Ōnishi did not use a kaishakunin, the customary second chosen to behead an individual who has performed seppuku. Ōnishi's attempt to slit his own throat was not as successful and when found he declined assistance and chose instead to suffer fifteen hours of pain as penitence to those many special attack pilots. Ōnishi's seppuku sword is at the Yushukan Museum in Yasukuni Shrine, in Tokyo. Three days after the war ended, the Ohka concept's creator, now Lt (jg) Mitsuo Ohta, an air reconnaissance officer, not a kamikaze pilot, left the Konoike Ohka air wing base and flew off in a Zero over the Pacific. He was never seen again.

Number Built

A total of 852 Ohkas were built by the following major contractors with the collaboration of a series of subcontractors:

Dai-Ichi Kaigun Koku Gijitsusho, Yokosuka:
155 Ohka Model 11
50 Ohka Model 22
45 Ohka Model K-1
2 Ohka Model 43 K-1 KAI
Dai-Ichi Kaigun Kokusho, Kasumigaura:
600 Ohka Model 11

Post-War 'Victor's' Ohka Display

Preparing Ohkas for transport from Okinawa for shipment to America for examination and display. (*USN*)

Ohka examined by the Navy Air Material Unit, 4th Naval District, Hickam Field, Hawaii, during June 1945. (*USN*)

Okha Model 11 on Calcutta India docks awaiting shipment by the No. 54 RAF Embarkation unit to Britain during 1946. The Japanese ID number has been painted but this is probably one of the four on static display in Great Britain today. (*RAF*)

The Ohka was displayed at Wright Field in July 1945, where captured enemy aircraft were on display. The Ohka (note a rocket motor on ground) is seen at the arrow and next to the gigantic Junkers Ju 290, which after being flown across the Atlantic was scrapped in 1946. (*USAAF*)

A 43B MXY7 K-2 at NAS Norfolk 1947 as a beginning to its long journey to restoration at the National Air and Space Museum. (*USN*)

A St Louis father shows his son an Ohka at a travelling exhibit at Lambert Field in 1947. Note the spurious Hinomaru painted on its fuselage. (*USN*)

Fleet Admiral Chester Nimitz, USN, during a triumphant return to Washington, DC for a parade in his honour down Pennsylvania Avenue in October 1945. Here, a captured Japanese Suicide Baka Bomb is shown to the crowds. (*USN*)

Surviving Ohkas

Static Display

India

Model 11 at the Indian Air Force Museum in Palam, New Delhi.

Japan

Model 11 on static display at Iruma Air Force Base in Iruma, Saitama.
Model 11 on static display at the Kawaguchiko Motor Museum in Narusawa, Yamanashi.
Model 11 on static display at Usashi Heiwa Museum in Usa, Oita.

United Kingdom

Model 11 on static display at the Fleet Air Arm Museum in Yeovilton, Somerset.
Model 11 on static display at the Imperial War Museum in London.
Model 11 on static display at the Royal Air Force Museum Cosford in Shropshire.

United States

Model 11 on static display at the National Museum of the Marine Corps in Triangle, Virginia.
Model 11 on static display at the Planes of Fame Air Museum in Chino, California.
Model 11 on static display at the Yanks Air Museum in Chino, California.
Model 11 on static display at the Pima Air and Space Museum in Tucson, Arizona, on loan from the RAF Museum, UK.
Model 22 on static display at the Steven F. Udvar-Hazy Center of the National Air and Space Museum in Chantilly, Virginia.
Model 43B K-1 Kai Wakazakura on static display at the Pima Air and Space Museum in Tucson, Arizona. It is on loan from the National Air and Space Museum.
K-1 on static display at the National Museum of the United States Air Force in Dayton, Ohio.
K-1 on static display at the National Museum of the US Navy, Washington, D.C.
K-2 stored at the Steven F. Udvar-Hazy Center of the National Air and Space Museum in Chantilly, Virginia.

Replicas on Display

Japan

Model 11 on static display at the Yushukan Museum of the Yasukuni Shrine, Tokyo.

Japanese Museums and Monuments Honouring the Kamikaze

Kanoya Special Attack Corps War Dead Memorial Tower

The Fifth Air Fleet used Kanoya Airbase as its headquarters during the Battle of Okinawa in the spring of 1945. Kanoya also served as the main sortie base for special (suicide) attacks on Allied ships off Okinawa, and 908 members of Special Attack Corps units based at Kanoya lost their lives. In 1958, Kanoya City and the Japanese Maritime Self-Defense Force (JMSDF) Kanoya Base built the Special Attack Corps War Dead Memorial Tower to honour men who died in suicide attacks after taking off from Kanoya. Funds used to build this tower in Kotsuka Hill Park came not only from these two groups but also from local residents and people throughout Japan. A white dove sits on top of the tower, and a bronze plaque to the right side of the tower has inscribed the names and squadrons of the men who died in special attacks.

Kanoya Ohka Monument

This stone tablet monument was erected in 1978 led by Kyusaku Kojo, a kamikaze Special Attack Corps Ohka Unit member. The tablet memorialises the pilots of the Special Attack Corps who volunteered from Konoike Airbase and other bases who mobilised at Kanoya Airbase in Kyushu at the southern tip of Japan.

Kanoya Special Attack Corps War Dead Memorial Tower. (*JMSDF*)

Kanoya Ohka Monument. (*JMSDF*)

Japanese Kamikaze Museums With Exhibits

Most museums with exhibits to honour members of special attack forces are located at sites of former IJN or IJA bases and present a separate history of either the Imperial Japanese Navy or Army special attack forces. Almost all of these locations also had special attack force memorials constructed prior to the opening of the museum exhibits. These exhibits feature photos and letters of individual pilots and kamikaze units and training classes. The photos of individual pilots are exhibited with each pilot's basic biographical information, such as name, unit, date of death, age at death, and home prefecture. All museums display numerous letters, poems, and diary entries, most written on the eve of the final mission or soon before. These letters have the deepest emotional effect on museum visitors. Since the primary goal of the special attack forces exhibits is to memorialise the pilots who sacrificed their lives to defend their country, the museums do not present controversial or negative aspects of Japan's history of suicide attacks.

Chiran Peace Museum for Kamikaze Pilots

Chiran, which served as the site of the former Chiran Army Airbase the main special (suicide) attack sortie base for Japanese Army air attacks on Allied ships around Okinawa, has become the principal place that Japanese people associate with kamikaze pilots, even though the kamikaze Special Attack Corps was part of the Japanese Navy rather than Army. The Chiran Peace Museum for Kamikaze Pilots was known as Chiran Tokko Ihinkan (Chiran Special Attack Items Museum) from its opening in 1975 until the enlargement of the museum building to 17,000 sq ft in 1986, after which it was designated as the Chiran Peace Museum for Kamikaze Pilots. Chiran also has several statues and memorials related to Special Attack Corps pilots, and stone lanterns dedicated to the pilots line the town's main street and the road leading to the museum. The museum contains photographs of the pilots displayed in the chronological order of when they died. Also included are their family records, personal effects, such as hachimaki headbands, Hinomaru flags, inscribed with messages of encouragement from family and friends, uniforms, farewell letters and weapons.

Chiran Peace Museum for Kamikaze Pilots. (*Chiran Tokko Ihinkan*)

Chapter Six

Kawanishi Baika (Plum Blossom)

The Kawanishi Baika ('Plum Blossom') was a pulsejet-powered kamikaze aircraft under development for the Imperial Japanese Navy towards the end of the war.

German Influence

Under the Japanese-German Technical Exchange Agreement of 1943, the two Axis allies had agreed to share technical information. By 1944, Japan was to rely heavily upon this Technical Exchange Agreement, obtaining manufacturing rights, intelligence, blueprints, and even actual airframes for several of Germany's new air weapons. These included the Me 163 Komet rocket fighter (which culminated in its development as the Mitsubishi J8M Shusui), the BMW 003 axial-flow jet engine (which was revised to Japanese standards as the Ishikawajima Ne-20), the Me 262 jet fighter (partially developed as the Nakajima J9Y *Kikka*), and data on the Fieseler Fi 103R series (Reichenberg) and its Argus pulsejet engine, which became a prototype for the Kawanishi Baika.

By October 1943, US intelligence contended that the Japanese had been informed of the V-1 and in November 1944 that Japan had received a copy, as would be verified by a captured post-war cargo manifest from the Japanese submarine I-29 that catalogued a V-1 fuselage as part of the delivery. During 1953 Technical Commander Eiichi Iwaya, the Japanese naval officer who carried the Me 163 and BMW 003 data back to Japan via submarine, published a book on wartime Japanese technology, *Koku Gijutsu No Zenbo,* stating that he brought the data on the Fieseler Fi 103R (Reichenberg) and Argus As 014 pulsejet engine used to power the Fi 103R to Japan via a submarine. The pulsejet-powered Kawanishi Baika was intended as a replacement for the rocket-powered Ohka. The Baika bore a distinct resemblance to their German precursor, nonetheless, the only actual result of the Reichenberg/Argus pulsejet cooperation would be the manufacture of the Maru Ka-10 pulsejet engine Argus knock-off prototype, which was planned to power the never-to-be Baika.

Japanese Development

On 2 July 1944, the Kaigun Koku Hombu (Imperial Japanese Navy Aviation Bureau of the Ministry of the Navy) directed Kawanishi Kokuki K.K. to produce the Baika (Plum Blossom) special attack aircraft that was to be a replacement for the Kugisho Ohka 11 and 22 as well as the special attack version of the Nakajima Kikka, the Luftwaffe Me 262 jet fighter reproduction, which would have been too expensive to produce and too valuable tactically to waste as a kamikaze. Subsidised by Kawanishi, Professors Ichiro Tani and

Taichirb Ogawa of the Aeronautical Institute of the Tokyo Imperial University, initiated a study to fulfil this directive.

Kawanishi Kokuki K.K. was founded as Kawanishi Engineering Works in 1920 as an extension of the Kawanishi conglomerate. During 1923 the company initiated an airline, Nippon Koku K.K. (Japan Aviation Co. Ltd), which designed and built several aircraft for its use. Kawanishi Engineering Works formed Kawanishi Kokuki K.K. in 1928. However, in 1929 the Japanese government shut down Nippon Koku and transferred its routes to the government-owned Nippon Koku Yuso K.K. (Japan Air Transport Co. Ltd). While Kawanishi was best known for its seaplanes, such as the Kawanishi H6K (Mavis) and H8K (Emily) flying boats, its N1K-J (George) land-based fighter, derived from its N1K1 (Rex) floatplane fighter, was considered one of the outstanding Japanese fighters of the war. After the war the company was recreated as Shin Meiwa Industries (later ShinMaywa) and continued to produce flying boats such as the PS-1 and US-2.

On 5 August 1945, a conference was convened at the Aeronautical Institute of the Tokyo Imperial University and attended by Admirals Wata and Katahira from the Kaigun Koku Hombu, Professors Naganishi, Ogawa, and Kihara of the Aeronautical Institute, and Chairman Katachiro and Chief Designer Tamenobu Takeuchi of the Kawanishi Company. As a result, the Baika was selected over the rival Kugisho Ohka Model 43B, as the latter was considered as too complex to be built quickly in large numbers, especially since it used the Ne-20 turbojet, which was to be earmarked for powering the Nakajima Kikka.

At the conclusion of the meeting, Kawanishi was granted an order for one Baika prototype and ten two-seat trainers with a deadline of September 1945 to come up with a finalised design and production plan and mass production to begin during October 1945. Due to the inexorable American bombing of Japanese industry and the huge reduction of the imports of the vital raw materials needed to maintain the Japanese military machine by USN submarines and Allied air forces, the Baika aircraft was to be fabricated from as many non-critical war materials as possible. It was also to be of straightforward design to be produced unskilled or semi-skilled labour in small, dispersed workshops. Beginning on 8 August 1945, two days after the A-bomb was dropped on Hiroshima, a team of sixty men was scheduled to be gathered at Kawanishi Kokuki Kabushiki Gaisha at Naruo to commence production documentation for the Baika. On 11 August, the first ten designers arrived and the second group of twenty came on the 15th, with the third and last group of thirty scheduled for 20 August, including the remaining engineers. However, on 15 August the armistice was announced, and the Baika project ended before it had left the drawing board. Since the Baika never progressed beyond the design stage, the final production details were never finalised.

Baika Types

Several Baika types were proposed based on their take-off or launching methods. (Note: these designations of Baika Types I–III were not applied by the Japanese but in post-war descriptions.)

Type I

The Type I was intended for conventional take-off under its own power on a landing gear from an airfield using three 572lb (260kg) thrust Type-A rockets (from the Ohka Type 43) located at the wing roots and at the central axis of the fuselage to achieve the ignition speed of 225mph (360kmph) of the pulsejet located above and behind the cockpit. The main landing gear and booster rockets were to be jettisoned after take-off. Due to the pulsejet's high fuel consumption, this Baika had a range of only 125 miles (200km) at a cruising speed of 345mph (556kmph) at sea level. By not jettisoning their landing gear, these Baikas could also be used for training pilots before they converted to the combat-launched examples.

Type II

Although not carried by an aircraft, the Baika Type II was also unique, being carried by a submarine. In order to compete with the proposed submarine-carried Ohka Type 43A, the Sichuan West Company designed this Baika version, which could be launched using the same system as the Ohka 43 Type A. The wing folding mechanism was also similar to that of the Type A. The Type II was similar to the Type I, but with its pulsejet moved forwards. A modified take-off trolley was developed that was to be powered by a less-powerful solid-fuel rocket engine than the Ohka version, producing a thrust of 1,764lb (800kg) for nine seconds. The warhead was a conventional 250kg bomb with forward- and a rear-impact fuses.

Type III

The pulsejet was mounted ventrally and this version had no landing gear as it was intended to be air-launched, like the Ohka, by the twin-engine Mitsubishi G4M Betty or Yokosuka P1Y Frances medium bombers, or the four-engine Nakajima G8N Rita heavy bomber under development.

Baika Described

The Kawanishi Baika was largely conventional in layout, with low-set monoplane wings, a mid-position cockpit, standard empennage, a retractable landing gear, with a pulsejet engine mounted over the fuselage. The Baika fuselage was to be slim and circular in cross section; like that of the German Fi 103 (V-l) flying bomb but more curved, and significantly shorter. Originally the fuselage was to be fabricated of aluminium structure and cladding but due to the scarcity of the metal, the construction was to be wholly of wood, except for steel joints. The low wing was a change from the mid-winged layout of the V-1. The wings were tapered with round tips and equipped with standard slotted ailerons. The wood structure was clad with plywood covering (foldable in the Type II). The tail surfaces were of wooden structure with plywood covering. The main landing gear was taken from the Nakajima Ki-115 Tsurugi kamikaze. The cockpit was mounted at the centre of the aircraft and was integrated better into the fuselage than on manned versions of the V-1 Reichenberg. The cramped cockpit was covered with a canopy that offered good visibility, which could be opened to one side or slid aft depending on the several engine locations that were proposed. The engine instruments included a fuel gauge, fuel level indicator, and rpm counter, while the navigation instruments included an airspeed indicator, altimeter, compass, and turn-and-bank indicator.

Instead of integrating the Type III with the Yokosuka P1Y1 Ginga (Frances) by reducing the wingspan so that it could be carried between the main undercarriage, the final design weighed half the that of the Ohka 11 and could be installed in a more rearward position within the Ginga bomb bay. It also could be towed by the future Yokosuka Tenga jet bomber. To allow the ignition of the pulsejet during flight, the aircraft needed to be exposed to the air stream outside the mothership carrier, so its original location was changed to under the fuselage centreline of the Baika. The warhead in the internal nose was to be a Type 97 torpedo with 150kg of Torpex HE or a 550lb (250kg) GP bomb. At this point of the war, spring 1945, the Japanese politicians under the heavy bombing that virtually destroyed Tokyo were more interested in causing a high number of Allied casualties and, rather than attack heavily protected and armoured warships, believed that it would be better to try to destroy the lightly protected troop transports that were to invade the homeland using a small 550lb warhead instead of the 2,640lb (1,200kg) warhead of the Ohka 11, which never sank a warship.

Specifications

Kawanishi was to meet the following specifications for the Baika with two main factors to be considered: simplicity of design, with its basic dimensions to be kept as small as possible, and ease of operation. Soon after the original specifications were determined, the range requirement was abandoned and the armour plate was removed, leaving more room available for an increase in the warhead size to 550lb (250kg). While this resulted in a range reduction from 173 miles (278km) to 80 miles (130km), this was not seen as unfavourable as the probable distances flown to combat would be somewhat less than 80 miles (130km). Initially, the Baika was to include 0.315in (8mm) pilot armour protection, and although this only protected his back, it was a means to allow for some degree of protection from interceptors firing from aft rather than ground fire.

Kawanishi Baika: Specifications

Crew: 1
Layout: Pulsejet-powered monoplane
Length: 22ft 10in (6.97m)
Height: 13ft 1in (4m)
Wingspan: 21ft 7in (6.58m)
With folded wings, of no more than 11.8ft (3.6m)
Wing area: 81.6 sq ft (7.58 sq m)
Wing loading: 39lb/sq ft (188kg/ sq m)
Empty weight: 1,653lb (750kg)
Gross weight: 3,153lb (1,430kg)

Fuel capacity: 158.5-gallon (600-litre) tank behind pilot
Powerplant: 1 × Maru Ka-10 pulsejet engine (794lb thrust)

Performance
Maximum speed: 403mph (648kmph)
Cruise speed: 301mph (485kmph)
Launch speed: 225mph (360kmph)
Stall speed: 69mph (111kmph)
Maximum dive speed: 460mph (740kmph)
Range: 173 miles (278km) original to 80 miles (130km)
Service ceiling: 6,600ft (2,000m)
Time to altitude: 6,562ft (2,000m) in about four minutes

Armament
Warhead (Internal Nose): Type 97 torpedo warhead with 150kg of Torpex HE or a 550lb (250kg) GP bomb

Armour protection: 0.315in (8mm) armour plate behind the pilot

Note: The currently accepted illustrations of the Baika come from the 1953 published book *Koku Gijutsu No Zenbo*, in which Technical Commander Iwaya provided drawings of all three versions of the Baika.

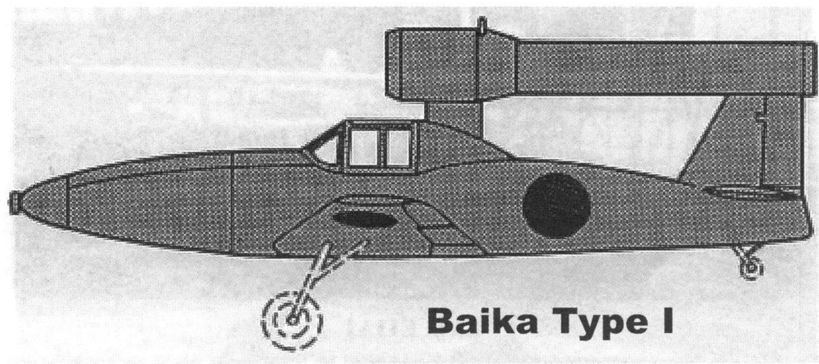

The Baika Type I was a conventional aircraft design with a landing gear and was intended for conventional take-off under its own power from an airfield using three booster rockets to assist until the overhead pulsejet began to provide thrust. (*Author's collection*)

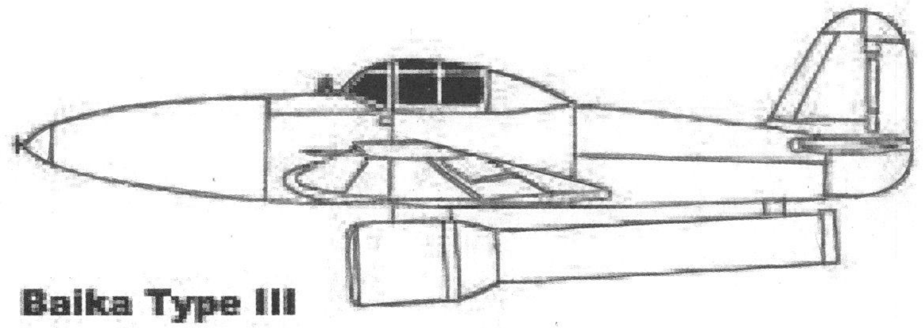

The Baika Type III had its pulsejet mounted ventrally to be accommodated under the mothership as it was intended to be air launched, like the Ohka. (*Author's collection*)

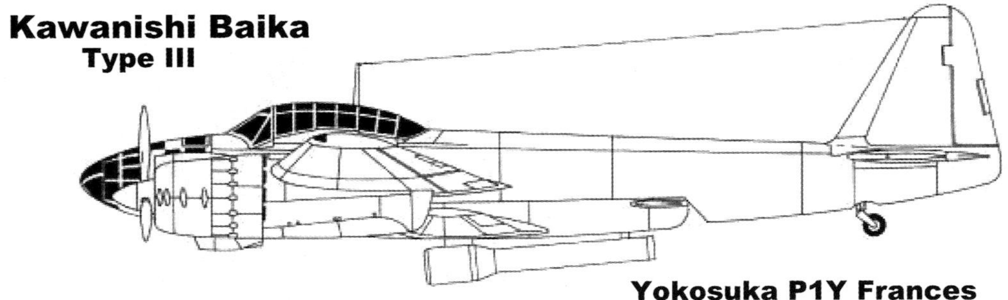

The Baika Type III was intended to be air launched by a such as the twin-engine Mitsubishi G4M Betty or Yokosuka P1Y Frances (shown) medium bombers, or the four-engine Nakajima G8N Rita heavy bomber under development. (*Author's collection*)

The Maru Ka-10, the Japanese Pulsejet Version of the Argus 014

The Baika's Maru Ka-10 pulsejet was designed by Professors Ichiro Tami and Taichiro Ogawa under licence by the Aeronautical Institute of the Tokyo Imperial University from the German Argus As 109-014 pulsejet from the technical plans that had been delivered to Japan via submarine in 1944.

The choice to use the pulsejet had several main benefits at this final phase of the war, as Japan had difficulty supplying fuel for its piston-driven operational aircraft. Even pre-war, Japan was almost totally dependent on imported oil and since its imports from the recaptured Dutch East Indies had been significantly reduced, the pulsejet's use of low-grade petrol freed up the more refined aviation fuel for combat aircraft. Initial tests of the Ka-10 were performed using benzol (a coal-tar product consisting mainly of benzene and toluene) as a fuel. However, the engine was designed to run on various fuels, including heavy kerosene and pine oil. Second, the simplicity of the pulsejet design meant it could be built in large numbers by relatively unskilled labour in home workshops throughout Japan at a lower cost per unit than a turbojet or piston engine. Thirdly, Ka-10 pulsejets were low maintenance and were relatively dependable over short distances.

However, the pulsejet had major flaws. It was not fuel efficient and suffered from having a short service life, mainly due to problems with the fuel valve system. Both these failings were considered as unimportant for a low-mileage, one-way suicide aircraft. The Baika's pulsejet engine would have had a high noise level, as did the Germans' well-named 'buzz bomb', and could have provided enough advance warning for detection and to establish countermeasures. The significant vibration caused by the operating engine could stress the Baika's structure, but probably not enough for the short distances it was to fly. When considering the benefits and flaws of the one-way Baika versus the reusable German Fi 103R Reichenberg, the Baika's pulsejet benefits far outweighed the disadvantages.

A small test model was completed in early 1945 and tested until June, after which the standard working version was completed. It began testing at the end of July and continued until the end of the war in August. The post-war US Army Special Weapons branch reported that five Ka-10s were bult.

The Maru Ka-10 was the Japanese pulsejet version of the German Argus 014 devised from the technical plans that had been delivered to Japan via submarine in 1944. The photo depicts a Ka-10, which was part of a post-war US Navy assemblage of captured Japanese aircraft engines. (*USN*)

Specifications Maru Ka-10 Pulsejet

General Characteristics

Type: Pulsejet
Length: 12.33ft (3.75m)
Diameter: 1.8ft (0.55m)
Dry weight: 337lb (153kg)

Components

Compressor: Constant volume explosion chamber
Fuel type: Benzole, kerosene, turpentine, pine oil, and various low-quality hydrocarbon fuels

Performance

Maximum thrust: 794lb (360kg) at 460mph (740kmph) at sea level
Thrust-to-weight ratio: 2:35

Chapter Seven

Mizuno Shinryu II (Divine Dragon)

Jinryu (Divine Dragon) Rocket Glider: Shinryu II Precursor

During November 1944, the Kaigun Koku Hombu (Naval Air Command Navy Aviation Bureau) began their investigation into developing a suicide glider to repel the anticipated Allied fleet's invasion of the Home Islands. The Bureau assigned the Yokosuka Naval Aircraft Workshop (Kaigun Koku Gijutsu-Sho) led by Shigeki Sakakibara to build the prototype glider, which was designed by Yoshio Akita. It would not be until May 1945 that Akita finalised the design and Sakakibara would direct several crews that were each to build a part of the glider. To conserve Japan's limited supply of aluminium for other more vital military purposes, the glider was to be constructed with as much wood as possible. By using wood, the glider could be fabricated in small workshops using only woodworking tools.

The Mizuno Company, Osaka, was contracted to build several military versions for testing. Mizuno was a pre-war Western sports paraphernalia company, such as baseball equipment, golf clubs, and skis, which had changed during the war to the manufacture of several military gliders. (After the war Mizuno once again came to the forefront of the Japanese and international sporting goods industry, producing sportswear, athletic shoes, and equipment for many sports.) These military versions were sleek but very simple open-cockpit, high-wing monoplane suicide gliders that could be easily flown by inexperienced pilots. The gliders, armed with 220lb (100kg) warheads, would be launched by three Toku-Ro.1 Type I rocket boosters from caves or shore positions, manned by pilots who would guide them into Allied ships or tanks during an Allied invasion of the Home Islands. After the handling and flight characteristics of the Jinryu glider version were proven and modified by adding some strengthening, its testing advanced to the next phase of powered rocket flight. However, ground testing of the rocket motors disclosed serious quality problems and it was also decided that the Jinryu would be unsuited for

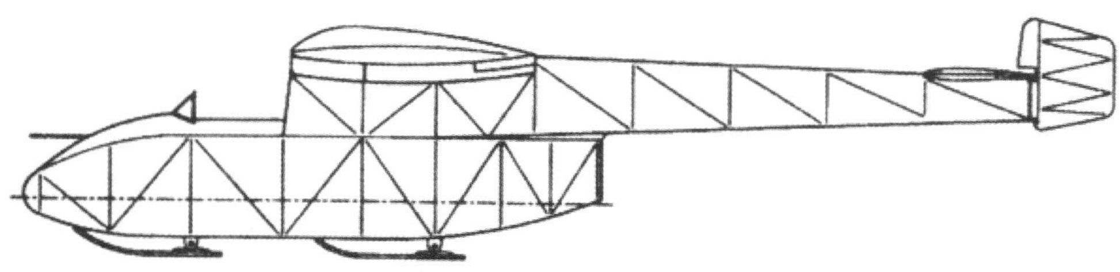

(*Author/Lansdale*)

Rare photo of the Jinryu rocket glider. (*Author/Lansdale*)

suicide missions as its rocket-powered flight characteristics would make it a challenging aircraft to fly by poorly trained suicide pilots. The five completed Jinryu gliders would never fly under rocket power and after the failure of the rocket motors during ground tests the war ended before more suitable and reliable ones could be developed and tested. Thus, the Jinryu (Divine Dragon) rocket/glider design was to be replaced by an interceptor, designated as the Shinryu II (Divine Dragon), with a much-revised aerodynamic design and a different rocket power plant.

Shinryu II (Divine Dragon)

Once the Jinryu glider version encountered problems, the Kaigun Koku Hombu became interested in developing a point defence fighter that could climb quickly to counter the B-29 Superfortresses that were ravaging Japanese cities. A group was formed to create a new rocket-powered aircraft design, the Shinryu II, rather than a glider. Two engineers were retained from the Jinryu project: Shigeki Sakakibara, the lead designer, and Yoshio Tonsho, who would oversee the construction of the prototype, while Yujiro Murakami was assigned to aerodynamic testing.

Unlike the Jinryu, the Shinryu II was designed as an interceptor from the beginning, becoming second canard design following the Kyushu J7W Shinden. Its main wings had a planform like a cropped delta to ensure stability and good handling. For power, the Shinryu II was to use four problematic Toku-Ro.1 Type 2 rocket engines located in the rear fuselage, with each engine providing a thirty-second burn time for a total thrust of

1,322lb (600kg). Two rockets would be used for take-off while the other two would be used for flight. A nose skid was provided with a basic spring suspension to absorb the landing forces, while a non-sprung skid assembly was supported by two struts under each wing.

For take-off the Shinryu II was to use a two-wheeled dolly that the pilot would jettison once airborne. In addition to this runway take-off method, other means for launching were considered, including towing and air launching the Shinryu II like the Kugisho Ohka, carried by a modified Mitsubishi G4M Betty or Yokosuka P1Y Frances bombers. Using either air launch method would have conserved two of the rocket engines, which would have been exhausted during ground take-off and no use in reaching the high-altitude B-29s. The pilot could then use the rockets to maintain altitude, cruise, and benefit from his aircraft's wingspan and wing area to stay airborne for extended periods. For armament the Shinryu II was to be equipped with eight rockets, with four tubes, one on top of the other and angled downwards, attached to the inside of the rear landing skid. These would probably be fired as a cluster in a spread pattern while diving on the Superfortress formations. Once the Shinryu II's fuel and ammunition were expended, its pilot would glide back to its base to be recovered, refuelled, and rearmed to re-enter combat.

The Shinryu II's suicide mission objective has been ventured as being an anti-shipping role, like the Ohka, and, secondarily, but improbably, to attack, important small, fortified targets or armoured (tanks) ground targets. For anti-shipping operations a 220lb (100kg) explosive warhead would be mounted in the nose. Once the Shinryu II's rocket armament

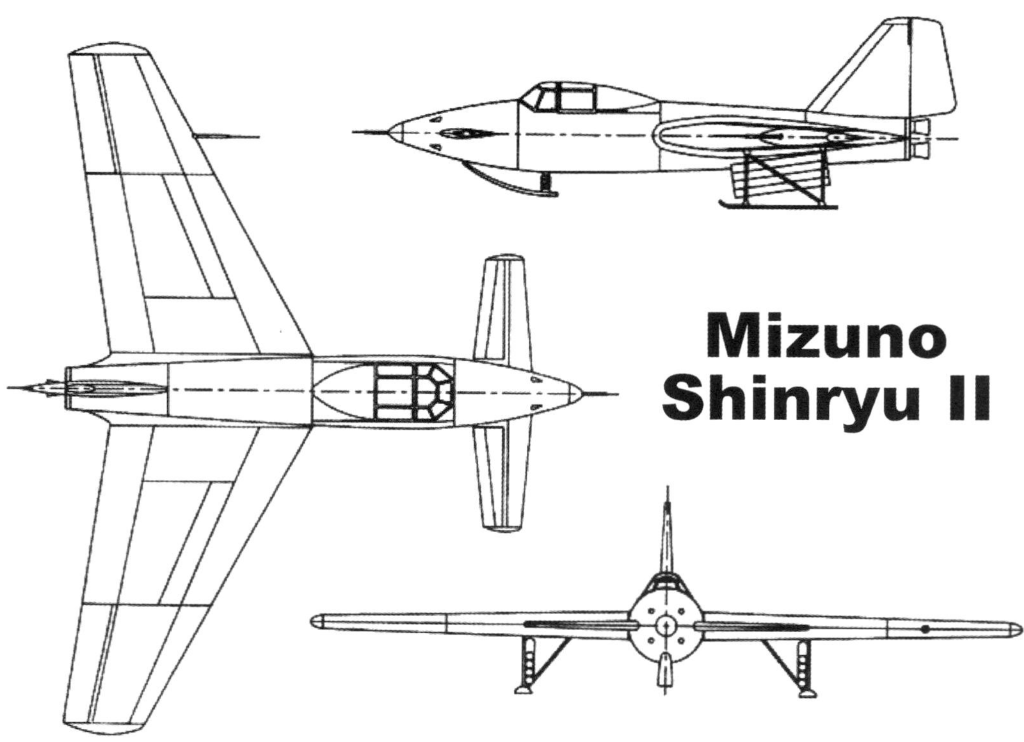

(*Author/Lansdale*)

and fuel was expended, its pilot could elect to crash his aircraft into a final target, exploding an impact-fused explosive warhead. However, the Shinryu II was far more complicated and expensive to build than the Ohka and since it was designed and constructed for manoeuvrability and high altitude (30,000ft+ with a proposed pressurised cockpit) operation, and with a means to land, it's suicide role would be improbable as it would be more far more valuable as an interceptor. The Shinryu II would never be built and remain a drawing board concept with the end of the war.

Mizuno Shinyu II: Specifications

Crew: 1
Length: 24ft 11in (7.6m)
Height: 5ft 11in (1.8m)
Wingspan: 23ft (7m)
Wing area: 120 sq ft (11 sq m)
Powerplant: 4 × Toku-Ro I Type II solid-fuel rockets (340lb thrust each)

Performance
Maximum speed: 190mph (300kmph)
Cruise speed: 68mph (110kmph)
Range: 2.5 miles (4km)
Service ceiling: Ground Launch: 1,300ft (400m); Air Launch: 30,000ft (9,144m)

Armament
Rockets: 8 × unguided rockets
Warhead: 1 × 220lb (100kg) explosive warhead

Bibliography

Books

Andersen, Roy, *Three Minutes off Okinawa: The Sinking of the Radar Picket Destroyer the U.S.S. Mannert L. Abele by Japanese Kamikaze Aircraft*, Jana Press, 2007

Appleman, Roy; Burns, James; Gugeler, Russell; Stevens, John; *The War in the Pacific: Okinawa: The Last Battle*, Center of Military History, US Army, Washington, D.C., 1948

Axell, Albert, and Kase, Hideaki, *Kamikaze: Japan's Suicide God*s, Harlow, Longman, NY, 2002

Christopher, John, *The Race for Hitler's X-Planes*, History Press, UK, 2013

Cooksley, Peter, *Flying Bomb, The Story of Hitler's V-Weapons in World War II*, New York: Charles Scribner's Sons, 1979

Cressman, Robert, *Official Chronology of the U.S. Navy in World War II*

Dictionary of American Naval Fighting Ships, Naval History & Heritage Command, Washington, D.C., 1999

Detweiller, Donald, *Naval Armament Vol. 1*, Taylor and Francis, UK, 1980

Dobinson, Colin, *AA Command: Britain's Anti-aircraft Defences of World War II*, Methuen, UK, 2001

Ellis, Ken, *Wreck & Relics*, Crecy, UK, 2012

Engelmann, Joachim, *V-1: The Flying Bomb*, Schiffer, PA, 1997

Evans, David, (Editor and translator), *The Japanese Navy in World War II: In the Words of Former Japanese Naval Officers*, Naval Institute Press, MD, 1986

Francillon, Rene, *Japanese Aircraft of the Pacific War*, Putnam & Company, UK, 1979

Francillon, Rene, *Mitsubishi G4M Betty and Ohka Bomb*, Aircraft in Profile, Vol. 9, Profile Publications, UK, 1971

Frank, Richard, *Downfall: The End of the Imperial Japanese Empire*, Random House, NY, 1999

Georg, Friedrich, *Hitler's Miracle Weapons: The Secret History of the Rockets and Flying Crafts of the Third Reich: Volume 2 – From the V-1 to the A-9*, Helion, UK, 2005

Hoyt, Edwin, *The Kamikazes,* Arbor House, NY, 1983

Hulver, Richard and Waldman, Martin, *Battle of Okinawa: Historic Overview & Importance*, Naval History and Heritage Command, Washington, D.C., 13 May 2020

Inoguchi, Rikihei; Tadashi. Nakajima; and Pineau, Roger, *The Divine Wind: Japan's Kamikaze Force in World War II*, Naval Institute Press, Md, 1988

Irons, Roy, *Hitler's Terror Weapons: The Price of Vengeance*, Harper Collins, NY, 2003

Kay, Anthony, *Buzz Bomb*, Monogram Aviation Publications, UK, 1977

King, Benjamin; Kutta, Timothy, *Impact: The History of Germany's V-Weapons in World War II,* Sarpedon, NY, 1998

Maloney, Edward, *Kamikaze*, Aero Publishers, Aero Publishers, CA, 1966

Mikesh, Robert; Abe, Shorzoe, *Japanese Aircraft, 1910–1941*, London, Putnam Aeronautical Books, UK, 1990

Morison, Samuel Eliot, *History of United States Naval Operations in World War II, Vol. XII: Leyte, June 1944–January 1945*, Little, Brown and Company, MA, 1958

Morison, Samuel Eliot, *History of United States Naval Operations in World War II, Vol. XIV: Victory in the Pacific, 1945*, Little Brown and Company, MA, 1960

Norman, Friedman, *The Naval Institute Guide to World Naval Weapon Systems*, Naval Institute Press, MD, 2006

Oliver, John, *The V-1, The Machine and its Men,* CreateSpace Independent Publishing Platform, NY, 2018
O'Neill, Richard, *Suicide Squads: The Men and Machines of World War II Special Operations*, The Lyons Press, Washington DC, 2001
Prados, John, *Combined Fleet Decoded: The Secret History of American Intelligence and the Japanese Navy in World War II,* MD, Naval Institute Press, 1995
Reitsch, Hanna, *The Sky My Kingdom: Memoirs of the Famous German World War II Test Pilot*, Casemate, UK, 2009
Reitsch, Hanna, *Flying is My Life,* Putnam, NY, 1954
Rielly, Robin, *Kamikaze Attacks of World War II: A Complete History of Japanese Suicide Strikes on American Ships, by Aircraft and Other Means*, McFarland, NC, 2010
Sheftall, M.G., *Blossoms in the Wind: Human Legacies of the Kamikaze*, New American Library, NY, 2005
Shobo, Ushio, *Kamikaze Special Attack Forces*, Special No. 108, Japan, 1986
Shobo, Atene, *Navy Battle Record of Special Attack Units*, Maru, Japan, 2001
Skorzeny, Otto, *My Commando Operations: The Memoirs of Hitler's Most Daring Commando*, Schiffer, PA, 1997
Thomas, Andrew, *V-1 Flying Bomb Aces. Aircraft of the Aces*, Osprey, UK, 2013
Thomas, Graham, *Hitler's Terror from the Sky: The Battle Against the Flying Bombs*, Pen & Sword, UK, 2009
Wolf, William, *The 13th Fighter Command in World War II: Air Combat over Guadalcanal and the Solomons*, Schiffer, PA, 2000
Young, Richard, *The Flying Bomb*, UK, Ian Allan, 1978
Zaloga, Steven, *Kamikaze: Japanese Special Attack Weapons 1944–45*, New Vanguard #180, Osprey, UK, 2011
Zaloga, Steven, *German V-Weapon Sites 1943–45*, Osprey, UK, 2008

Magazine Articles

Hone, Trent, 'Countering the Kamikaze', *Naval History Magazine*, October 2020
Popular Science, 'Japanese Gamble On Human Bombs', *Popular Science*, August 1945
Momiyama, Thomas, 'Racing Against Invasion', *Air Power History*, summer 2009
Naito, Hatsuho, 'Memoir of a Kamikaze Squadron Survivor: How the Thunder Gods Prepared For Suicide', *Air & Space Magazine*, 30 April 1991
Wolf, William, 'Suicide Samurai', *Wings*, February 1977
Wolf, William, 'V for Vengeance', *Airpower*, March 1978
Yokoi, R. Adm. Toshiyuki, 'Kamikazes and the Okinawa Campaign', *USNI Proceedings*, May 1954
Yokoi, R. Adm. Toshiyuki, 'Thoughts on Japan's Naval Defeat', *USNI Proceedings*, October 1960

Reports and Papers

Albert F. Simpson Historical Research Center (AFSHRC), V-1 and Ohka files and photos, Maxwell AFB, AL, 1975
CIC (Combat Information Center), Baka, *Flying Warhead,* US Office of the Chief of Naval Operations, June 1945
Luftwaffe, *FZG 76 Geräte-Handbuch*, Luftwaffe, 1944
Headquarters of the Commander-in-Chief, US Fleet (COMINCH), *Antiaircraft*
Headquarters of the Fleet, US Navy, 'Antiaircraft Action Summary: Suicide Attacks, April 1945', COMINCH P-009, 30 April 1945
Lansdale, James, Japanese aircraft and Ohka files and photos, 1975
National Museum of the United States Air Force (NMUSAF) Research Center, Reichenberg files and photos, Wright-Patterson Air Force Base, OH, 2012
Naval History and Heritage Command, *1945: Battle of Okinawa, The Most Difficult Antiaircraft Problem Yet Faced By the Fleet,* NHHC, Washington, D.C., 2020
Naval History and Heritage Command, *Battle of Okinawa: Okinawa Highlights: 12–19 April 1945*, NHHC, Washington, D.C., ND

Timenes, Nicolai, *Defense Against Kamikaze Attacks in World War II and its Relevance to Anti-Ship Missile Defense, Volume I: An Analytical History of Kamikaze Attacks Against Ships of the United States Navy During World War II*, Operations Evaluation Group, Center for Naval Analyses, Study 741, CA, 1970

United States Strategic Bombing Survey, *The Campaigns of the Pacific War*, US Government Printing Office, Washington, D.C., 1946

US Navy, *Action Summary: World War II,* Information Bulletin No. 29, 8 October 1945

US Navy, Battle Experience, *Radar Pickets and Methods of Combating Suicide Attacks Off Okinawa*, Washington, D.C., March–May 1945

US Navy H-044-2: *Floating Chrysanthemums: The Naval Battle of Okinawa,* Washington, D.C., 1945

US Navy H-046-3: *Kikusui No. 6 and Its Prelude: The Epic Fight of USS Hugh W. Hadley (DD-774),* 11 May 1945

US Navy H-Gram 046: *Chrysanthemums from Hell,* 7 May 2020

Index

Part I: German Manned Parasite Suicide Aircraft

Part Two: Japanese Manned Suicide Composites